Teach Yourself VISUALLY™

Jewelry Making & Beading

Visual®

by Chris Franchetti Michaels

1807
WILEY
2007

Wiley Publishing, Inc.

For general information on our other products and services or to obtain technical support please contact our Customer Care Department within the U.S. at (800) 762-2974, outside the U.S. at (317) 572-3993 or fax (317) 572-4002.

Wiley also publishes its books in a variety of electronic formats. Some content that appears in print may not be available in electronic books. For more information about Wiley products, please visit our web site at www.wiley.com.

Library of Congress Control Number: 2007921821

ISBN: 978-0-470-10150-6

Printed in the United States of America

10 9 8 7 6 5 4 3

Book production by Wiley Publishing, Inc. Composition Services

Wiley Bicentennial Logo: Richard J. Pacifico

Praise for the Teach Yourself VISUALLY Series

I just had to let you and your company know how great I think your books are. I just purchased my third Visual book (my first two are dog-eared now!) and, once again, your product has surpassed my expectations. The expertise, thought, and effort that go into each book are obvious, and I sincerely appreciate your efforts. Keep up the wonderful work!

—Tracey Moore (Memphis, TN)

I have several books from the Visual series and have always found them to be valuable resources.

—Stephen P. Miller (Ballston Spa, NY)

Thank you for the wonderful books you produce. It wasn't until I was an adult that I discovered how I learn—visually. Although a few publishers out there claim to present the material visually, nothing compares to Visual books. I love the simple layout. Everything is easy to follow. And I understand the material! You really know the way I think and learn. Thanks so much!

—Stacey Han (Avondale, AZ)

Like a lot of other people, I understand things best when I see them visually. Your books really make learning easy and life more fun.

—John T. Frey (Cadillac, MI)

I am an avid fan of your Visual books. If I need to learn anything, I just buy one of your books and learn the topic in no time. Wonders! I have even trained my friends to give me Visual books as gifts.

—Illona Bergstrom (Aventura, FL)

I write to extend my thanks and appreciation for your books. They are clear, easy to follow, and straight to the point. Keep up the good work! I bought several of your books and they are just right! No regrets! I will always buy your books because they are the best.

—Seward Kollie (Dakar, Senegal)

Credits

Acquisitions Editor
Pam Mourouzis

Project Editor
Donna Wright

Copy Editor
Marylouise Wiack

Technical Editors
Virginia Blakelock and Carol Perrenoud

Editorial Manager
Christina Stambaugh

Publisher
Cindy Kitchel

Vice President and Executive Publisher
Kathy Nebenhaus

Interior Design
Kathie Rickard
Elizabeth Brooks

Cover Design
José Almaguer

Photography
Matt Bowen

Special Thanks...

To the following artisans for granting us permission to show photographs of their designs:

- Sherri Haab (www.sherrihaab.com)
- Linda Chandler and Christine Ritchey (www.jewelrybylinda.com)
- Preston Reuther (www.wire-sculpture.com)
- Sarah Moran (www.z-beads.com)
- Lisa Shea (www.lisashea.com)
- Lori "Trixxie" Juergens

About the Author

Chris Franchetti Michaels is a writer and jewelry artisan specializing in beaded designs, wire-work, and metal fabrication. She is the editor of the BellaOnline.com Jewelry Making website and has appeared on several episodes of the DIY Network television show *Jewelry Making*. Her designs are featured in two recently published print compilations of notable jewelry-making and beading projects. Some of Chris' projects are available for purchase as kits on her website www.chettibeads.com.

Acknowledgments

I would first like to thank Shari Bonnin and Marilyn Allen, whose recommendations and encouragement brought this project into existence. I will always remember and appreciate the contributions of Pam Mourouzis, Donna Wright, Marylouise Wiack, Matt Bowen, and the other team members whose many hours of work helped to make my vision for the book a reality. Thank you also to Lisa Shea for giving me a wonderful opportunity to develop my skills by writing online, and for always thinking of ways to promote my jewelry. Finally, and most importantly, many heartfelt thanks go to my family: Peg Franchetti, Victoria Franchetti Haynes, Don Linebarger, Robyn Haynes, the Brunos, the Bugatos, and my ever-patient and devoted husband, Dennis Michaels. Their love and support gave me the strength to complete this book during what was otherwise the most difficult of times.

Table of Contents

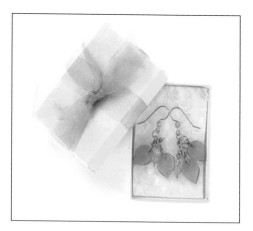

chapter 3 Basic Bead Stringing Techniques

chapter 4 More Advanced Bead Stringing Techniques

chapter 5 Bead Weaving

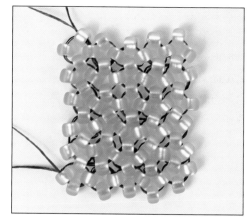

chapter 6 Basic Wirework

chapter 7 More Advanced Wirework Techniques

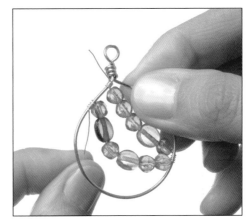

chapter 8 Using a Wire Jig

chapter 9 Macramé Knotting and Beading

chapter 10 Easy Projects

chapter 11 **Intermediate Projects**

chapter 12 Expanding Your Horizons

chapter 1

Introduction to Jewelry Making and Beading

Are you interested in learning how to make jewelry and work with beads, but unsure where to begin? Let this book guide you through the basic skills and techniques you will need to create the most popular styles of jewelry and beadwork. In this chapter, you will learn about the essential tools, equipment, and supplies used for common tasks. Then you can set up your work area and start exploring this creative hobby.

Become a Jewelry Artisan

Jewelry making and beading are very personal and rewarding crafts. With some basic supplies and a little creativity, you can adorn yourself, and the people in your life, with beautiful objects that communicate your inner feelings and your sense of style.

People have been crafting jewelry and beading for thousands of years. Throughout human history, jewelry and beads have symbolized social status, wealth, and spiritual beliefs. Some cultures even attribute magical powers to their jewelry and gemstones. Today, many people still view jewelry as more than mere decoration; they use it to symbolize love and commitment, religion, politics, life experiences, the birth of children, and important memories. Our choice of jewelry conveys important information about us. It helps us—and those around us—to understand who we are.

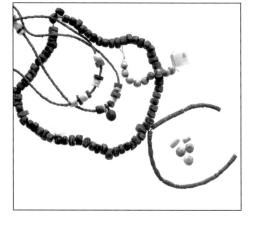

When you begin making your own jewelry and beaded artwork, you will use many of the same techniques that ancient crafters used thousands of years ago. Your designs will be special because you made them by hand to your own specifications. You will experience the satisfaction of making jewelry you really love (and that fits you), while avoiding the cheaply made, mass-produced jewelry that you see at so many retail stores.

You can also save money by making your own jewelry. Using the basic techniques covered in this book, you can affordably make jewelry that is very similar to expensive designer jewelry from department stores and boutiques. You will also find that gift-giving becomes far less challenging for the jewelry and beadwork lovers on your gift lists.

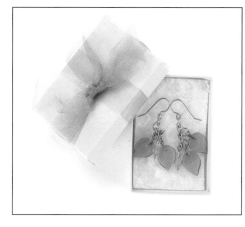

One of the most rewarding aspects of jewelry making and beading is that your creations can serve any purpose and match any style that you choose. If you love fashion, you can be your own personal fashion jewelry designer. If you're interested in a particular culture, religion, spiritual path, or time in history, your designs can reflect what's important to you. You can even reassemble your old jewelry into new, updated designs.

As you work through this book, allow yourself plenty of time to experiment and play with new techniques. You may master some skills quickly, but others will take practice. Be patient, and keep in mind that you will be able to complete projects faster over time. Enjoy each new accomplishment, and use your newfound talents to bring more creativity and enrichment into your life.

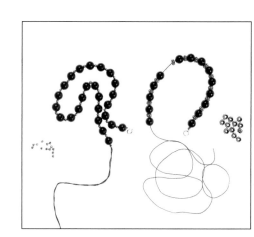

Beads and Beading Supplies

Beads are the most popular and widely available jewelry-making components. You can find them at craft stores, bead shops, and on the Internet. (See pages 282–283 for a list of bead resources.) Typically, beads are categorized by material, shape, and size.

Common Bead Materials

GLASS BEADS

Glass beads are available in just about any color and style you can imagine. Their quality is often linked to where and how they are made. For example, many glass beads currently made in China and India are less consistent in size and color than glass beads from Europe; however, they typically are less expensive than European beads.

Some of the most popular glass beads from Europe are made in the Czech Republic. These are often referred to as *Czech glass beads*. Some Czech glass beads are *pressed*, or manufactured in molds. You can find them in a lot of fun shapes like flowers, animals, and even fruit. Other Czech glass beads are *fire polished*. Fire polishing is a special process that gives glass extra shine and sparkle. But fire-polished glass beads are not quite as eye-catching as *crystal beads*. Crystal is glass that contains a small amount of lead. The lead makes the glass softer so that it can be cut into more precise shapes. It also changes the way light reflects within the glass, creating extreme shine. The highest-quality crystal beads are made in Austria and Czech Republic, but less expensive variations are also manufactured in China.

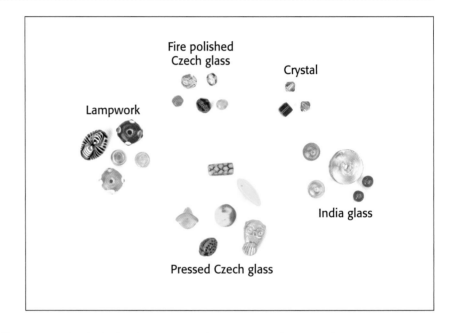

Fire polished Czech glass

Crystal

Lampwork

India glass

Pressed Czech glass

Seed beads are tiny glass beads that are commonly used to create woven beaded fabric. You can also use them to make thin, beaded strands. As with larger beads, seed beads vary in quality depending on how and where they were made. You will learn more about bead weaving and selecting quality seed beads in Chapter 5.

Although most glass beads are made by machine, some are individually handmade. *Lampwork beads* are an especially popular style of handmade glass beads. They are crafted by manually applying molten glass to metal rods.

Other beads are created by a combination of mechanical and handmade methods. For example, some manufactured glass beads are *hand faceted*, or cut to have multiple flat surfaces, to mimic the look of gemstone beads.

GEMSTONE BEADS

Most gemstone beads are made from *semiprecious* natural stone. Semiprecious stone is more abundant, and less costly, than the *precious* gemstones used in fine jewelry settings. Agate, jade, quartz, jasper, and turquoise are examples of common semiprecious stones. You can also find semiprecious varieties of more expensive stones like ruby, amethyst, emerald, and citrine.

Gemstone beads are usually shaped by hand. Like glass beads, their quality and cost often depend on where they were made. Some of the most affordable gemstone beads are made in India. They are colorful and beautiful, but their shapes and sizes are less consistent than more expensive gemstone beads from China.

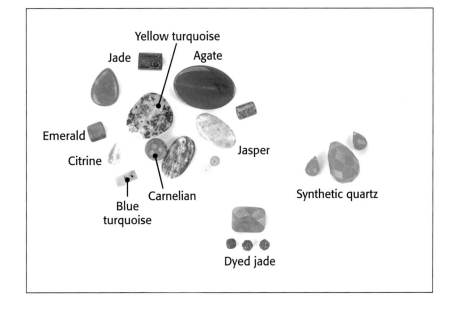

Many gemstone beads are *treated*, which means that they may be dyed, oiled, heated, irradiated, or injected with waxes. Treatments improve the look of lower-quality stones, but treated stones remain less valuable than higher-quality, untreated stones. Treated gemstone is not the same as *synthetic* gemstone. Synthetic gemstone beads are not really made from stone; they are another material made to look like stone. Many synthetic stones—especially synthetic quartzes—are made from glass. They can be very beautiful, but they are typically considered inferior to natural stone.

CONTINUED ON NEXT PAGE

CERAMIC BEADS

Ceramic beads are made from earthen clay. They can have a simple, natural look or be highly decorative. Colorful ceramic beads are usually painted, printed, or glazed. With *painted* ceramic beads, the paint is brushed on or the beads are dipped into paint. A coat of lacquer may be applied to seal the paint in place. *Printed* ceramic beads are either stamped with paint or have designs *transferred* onto them from other surfaces. Transferred designs are usually applied using heat, but otherwise they are similar to stamps. Printed and transferred designs are less time-consuming to create, and more regular in appearance, than hand-painted designs. *Glazed* ceramic beads are coated with colored or clear glass.

Some ceramic beads are shaped by hand, and others are molded, carved, or *impressed*. Impressed beads have indented or three-dimensional designs made by pressing a mold or modeling tool onto the clay before it hardens.

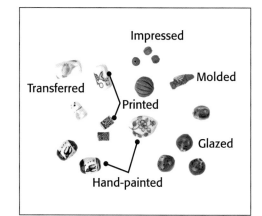

METAL BEADS

Metal beads can be made of precious metal or base metal. *Precious metal* is less abundant and more expensive than base metal. The most common precious metals used in handmade jewelry are sterling silver and gold. *Base metal* refers to any of the more common, less expensive metals like copper, brass, nickel, tin, or aluminum—or to any mixture, or *alloy*, of more than one type of base metal. Base metal beads are often finished or plated. *Finishing* is a technique used to change the color of the surface of metal to make it look more like another metal. It can also be used to darken metal, making it look *oxidized*, or antiqued. *Plated* metal is coated with a very thin layer of another metal. Common examples are silver-plate and gold-plate. Plated beads have a nice look, but their plating can wear off relatively easily.

Most solid metal beads are *cast*, or molded. Hollow metal beads are often made of two stamped sheets of metal joined together at the seam. Handmade metal beads are usually made from precious metals, and they are significantly more expensive than cast beads because of the time and effort required to make them. Most handmade metal beads are fabricated using traditional, advanced jewelry-making techniques. Others are hand-formed from metal clay. (For more information on metal fabrication and metal clay, see Chapter 12.)

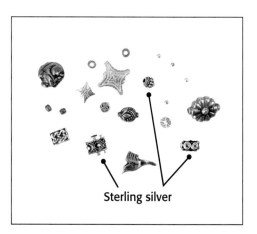

PLASTIC BEADS

While some plastic beads are inexpensive and of low quality, others are pricey and highly collectible. Beads made from hard vintage plastics like *Bakelite* and *celluloid* are especially sought after. *Artificial resin* is a soft plastic used to make bright, colorful beads, or to replicate natural materials like amber and cinnabar. (In fact, modern beads called "cinnabar" are usually made from red or black resin, because natural cinnabar is highly toxic.) Some basic plastic, or *acrylic*, beads are coated to look like metal beads. Others look like carved bone, tortoise shell, or pearls.

Many handmade plastic beads are made from *polymer clay*, which is a heavy plastic that can be shaped easily and layered to create interesting artistic effects. (For more information on polymer clay, see Chapter 12.)

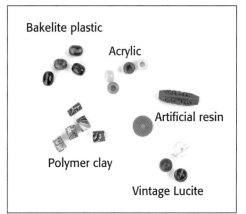

ORGANIC BEADS

Historians believe that the first beads ever made were crafted from small seeds or tiny pieces of shell. These materials are *organic* because they come from living things. Pearl is an all-time favorite organic bead material. Pearls are formed by little water creatures called *mollusks*. When an irritant, like a piece of sand, gets trapped in the mollusk's tissue, it deposits layers of a substance called *nacre* around the irritant. Multiple layers of nacre create a pearl. Most pearls are *cultured*, meaning that irritants were manually placed into mollusks' tissues to create them. *Natural* pearls are pearls that form without any human intervention. They are very rare and expensive, and so the pearls you use in jewelry will likely be cultured. Pearl beads are often dyed, but they can also have a natural white, cream, or tan color. There are many different qualities, or *grades*, of pearl beads. Even the lower-grade, inexpensive varieties can look stunning in jewelry.

Other organic bead materials include wood, seeds, shell, amber, bone, and horn. *Amber* is a very lightweight material made from the natural resin of ancient trees. Bone and horn beads typically derive from the byproducts of large livestock like cows and sheep. Beads made from these materials are usually handcrafted, and many are hand carved.

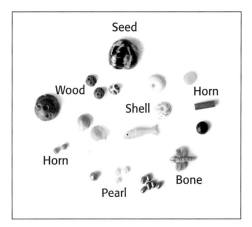

CONTINUED ON NEXT PAGE

Bead Shapes

Beads are available in many shapes. Here are the most common shapes you will encounter when bead shopping.

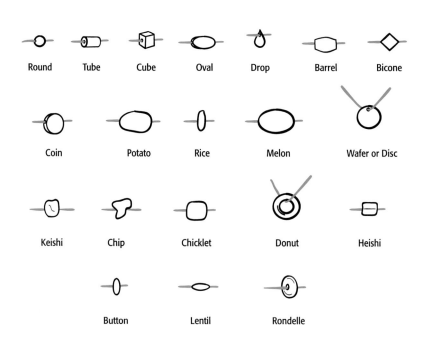

Round Tube Cube Oval Drop Barrel Bicone

Coin Potato Rice Melon Wafer or Disc

Keishi Chip Chicklet Donut Heishi

Button Lentil Rondelle

FAQ

What are bead caps?

Bead caps are small, cup-shaped components that adorn the ends of beads. You can string on bead caps before and after a bead to give it a more ornate appearance. Bead caps are usually made of metal, and they can be plain or elaborate in their styling. For best results, select bead caps that fit snugly so that they almost appear to be part of the beads that they contain.

Bead Sizes

With the exception of tiny seed beads, bead sizes are typically described in millimeters. (To learn about the unique sizing classifications for seed beads, see page 95 in Chapter 5.)

The size of a round bead is its *diameter*, which is the same measurement as either its *length* (the distance between the two openings of the drill hole) or its *width* (the distance between the other two sides of the bead). The sizes of other shapes of beads are often described by both their length and width. Typically, length is the first measurement given, but sometimes width is provided first. (For this reason, it's important to examine the bead in question to understand its width versus length.) Here are some examples of common bead sizes.

CONTINUED ON NEXT PAGE

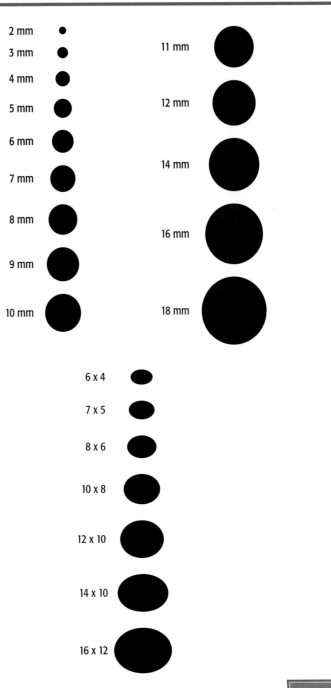

Pendants and Charms

You can use pre-made pendants and charms in just about any type of jewelry you make. They are sold at most bead shops and jewelry supply stores, and you can even take them off of old jewelry and reuse them for new designs.

Pendants are usually larger than charms and serve as focal pieces for necklaces. They can be made from any material that beads are made from. The little devices that hold pendants onto necklaces are called *bails*.

Charms are typically used as accent pieces rather than focal points. You can use a single charm in a design, or a collection of many. Charms usually attach to jewelry with split rings or jump rings (see page 27).

Bead Stringing Materials

You can string beads on many different materials. Here's a brief look at the most common stringing materials used for beading. You will learn more about them in Chapters 3, 4, and 5.

BEADING WIRE AND MEMORY WIRE

Unlike regular metal wire, *beading wire* is soft and flexible. It's made up of many tiny metal strands woven or wound together. Most beading wire is covered with a thin layer of nylon plastic. To learn more about the types and sizes of beading wire, see "Select a Stringing Material" in Chapter 3.

Memory wire is hard, single-strand steel wire designed to hold a circular shape. You can use it to make beaded coil bracelets, necklaces, and rings that don't require clasps.

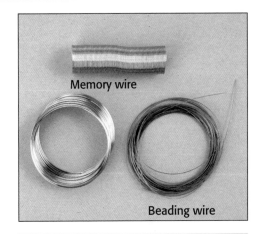

Memory wire

Beading wire

CORD AND RIBBON

Cord is non-metal material that often consists of smaller strands woven together. Silk, nylon, cotton, and satin are popular types of multiple-strand cord. Leather, suede, and rubber are typical single-strand cords. Stretch cord can have single or multiple strands. Most cord is sized in millimeters or inches according to its diameter, but some manufacturers use their own sizing system using numbers or letters. *Ribbon* for beading is usually made of soft fabric, like organza or satin.

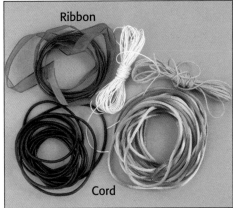

Ribbon

Cord

BEADING THREAD

Beading thread is a special synthetic thread designed for beading. It has a very small diameter and can fit through tiny bead holes. Like cord, it is often composed of multiple strands. Beading thread is usually stronger and smoother than thread used for sewing. To learn about beading thread sizes, see "Select Beads, Thread, and Needle" in Chapter 5.

CONTINUED ON NEXT PAGE

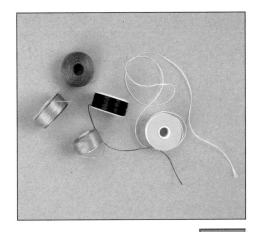

Beading Tools and Supplies

Although beads and stringing material are the basic necessities of any beading project, there are other tools and supplies that can make your beadwork easier and help you create more complicated designs. Here's a look at some items that you may find useful. You will learn more about working with many of them in Chapters 3, 4, and 5.

BEADING MATS, BEADING DISHES, AND BEAD BOARDS

Because many beads are round, they can easily roll away from your work area. You can keep better track of your beads by working on a *beading mat*. A beading mat can be any flat surface that is textured to keep beads from rolling. It can be as simple as a terry cloth hand towel or as fancy as a specially engineered, rubberized mat from a bead shop. Textured foam drawer-liner material also makes a nice bead mat, and you can find it at most drug stores.

When you work with tiny seed beads, you may find it more helpful to keep them on a ceramic dish or in a shallow, smooth bowl. This makes it easier to pick up the beads using a beading needle.

A *bead board* is a three-dimensional tray with long grooves for holding and arranging beads. Most bead boards are made of plastic with a velvety coating that helps beads stay in place. Bead boards are available in a variety of shapes and sizes, and they usually have measurement marks to help you gauge the lengths of your designs.

TAPE AND CLAMPS

There may be times when you want to string some beads before you permanently secure the end of your stringing material. You can keep your beads from falling off the string by temporarily securing it with a piece of masking tape or a clamping device. *Alligator clips* are small metal clamps traditionally used for electrical work. They are especially useful for clamping cord. You can also find clamps made specifically for beading called Bead Stoppers at some bead shops and jewelry supply stores.

MEASURING TOOLS

It's a good idea to have a ruler and a measuring tape on hand for measuring the lengths of beaded strands, sizing beads and other components, and helping with jewelry sizing. You can also use a sliding *brass measuring gauge* to determine the dimensions of beads and components. Brass measuring gauges have marks that line up to show you the sizes of items in millimeters and inches. They are relatively inexpensive and provide very accurate measurements.

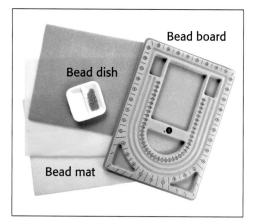

Bead board

Bead dish

Bead mat

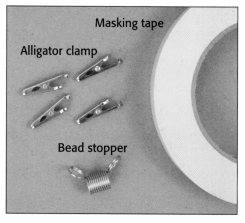

Masking tape

Alligator clamp

Bead stopper

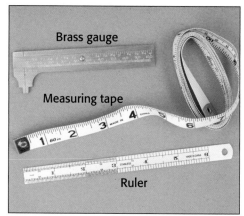

Brass gauge

Measuring tape

Ruler

SHARP SCISSORS OR NIPPERS

A good pair of small, sharp scissors will help you cleanly cut and trim soft stringing materials like cord, ribbon, and thread, and even smaller sizes of beading wire. For larger beading wire, or to cut soft materials more quickly, you can use a pair of short-bladed cutters called *nippers*. Try to avoid using your beading scissors or nippers on anything other than bead-stringing material; hard or rough materials can damage or dull them.

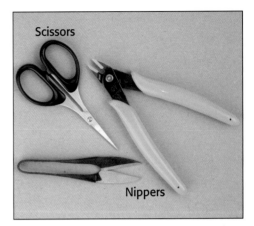

Scissors

Nippers

PLIERS FOR CRIMPING

You can secure the ends of beading wire with little collapsible beads or tubes called *crimps* (see "Crimp Beads and Crimp Tubes" on page 26). To attach crimps, you need a pair of chain nose pliers or specially designed crimping pliers. *Chain nose pliers* are short needle nose pliers with smooth jaws. Although similar pliers are sold at hardware stores, it's best to purchase them at a bead shop or jewelry making supply store. *Crimping pliers* are usually available where other beading supplies are sold. (To learn more about crimping pliers, see page 50 in Chapter 3.)

NEEDLES AND THREAD CONDITIONER

Some bead-stringing materials are stiff enough that you don't need a needle to string them with beads. This is true for beading wire and many types of cord. But for very thin or soft cord, or with beading thread, a needle can make bead stringing much easier. There are several types of needles used for stringing beads. The one you select for a given project depends on the stringing material and beads that you use. (For more information on needles, see page 54 in Chapter 3, "Needles Used with Cord" and page 97 in Chapter 5, "Selecting a Needle for Beading Thread".)

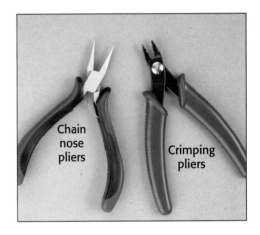

Chain nose pliers

Crimping pliers

Before you string beads onto a strand of beading thread, it's also a good idea to treat the thread with beeswax or thread conditioner. *Beeswax* is sold in blocks at most bead shops. When you rub it along a piece of thread, a layer of wax adheres to the thread to protect it from moisture and to slightly stiffen it, making it easier to work with. However, some beaders avoid beeswax because it can attract dirt and make thread feel sticky.

Thread conditioner is an alternative to beeswax. It is usually sold in small plastic boxes at bead shops and fabric stores. You apply it by gently pressing the thread into the container with your finger and pulling the thread through the conditioner until it is completely coated. Thread conditioner is thought to make thread stronger and to reduce tangling. It is not as sticky as beeswax and it is less likely to attract dirt.

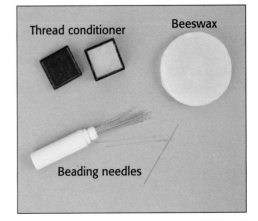

Thread conditioner

Beeswax

Beading needles

CONTINUED ON NEXT PAGE

KNOTTING AWLS AND KNOTTING TOOLS

A *knotting awl* helps you position knots against beads. You can find one at most bead shops, or you can use a regular darning needle as a substitute. Narrow tweezers or *knotting pliers* are also useful for sliding tiny knots against beads. Another option is a *specialty knotting tool*, which mechanically maneuvers the stringing material as you make knots. (You will learn how to use an awl and specialty knotting tool in Chapter 4.)

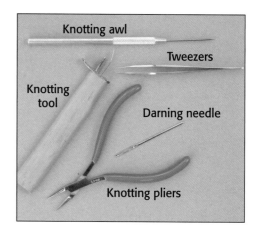

Knotting awl

Tweezers

Knotting tool

Darning needle

Knotting pliers

GLUE AND TOOTHPICKS

Glue is often used to help secure knots at the ends of stringing material or to attach components to base findings (see "Jewelry Findings" on page 26). One of the most popular glues for jewelry making is E6000. This thick, clear glue can take time to dry, but it remains flexible and moisture proof when it sets. You can find it at bead shops, jewelry making supply stores, and hardware stores. It's a good idea to keep some toothpicks on hand for applying the glue to small areas, and some paper towels for wiping up glue messes.

Instant bond glue is also used in jewelry making. This is the glue that you typically find in little squeeze bottles at grocery and drug stores. As its name implies, instant bond glue sets very quickly. However, it also becomes brittle and may crack and break. For some applications, especially securing small knots, you can use clear nail polish as an alternative to E6000 or instant bond glue. Whichever glue you choose, always apply it in a well-ventilated area and avoid breathing in fumes.

Instant bond glue

STRAND HOLDERS

Some beading techniques require that you hold or secure multiple strands temporarily while you work. One way to do this is to loop strands through a thin, generic shower curtain ring. (You may see these rings holding strands of beads at bead shops.) They are available from many jewelry making suppliers and are relatively inexpensive. As an alternative, try using a *stitch holder* for knitting. Stitch holders are made of thick metal wire or plastic and look like big safety pins. You can find them at yarn shops and fabric stores. Many other items can be used as strand holders, including small *carabiners* (often sold as key chains), or even simple twisted loops of wire.

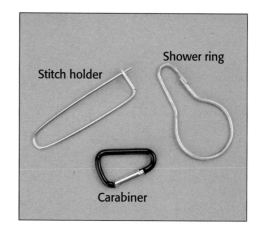

Stitch holder

Shower ring

Carabiner

BEAD REAMERS

Bead reamers are hand tools with rough, pointed ends. You use them like sandpaper to *debur*, or smooth out, the holes in some beads before stringing them. Reaming removes jagged edges that might otherwise damage your stringing material. You can also use reamers to slightly enlarge holes on beads made from softer materials. Bead reamers work best on beads made of stone, organic material, plastic, or ceramic. For best results, keep the tip of your bead reamer moist with water while using it.

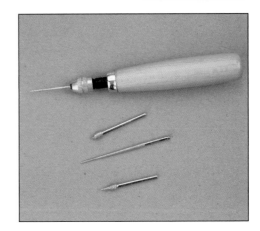

BEADING LOOM

Beading looms are small, specialized looms designed for weaving long lengths of beaded fabric. They are available in a variety of types and sizes. Most have long, rectangular frames with a bar at each end for securing beading thread. You can find beading looms at most bead shops and from suppliers who specialize in seed beads and bead-weaving supplies.

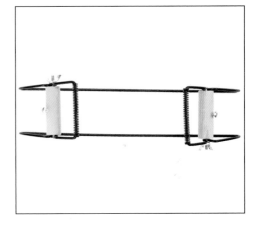

STORAGE AND ORGANIZATION

Perhaps the greatest challenge when it comes to bead stringing is keeping track of the many beads and components that you collect over time. Some may be left over from previous projects, while others are waiting for the right project to come along. You can store beads in small reusable containers like baby food jars and prescription bottles, or you can purchase modular plastic or acrylic containers made especially for beads. Try to store items in clear containers so you can easily see them. Use a spoon or *bead scoop* to collect beads and place them back into their containers when you're finished with them. You can organize your containers by the type, color, or material of the items they contain.

Bead scoop

Wire and Wirework Supplies

Wirework involves shaping metal wire into useful and decorative components and designs. To make wire jewelry, you need the right type of wire and some simple tools to help you manipulate it. This section provides an introduction to wire and common wirework tools. You will learn more about using them in Chapters 6, 7, and 8.

Wire and Tools

JEWELRY WIRE

You can make wire jewelry with any base-metal or precious-metal wire that is soft and easy to bend. (Do not confuse wire used for wirework with beading wire used for bead stringing, which is defined in Chapter 3.) The most popular base metals for wirework are copper, plated copper, nickel, and brass. Precious-metal wire jewelry is often made from sterling silver, fine silver, or gold-filled wire. *Sterling silver* is an alloy that contains at least 92.5% silver and no more than 7.5% base metal (usually copper). *Fine silver* contains at least 99.9% pure silver, and may contain .1% or less base metal. (Fine silver wire is used primarily for advanced projects that require extremely soft wire, like the wire knitting and crochet techniques described on page 274 in Chapter 12.) *Gold-filled wire* has a core of base metal covered with a layer of real gold. Gold-filled wire contains much more gold than *gold-plated* wire, which has a very thin wash of gold on its surface. Wire is available in different sizes, called *gauges*. See page 122 in Chapter 6 for a comparison of wire gauges and recommended uses for them.

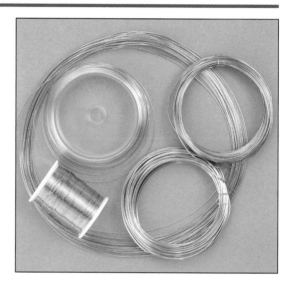

FAQ

What is wire *temper*?

Temper refers to the hardness, or stiffness, of wire. Wire with *soft temper* is easier to bend than wire with *hard temper*. Base-metal wire is typically sold with soft temper; but when you buy sterling-silver wire, you often have a selection of tempers to choose from. Sterling-silver wire with *dead-soft* temper is the most versatile for jewelry making because it's the easiest to work with. However, you may want to use *half-hard* sterling wire when you'd like your finished component to be relatively stiff. For example, jump rings or ear wires are more durable when they're made from wire with half-hard temper.

You can also change the temper of dead-soft wire by hammering it. When you tap on wire with a hammer, the molecules align so that the metal becomes stiffer. To learn more about hammering tools and supplies, see pages 20–22.

CHAIN NOSE PLIERS

As you learned on page 15, chain nose pliers are a type of short needle nose pliers. They are the most versatile tool in wire jewelry making. Their jaws are thinner at the tips and wider at the base. Some have straight noses, and others are bent at an angle. It's important to use chain nose pliers that have smooth jaws—not serrated jaws—for wirework. Serrated (or textured) jaws can create undesirable impressions on soft metals. Chain nose pliers are available in a range of sizes, but any standard pair will do when you're just getting started. If you advance to more intricate wirework using tiny-gauge wire, you may want to invest in a pair with especially narrow tips.

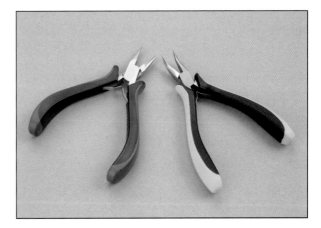

FLAT NOSE PLIERS

Flat nose pliers have long rectangular jaws. As with chain nose pliers, it's important to use a pair with smooth jaws. Flat nose pliers are available in different widths and lengths, but any standard beginner's pair works well for most applications.

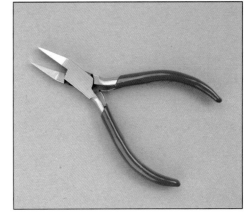

ROUND NOSE PLIERS

Round nose pliers have jaws that are rounded into solid cylinders. You can find round nose pliers with very long noses at the hardware store, but shorter-nose versions are better for jewelry making. They are available at most bead shops and jewelry making supply stores.

CONTINUED ON NEXT PAGE

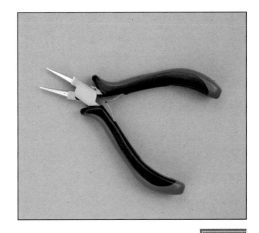

NYLON JAW PLIERS

Nylon jaw pliers are special pliers with plastic jaws. Most models have removable plastic inserts so that you can replace them when they wear out. Because their jaws are softer than metal, nylon jaw pliers do not scratch or mar wire like regular pliers do. In jewelry making, they are most commonly used to straighten wire that has become bent or kinked. For details on using them, see page 135. Nylon jaw pliers are available at most jewelry making supply stores.

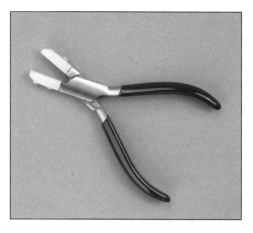

SIDE CUTTERS

Side cutters are special types of wire cutters that are designed to make flat, or *flush*, cuts on wire. They are the best cutters to use on jewelry wire, because you typically want the ends of your wire to be flat, rather than jagged. However, be aware that side cutters only create a flush cut with one side of their jaws; the other side creates a jagged cut. When you use them, make sure that the flat side of the cutters is pointing away from the end of the wire that you're trimming. The best side cutters for wirework are sold at jewelry making supply stores.

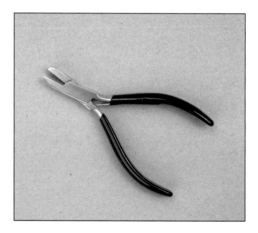

HAMMERS

The *chasing hammer* is a popular hammer for wirework. It's actually designed for hammering on other tools (called *chasing tools*) to create marks on sheet metal, but it also works well for flattening and hardening wire. The *face*, or flat surface, of a chasing hammer is smooth and slightly rounded, making it easier to taper wire by hammering it at a slight angle. Two other useful hammers are the *nylon head hammer* and the *rawhide hammer*. Both have soft faces that will not scratch or mar wire. They are useful for straightening and slightly stiffening wire without flattening it. You can find nylon head and rawhide hammers at most hardware stores, but it's a good idea to purchase other hammers from a jewelry making supplier.

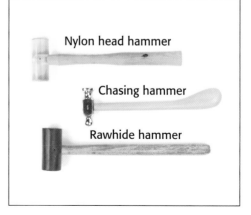

Nylon head hammer

Chasing hammer

Rawhide hammer

BENCH BLOCK AND BENCH PIN

A *bench block* is a smooth piece of hardened steel used as a surface for hammering. You place wire on top of the bench block and hold it in place while you hammer. To keep your bench block from moving while you hammer, try placing it on a rubberized bead mat.

A *bench pin* is a specially-shaped piece of solid wood that jewelers attach to their work benches. They use it to support pieces of metal while they cut or file them. Although bench pins are typically used for advanced metalsmithing, you can also use one when you make jump rings (see page 126 in Chapter 6). Some bench pins are designed to fit into pre-made slots found in most jewelers' benches, but others can be attached to any work surface using a clamp. (If you don't have a bench pin, try using a piece of scrap wood instead.) Bench blocks and bench pins are sold at most jewelry making supply stores.

Bench block　　　Bench pin

NEEDLE FILES

Needle files are small metal files that come in a variety of shapes. The most useful shape for wirework is the *flat needle file*. You can use this file to smooth the ends of wire after trimming it. Affordable needle files are stocked by many hardware stores. If you'd like one that lasts longer or is more comfortable to use, you can find a nicer one at a jewelry making supply store.

MANDRELS

Mandrels are used to wrap wire into particular shapes. The most common mandrels are metal rods for coiling wire or forming wire loops. You can purchase mandrels in various sizes and shapes at jewelry making supply stores, but you can also make your own. Household objects like pens, chopsticks, and prescription bottles can serve as mandrels. You can even make mandrels out of wooden dowels or small metal tubes from the hardware store. A *tapered mandrel* is a special type of mandrel that allows you to create wire shapes in a range of sizes. Shapes created near the end of the mandrel are smaller than those created near the base. A common type of tapered mandrel is the *ring mandrel*, which is used for making finger rings in specific sizes.

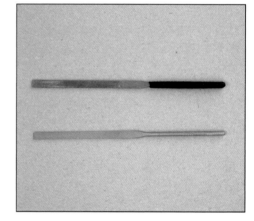

Ring mandrel

CONTINUED ON NEXT PAGE

WIRE JIG

A *wire jig* is a device for guiding wire into specific shapes. It consists of a flat surface, or *base*, and a number of *pegs* that fit into the base. Most modern pre-made jigs have moveable pegs that you can arrange in many different configurations. You can create jewelry components in useful shapes by wrapping wire around the pegs. When you make multiples of the same component, each will be the same shape and size. Jigs are available in many sizes and styles. Some are made of plastic, but the more durable models are made of metal. You can find them at some bead shops and most jewelry making supply stores.

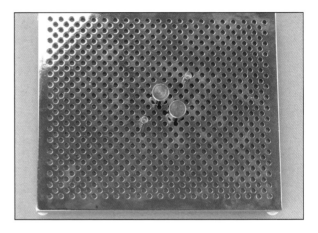

HAND DRILL

A *hand drill* is a manual drill that operates when you turn a crank handle on its side. If you'd ever like to twist two pieces of wire together for a decorative effect, a hand drill can speed up the process. You will learn how to do this on page 158 in Chapter 7. You can find a simple hand drill at most hardware stores.

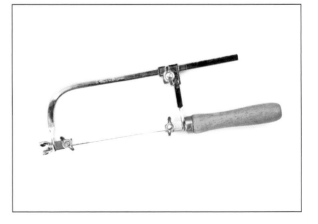

JEWELER'S SAW

A *jeweler's saw* is a special saw designed for intricately cutting sheet metal in advanced jewelry making. You can also use it to speed the process of making multiple wire *jump rings* (see page 128 in Chapter 6 for more information on how to make jump rings). Most hardware stores carry simple, affordable jeweler's saws.

STORAGE AND ORGANIZATION

Wire and wirework tools are usually easier to keep track of than beads, but it's a good idea to develop a system for keeping them organized. When you buy wire, it may be packaged in a coil or on a spool. Be sure to label each package with the material the wire is made of and its gauge. You may also want to keep scrap wire in labeled plastic boxes, organized by type of metal.

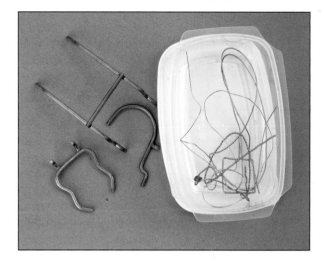

Keep your tools in a location where you can easily reach them as you work. You can store pliers and files on special stands available at jewelry making supply stores, or on heavy-duty magnetic strips that you hang on the wall. Smaller mandrels can be kept in a pencil holder or mug.

Hammers are best stored in a drawer or on a wall-mounted *pegboard*. You can find pegboard and pegboard accessories at most hardware stores. Accessories include special hooks for hanging hammers, and generic hooks that you can use to hang a jeweler's saw or coils of wire.

Macramé Knotting and Braiding Supplies

The basic necessities for making macramé and braided jewelry are knotting cord, knotting boards, and T-pins or tape.

KNOTTING CORD

You can make macramé knots and braids with any type of cord that has a large enough diameter to work with (typically 1–2.5mm). One of the easiest cords to knot, and the most popular for jewelry making, is *twine*. Twine is usually made from hemp, which is a plant with very strong fibers. Hemp twine has a natural brownish color, but it's also available bleached (cream colored) and dyed in an array of colors. Some types of hemp twine have a smooth texture, but others are rough and a little scratchy to wear. All hemp cord tends to soften and develop a smoother texture if it's worn for a while, especially when it's allowed to get wet.

Waxed linen, waxed cotton, and braided nylon are also popular cords used for macramé knotting and braiding. Smooth satin cord called *rattail* is a more colorful option. Leather and suede cord are more difficult to work with, but you can give them a try as your skills develop.

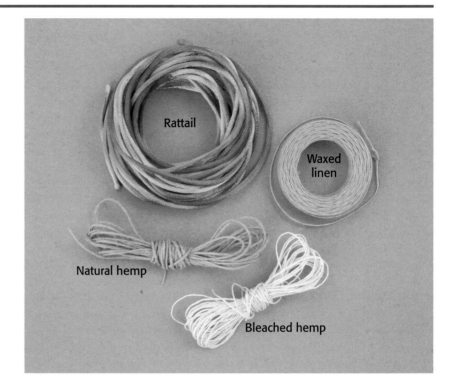

Rattail

Waxed linen

Natural hemp

Bleached hemp

KNOTTING BOARD

You can use a *knotting board* to secure your cords as you work. As you will learn in Chapter 9, you can buy a pre-made knotting board, make one yourself, or use an office clipboard as a substitute.

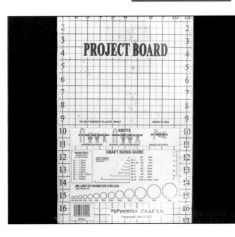

T-PINS AND TAPE

T-pins are sturdy, steel stickpins with tops shaped like the letter T. They are used by scientists to dissect things and pin down dead bugs, but they are also useful for securing, or *anchoring*, cords to a knotting board. If you don't have a knotting board, try using masking tape to anchor your cords instead.

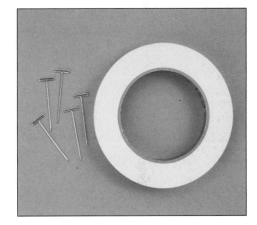

CORD DISPENSERS

When you buy cord for macramé knotting and braiding, it's often wound into a ball or around a spool. You can keep cord balls and spools clean and untangled by storing them in *cord dispensers*. A cord dispenser can be just about any container with a locking lid and a hole in its top or side for dispensing the cord. You can buy them pre-made from some stores that sell kitchen supplies, or you can make them yourself. Try cutting holes in the lids of storage tins, large jars (like peanut butter or mayonnaise jars), or small plastic storage boxes. You can also use ceramic teapots (pull the cord out through the spout) and upside-down flower pots (dispense the cord through the drain hole).

Jewelry Findings

Jewelry findings are components that serve practical purposes in designs. They attach jewelry parts, keep beads from falling off, and secure jewelry so that it can be worn on the body. Pre-made findings are sold along with beads and other supplies at bead shops and jewelry making supply stores. Most findings are made of metal, but they are also available in other materials. Here are the most common types.

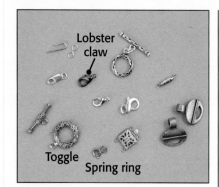

CLASPS

Clasps hold the ends of jewelry together. A clasp can be a simple hook or toggle, or it can be *mechanical*, with moving parts. *Lobster claws* and *spring rings* are examples of mechanical clasps. Most bead shops carry a large selection of clasps in various colors, finishes, and materials.

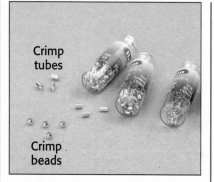

CRIMP BEADS AND CRIMP TUBES

Crimp beads and crimp tubes are used to secure the ends of bead-stringing wire. *Crimp beads* are rounded and look like tiny metal beads. *Crimp tubes* are tiny metal tubes. You attach crimps to beading wire by squeezing them with chain nose pliers or crimping pliers. To learn more about using crimping beads and tubes, see Chapter 3.

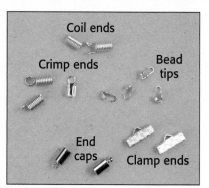

END PIECES

End pieces are metal components designed to secure the ends of various types of stringing material. They often include loops or rings for adding a clasp. Some attach to jewelry with glue, and others are folded-over or clamped down with chain nose pliers. End caps, coil ends, bead tips, clamp ends, and crimp ends are common styles of end pieces. To learn more about using them, see Chapter 3.

CONNECTORS AND SPACER BARS

A *connector* is a component with two or more rings or holes that can be used to connect strands in a design. Connectors can be functional or purely decorative. *Spacer bars* (also called *separator bars*) have a series of holes or rings that you can string over multiple strands to hold them together side-by-side.

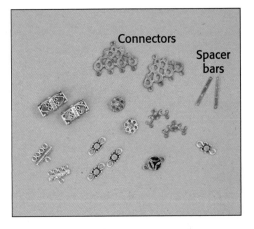
Connectors

Spacer bars

JUMP RINGS AND SPLIT RINGS

Jump rings are small wire rings used to connect jewelry parts. Most jump rings are *open*, which means that they are not soldered closed. You can open and close them using chain nose pliers. (You can also purchase *closed* jump rings, which are soldered and do not open.) *Split rings* are coiled wire rings that work like round key rings. You attach them by sliding components between their coils. Split rings are more secure than open jump rings because they cannot accidentally be pulled open; however, they also have a bulkier appearance than jump rings. If you decide to use split rings regularly, consider purchasing a pair of *split ring pliers* to help you attach them more easily.

Jump rings and split rings are usually sized by the gauge of wire they're made from and their outside diameter, called *OD*, or their inside diameter, called *ID*. (For example, an 18-gauge, 6mm OD jump ring is one that is made from 18-gauge wire and has an outside diameter of 6mm.) To learn more about jump rings and how to make your own, see Chapter 6.

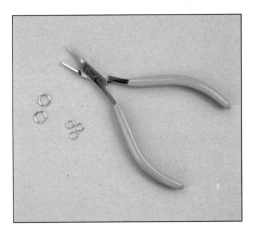

HEAD PINS AND EYE PINS

Head pins and eye pins are short lengths of wire used to create bead drops. *Head pins* typically have flat heads like nails, but some have metal balls, decorative shapes, or even set stones at the end. When you string a bead onto a head pin, the pin's head keeps the bead from falling off. You can then use round nose pliers to create a loop at the other end of the bead and attach the loop to another jewelry component. (See Chapter 6.) *Eye pins* have a small loop at one end instead of a solid head. You can attach charms or other bead drops to the loop for a more dramatic look.

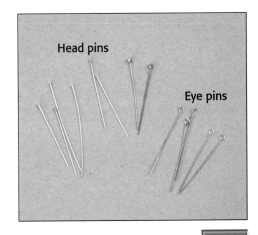
Head pins

Eye pins

CONTINUED ON NEXT PAGE

BAILS

Bails are the devices that hold pendants onto necklaces. Some pendants have bails already attached. For others, you will need to purchase bails separately or make them yourself. Bails can be as simple as large jump rings or as elaborate and decorative as the pendants they hold.

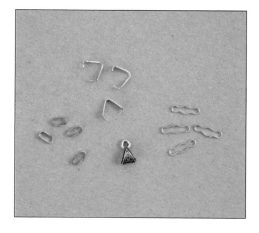

EARRING FINDINGS

Earring findings are components that allow earrings to be inserted through, or clamped onto, the earlobe. Just like clasps, they can be simple (like hooks) or mechanical (with moving parts). One of the most common and simple earring findings for pierced ears is the *French hook*. The most popular mechanical earring findings are called *lever backs*. You can also find *earring studs* with loops for attaching decorative components, as well as various styles of findings for non-pierced ears, including *clip-ons* and *screw backs*.

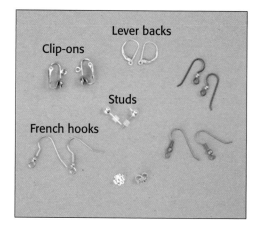

BAR PINS AND BASE FINDINGS

Bar pins are mechanical findings that you can glue onto other components to create pins and brooches. They are available in a range of sizes. Some come with attached bails so that you can make brooches that may also be worn as pendants. *Base findings* are bare pieces of metal or plain, pre-made pieces of jewelry that you can decorate by gluing, stitching, or wire-wrapping. They include sheet-metal discs, cuff bracelet bases, and pendant bases.

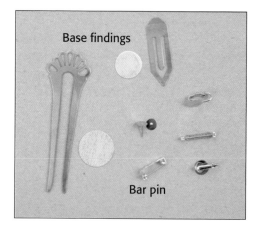

STORAGE AND ORGANIZATION

Over time you may collect a large number and variety of jewelry findings which, like beads and wirework supplies, need to be stored and organized. You can store most findings in the same small containers that you use to store beads. You can also keep them in a fishing tackle box or a divided storage bin from the hardware store. Be sure to label each container or compartment with the material the finding is made of, and any other useful information you'd like to remember about it. You can organize your findings by material, type, or style. Experiment to see which method works best, based on the kind of jewelry you most enjoy making.

TIP

Making Your Work Area Safe and Comfortable

Introductory jewelry making and beading are not high-risk activities, but it's a good idea to take some basic measures for safety and comfort. A first-aid kit will come in handy if you prick your finger with a beading needle, get scratched by a wire, or slice your finger while cutting jump rings. Make sure your work area has adequate ventilation (especially when you use glue), and keep the safety devices suggested in Chapter 6 (like eye and ear protection for wirework) within reach. Make sure your work area is well-lit, and use a magnifier to reduce eye strain. Sit in a comfortable chair and support your arms while you work. Finally, don't forget to consider the safety of children and pets. Jewelry components can be choking hazards, and some even contain small amounts of toxic lead that can be absorbed through the mouth. Pets are also especially susceptible to internal damage if they swallow cord, thread, or string. To avoid these dangers, keep your work area tidy and your supplies safely stored.

chapter 2

The Art of Design

You're now familiar with the tools, supplies, and materials used in jewelry making. This is a good time to start thinking about jewelry design. Although the tasks and projects in this book give you some design ideas, you'll probably want to invent some custom designs as well. This chapter covers the most important elements of design and how you can apply them to your jewelry making and beading.

Color Harmony

Some of the first decisions you make about a new design involve color. The colors of beads and other components that you select for a piece of jewelry should have *harmony;* that is, they should work well together visually. Colors that seem to "clash" do not have harmony; however, neither do colors that look dull or monotonous side-by-side. Here are some tools to help you select colors that harmonize.

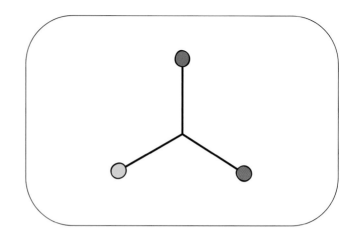

The Color Wheel

The traditional color wheel is a circular chart with equally sized sections of color positioned at regular intervals around the chart. It includes three types of colors: primary, secondary, and tertiary.

PRIMARY COLORS

Red, yellow, and blue are called *primary colors.* All other colors are a mixture of these three. Notice that primary colors look very solid and bold. The 3-part color wheel with the primary colors is shown above.

SECONDARY COLORS

Green, orange, and purple are called *secondary colors.* Each secondary color is a combination of two primary colors:

- Green is a mixture of yellow and blue.
- Orange is a mixture of yellow and red.
- Purple is a mixture of blue and red.

The secondary colors are positioned between their respective primary colors on the color wheel. They have a milder appearance than the primary colors, but they are still relatively bold.

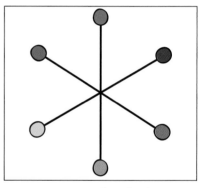

6-part color wheel

TERTIARY COLORS

A *tertiary color* is a mixture of one primary color and one secondary color. Tertiary colors have two-part names that indicate which two colors combine to form them. They are:

- Yellow-orange
- Red-orange
- Red-purple
- Blue-purple
- Blue-green
- Yellow-green

The tertiary colors are located between their respective primary and secondary colors on the color wheel. They are noticeably milder than the primary and secondary colors.

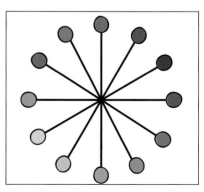

12-part color wheel

How to Use the Color Wheel

You can use the color wheel to identify sets of colors that harmonize. The two main categories of harmonizing colors are *analogous colors* and *complementary colors*.

ANALOGOUS COLORS

Analogous colors are sets of two or three colors positioned side-by-side on a 12-part color wheel. To use analogous colors in a design, select components that match, or are various shades of, those colors. Remember that you don't have to use equal parts of colors in a design. For example, one color may dominate, and another may occur only occasionally as an accent.

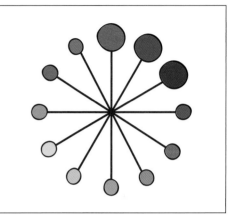

COMPLEMENTARY COLORS

Complementary colors are positioned directly opposite one another on the color wheel. These color sets show contrast without losing harmony. Consider using them when you'd like to create a bolder look.

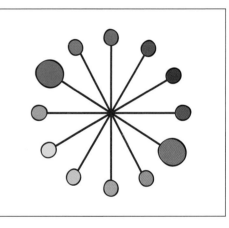

OTHER COLOR HARMONY RELATIONSHIPS

Although analogous and complementary colors are the simplest color combinations, you can also use a 12-part color wheel to find more complicated color sets. Movable color wheel charts from art supply stores are usually marked to show those alternative relationships, which include *split complementaries*, *triads*, and *tetrads*. Try experimenting with them for your most colorful designs. The artist's color wheel, shown here, is movable; you can spin it to quickly identify harmonious combinations of colors.

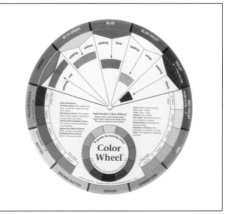

CONTINUED ON NEXT PAGE

Other Ways to Select Colors

You can find inspiration for color just about anywhere. Practice looking for harmonious color sets all around you, and try mimicking them in your designs. Many of the color combinations that you'll find appear in defined sets on the color wheel, but seeing them in a real-world context can help spark new ideas.

COLORS IN NATURE

Harmonious color schemes are especially prevalent in nature. You can find interesting color sets in leaves, flowers, stems, bark, wood, stones, and even water. Jewelry designs inspired by natural colors tend to remind people of nature, often subconsciously. They can invoke feelings of happiness and tranquility.

COLORS IN ARTWORK

When you notice a painting or other artwork with colors that you love, try incorporating those same colors into a jewelry design. Pay attention to how the colors are used in the artwork. Is one color used more than others? How many different shades of each color are used? Experiment with similar approaches in your designs.

FAQ

Can I make replicas of other jewelry designs, or would that be a violation of copyright?

Generally speaking, *copyright* is the legal right to create a particular design. When you complete a new, original piece of jewelry, you automatically hold its copyright. This means that no one else is allowed to copy that design without your permission. Of course, jewelry made by other artisans is also protected by copyright. You cannot copy another artisan's design unless he or she gives you permission.

Sometimes, artisans grant *limited* permission for anyone to copy their designs. This is often the case with project books and magazines. Typically, the artisan who designed a project grants limited permission for you to copy the design for personal use, but not for commercial use. (That is, you are not allowed to sell copies of the jewelry in the project.)

Copyright laws differ from country to country, and they can be complicated. For more information about how copyright laws apply to you, try searching the Internet or doing some research at your local library.

SYMBOLIC COLORS

If you'd like a design to communicate a message or represent something important to you, consider using symbolic colors. Color sets that symbolize nations, teams, or holidays are typical examples, but you can also use more subtle symbolic colors. For example, the color blue can symbolize peace or the winter season. You can design jewelry with obvious or subtle color associations to suit your mood and purpose.

STYLISTIC COLORS

Some colors are more appropriate for particular styles of jewelry than others. For example, if you'd like to give your jewelry a strong Victorian feel, you should use colors that were popular during that era (like soft blues, rose pinks, rusts, and grays). If you'd rather make trendy jewelry, use color schemes featured in current fashion or home décor magazines. Take some time to research the styles that interest you, and learn which colors work best for them.

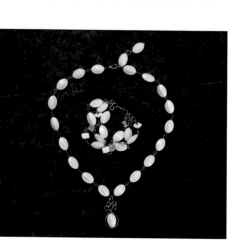

Weight, Texture, and Proportion

A jewelry design's *weight* and *texture* are influenced by the size of components that you use and the materials that those components are made from. Its sense of *proportion* is affected by the way you arrange different sizes of components within the design.

WEIGHT

Logically, heavier materials and components add more physical weight to jewelry than lighter ones. Heavier materials include metals, gemstone, and many ceramics. Wood, cord, bone, and plastics tend to be much lighter. When you plan a new design, think about how heavy it will be. Weight considerations can be specific to the type of jewelry you make. Here are a few examples.

Necklaces

Weight is especially important for necklaces because it affects how they *lay*. The lay of a necklace describes how it positions itself on the body when worn. For example, a lightweight pendant on a long necklace chain may not lie properly because it's not heavy enough to remain centered on the wearer's chest. Proper lay can be especially crucial for necklaces with fringe, drops, or tiers. With those designs, you may need to experiment with different components and weight distributions.

Bracelets

As a general rule, lighter-weight bracelets are more comfortable than heavier ones. Be aware that if one section of a bracelet is heavier than the rest, the heavier part may slide to the underside of the wrist when the bracelet is worn. If you would like the clasp to fall to the underside of the wrist, then you may need to make it slightly heavier than the rest of the bracelet. You can use a heavy, solid metal clasp, or add weight to a lighter clasp by adorning it with a bead drop or charm.

Earrings

Earrings that are too heavy are uncomfortable to wear, and they can even damage earlobes over time. You can control the weight of your earring designs by using smaller-gauge wire and small beads, and by limiting the number of larger beads or drops to one per earring.

Pins and Brooches

Improperly weighted brooches can tip forward and pull or stretch the fabric they're attached to. As a general rule, try to make your brooches relatively lightweight. For heavier pieces, attach the pin back higher up on the design rather than at its middle.

TEXTURE

You can add interest to any design by using varieties of textural components. Beads are especially effective for adding texture. Experiment by combining different types of beads and materials in your designs, especially when you use a limited color palette.

PROPORTION

Proportion refers to the relationship between individual parts of a design and the design as a whole. Size is a very noticeable element of proportion. For example, when you make a beaded design using different sizes of beads, its look will change depending on how you arrange the beads by size. Proportion can also apply to color; a design that is predominantly one color has a different feel than a design where two or more colors are used in equal amounts.

Try to achieve proportions that are pleasing to the eye. Consider using gradual transitions in size and color rather than sharp contrasts. Step back from a design and look for its *visual flow*, or how your eye moves along the piece. Are you smoothly drawn to the focal point of the design, or do you get distracted? Also think about a design's symmetry. Is it balanced, or does it seem somehow out of equilibrium? Don't worry if you find this challenging at first. Through practice and experimentation, your awareness of proportion will become second nature.

Motif and Pattern

Jewelry designs often contain repetitions of distinct elements or themes. You can achieve this effect by creating *motifs* and assembling *patterns*.

A motif is a self-defined element in a design; it has a pleasing and complete look all by itself. In jewelry design, a motif can be a grouping of beads, a setting of stones, or a stylistic piece like an ornate connector. By arranging motifs in a defined order, you create a pattern.

Motifs and patterns can be large or small, and simple or complex. You can repeat a single motif throughout a design or use an arrangement of different motifs. A motif may be defined by colors, textures, sizes, materials, or a combination of design factors. Here are some ideas of how you might use motifs and patterns in your jewelry projects. See if you can think of others as you work through this book and learn new techniques.

- Repeat a grouping of several beads of similar size and harmonious color.

- Repeat a grouping of beads of graduating size and harmonious color.

- Create two or three bead motif groupings and repeat them in the same order.

- Group together materials with certain textures, and repeat them throughout the design.

- Place a connector, accent bead, or drop at defined intervals within a design.

- Repeat the same series of knots between beads.

One of the best ways to harness your creativity is to keep an active record of your ideas. When you're ready to create a new design or shop for supplies, you can refer to your collection of ideas for instant inspiration.

CLIPPINGS AND PHOTOS

Make a habit of saving images and articles that catch your attention because of their design insight, color schemes, or information. Fashion and home décor magazines can be great sources of inspiration, and publications devoted to jewelry making and beading are full of colorful photos, free projects, and tips. (See page 284 in the Appendix for a list of popular titles.) Keep some scissors handy to clip images and articles as you find them. You can mount your clippings on photo-album pages or glue them onto paperboard sheets that you keep in a loose-leaf binder. If you use paperboard, you can also use the pages to jot down notes and design ideas related to each clipping.

DESIGN SKETCHES

Many jewelry artisans keep a sketch book for making rough drawings of designs before attempting to craft them. Sketches allow you to experiment with colors, motifs, and patterns using minimal time and resources. You don't need to draw well to make useful sketches; your pictures can be very rough, as long as they help you imagine and record your ideas. Try using a soft lead pencil (and a good eraser) for initial sketches. You can add color with colored pencils, pens, or even crayons. Experiment to find out which tools and techniques work best for you.

LIBRARY AND WEB-SITE NOTES

Today there are many books, magazines, and Web sites devoted to jewelry making and beading. As you collect information and design ideas from those sources, it can be challenging to keep them organized. You may want to devise a way to make it easier to find specific resources when you need them. One option is to keep a special journal just for that purpose. Record the titles of books, and list the page numbers of projects or techniques that you found especially interesting. With magazines, record the volume, issue number, or date along with your notes and page numbers. For Web sites, record or bookmark URL addresses. As an alternative, try keeping your notes and references on your computer or in an online blog.

3

Basic Bead Stringing Techniques

Basic bead stringing is a good place to begin your journey into jewelry making. The techniques are simple, and you can find all the beads and supplies you'll need at any local bead shop or craft store. In this chapter, you'll learn how to lay out a design and string beads using the most popular bead-stringing materials. You'll discover that the method used to finish the ends of a beaded strand depends on the type of stringing material you choose.

Lay Out a Design

You can save time and create more satisfying jewelry by laying out your beaded designs before you begin stringing.

Get Ready

ARRANGE THE BEADS AND FINDINGS

Using a bead board is a great way to lay out and organize your designs, whether you're following project instructions or creating a new design from scratch. It's much easier to rearrange beads when they are sitting on the board than to restring a beaded strand later.

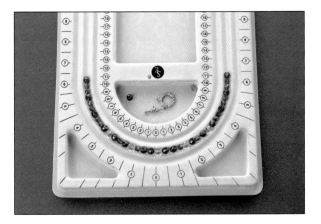

Most boards have measurement marks to help you keep track of strand lengths. It's not uncommon for these measurements to be slightly off, so it's a good idea to check the accuracy of your board's measurements with a tape measure before using it for the first time. If needed, you can make corrections by marking the board with a permanent marker.

Keep in mind the design principles from Chapter 2 as you arrange your beads and findings on the board. If you're creating a design that includes larger focal beads, try positioning those beads first; then fill in the design with your smaller accent and spacer beads.

If your design has a clasp, lay the clasp pieces on the board along with the beads. This way, you can see how the clasp design looks with your beads and how the clasp will affect the jewelry's length.

TIP

Bead Reaming

Design layout is a good time to inspect your beads for rough or sharp drill holes. Use a bead reamer to smooth the holes so that they won't damage your stringing material later.

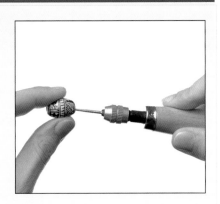

Simply choose a reamer with a tip that fits into the hole of your bead, and gently twist the reamer—or the bead—back and forth a few times. Some crafters keep the end of the reamer wet by dipping it into water occasionally while they work. This lubricates the reamer and may help it to last longer.

You can also use a reamer to slightly enlarge holes in pearls, which are very soft. Use care when reaming holes in glass beads to avoid chipping them.

DETERMINE THE JEWELRY LENGTH

You should decide how long you want your jewelry to be before you begin stringing beads. The length you choose depends on the size of the person who will wear it, and how you would like the jewelry to look. Here are some typical length measurements for necklaces, bracelets, and anklets.

	Style or Size	*Common Measurements*
Necklaces		
Women's	Collar	12–15 inches
	Choker	15–16 inches
	Pendant length	18–19 inches
	Matinee length	20–24 inches
	Opera length	28–32 inches
	Rope length	40–45 inches
	Traditional Lariat (has no clasp)	48+ inches
Men's	Choker	18 inches
	Medium length	19–23 inches
	Long	24+ inches
Bracelets		
Women's	Small	6–7 inches
	Medium	7½–8 inches
	Large	8½–9 inches
Men's	Small	8–9 inches
	Medium	9½–10 inches
	Large	10½–11 inches
Anklets		
Women's	Small–Medium	9 inches
	Medium–Large	10 inches
Men's	Small–Medium	11–12 inches
	Medium–Large	13–14 inches

Select a Stringing Material

As you may recall from Chapter 1, there are many bead-stringing materials. Some are very soft and require that you use a beading needle. A needle may be built into one end of the string, or you may need to attach one yourself. Other stringing materials are relatively stiff and do not require a needle.

By experimenting, you'll discover which materials you most enjoy working with, and which match your personal design style.

How to Select a Stringing Material

Start thinking about the type of stringing material you'll use during the design phase of your project. The type and size of stringing material you need depends on the textures, sizes, and weights of beads in your design and how you'd like your jewelry to look, feel, and wear.

Use the chart on the next page to become familiar with how the most popular bead-stringing materials can be used. To review the definitions of these materials, refer to Chapter 1.

FAQ

What is "tiger tail," and when would I use it?

Tiger tail is sometimes used as a generic name for all nylon-coated beading wire. However, it most commonly refers to early, lower-tech versions of the beading wire that most jewelry artisans use today.

Original tiger tail was a revolutionary stringing material because it was strong and didn't require a beading needle. Its main drawback was that it kinked easily. Not only did this affect the appearance and lay of some jewelry, but the kinked portions of cable tended to weaken and break. The newer beading wires are softer and more resistant to kinking than those early versions.

Basic tiger tail is still sold by many suppliers, and it's less expensive than the newer wires. You may want to use it for heavier necklaces, which are less likely to kink.

Material	Best for	Needle Required?	Special Considerations
Beading Wire	Most bead types, sizes, weights, and materials.	No.	Be sure to choose the correct weight and flexibility for your design.
Silk Cord	Lighter-weight glass, gemstone, or pearl beads.	Yes. Look for cards of silk cord with twisted-wire needles already attached.	Silk cord is prone to stretching and can be frayed and broken by sharp-edged or heavy beads. If the pre-attached needle breaks off before you finish stringing, it may be difficult to finish your project.
Braided Nylon Cord or Line	Lighter-weight glass, gemstone, and pearl beads; seed beads.	Maybe. Some brands and styles do not require a needle, and some do.	May be less prone to stretching and slightly more durable than silk, but may also be less flexible.
Linen Cord	Light- to medium-weight beads in most materials.	No.	Linen cord is available in a variety of colors and is popular for braiding and cord weaving. Purchase it pre-waxed for easy beading.
Cotton Cord	Most bead types, sizes, weights, and materials.	No.	Cotton cord is a nice alternative to leather cord. It is also available waxed.
Leather, Suede, and Rubber Cord	Beads with larger holes in most sizes, weights, and materials.	No.	The quality of leather cord varies, depending on how and where it is made. Typically, more expensive leather cord will be softer and smoother in texture. Less expensive leather may be rough and have a funny smell.
Satin Cord (Rattail)	Light- or medium-weight beads with larger, smooth holes.	Maybe. If needed, use a big eye or twisted wire needle.	Rattail is a very soft cord that can fray easily. It should only be used for very casual jewelry, or jewelry that will not be worn often.
Ribbon	Light- to medium-weight beads with larger, smooth holes.	Usually, yes. Use a big-eye needle for ribbon and similar large, but collapsible, materials.	Ribbon is available in a variety of sizes and weights. Make sure that the size and weight of your beads don't visually overpower the ribbon, or vice versa.
Stretch Cord	Lighter-weight beads with smooth holes.	Maybe. If needed use a twisted wire needle.	Stretch cord is especially prone to breakage because it must be stretched to take the jewelry on and off. Use the thickest cord possible, and size your pieces not to be worn tightly.
Memory Wire	Light- to medium-weight beads in relatively durable materials.	No.	Lower-quality memory wire may be susceptible to being stretched out and losing its shape. Also, some people find memory wire uncomfortable to wear.
Beading Thread	Seed beads.	Yes. Use a beading needle.	Beading thread is very thin and most commonly used for beaded lace and bead weaving. It can also be used for simple, strung jewelry, but be careful to use only very small, smooth, lightweight beads.

Select a Finishing Method

You probably already know how to thread a bead onto wire or string. A bigger challenge is deciding how to *finish* the ends of a beaded strand. Finishing refers to the techniques used to close strand ends so that the beads don't fall off, and so that you can attach a clasp. Usually, you will want to finish one end of a strand before you begin stringing beads. You'll finish the other end after all of your beads are strung.

How to Select a Finishing Method

The chart below indicates which finishing methods and findings are recommended for the most popular types of stringing material. You will learn how to apply each of these methods in the following sections of this chapter.

String Material	Common Finishing Methods
Beading Wire	Crimp beads, crimp tubes, crimp ends, or bead- or button-clasps*; the smallest sizes can also be knotted.
Silk Cord	French bullion wire, clamshell bead tips, or bead- or button-clasps*.
Braided Nylon Cord or Line	French bullion wire, clamshell bead tips, or bead- or button-clasps*.
Linen Cord	Fold-over crimp ends, larger clamshell bead tips, or bead- or button-clasps*.
Cotton Cord	Bullet ends, coil ends, or fold-over crimp ends, or bead- or button-clasps*.
Leather, Suede, and Rubber Cord	Coil ends, end caps, or fold-over crimp ends. Leather and suede cord can also be finished with bead- or button-clasps*, or with knot-and-loop closures.
Satin Cord	Fold-over crimp ends.
Ribbon	Fold-over crimp ends or clamps.
Stretch Cord	Knotting.
Beading Thread	Clamshell bead tips, or bead- or button-clasps*.
Memory Wire	Looping with round nose pliers or glue-on end caps.

* Bead- and button-clasps and knot-and-loop closures are more advanced techniques that are covered in Chapter 4.

TIP

Choosing a Clasp

There are a lot of pre-made clasp styles that you can use. When you choose a clasp, consider how the various styles of clasps function. Simple hook clasps are easy to use, but they may not be secure enough for lighter-weight bracelets or necklaces.

Toggle clasps have an elegant look, but you should provide a little extra length in your toggle-clasped designs (see the photo on the right). To close a toggle clasp, you need to pull its bar end into and completely through its loop end, and then allow the bar to rest back inside the loop. If your jewelry isn't long enough to accommodate this movement, it could weaken over time from being pulled too tightly.

Spring clasps and lobster clasps usually provide a secure closure, but larger fingers or arthritic hands may have difficulty using them. To minimize frustration, choose larger sizes of these clasps, especially for bracelets. In Chapter 1, you can review the various types of clasps that are available.

Before you begin a beading-wire project, you need to decide which wire to use, based on the types and sizes of beads in your design.

How to Select the Proper Beading Wire

Beading wire packaging is typically marked with up to three separate measurements. Here's a brief explanation of each.

NUMBER OF STRANDS

As explained in Chapter 1, beading wire is made up of many small steel strands that are wound together. Typically, the number of these strands determines the beading wire's flexibility. Beading wire that contains more steel strands is more flexible than beading wire with fewer strands.

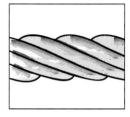

More-flexible beading wire has a softer feel and resists kinking better than less-flexible beading wire. However, more-flexible beading wire is usually more expensive than less-flexible varieties.

BEADING WIRE SIZE

Beading wire size is denoted by its diameter. Smaller-diameter beading wire is recommended for smaller, lighter-weight beads. Larger beading wire is preferred for larger-holed or heavier beads. If you use beading wire that is smaller than recommended for the beads you're using, your jewelry may break prematurely.

Beading wire diameter is usually measured in thousandths of an inch. You can find nylon-coated beading wire ranging from about .010 inch (very small) to about .024 inch (large).

Use the following chart as a general reference when deciding which wire to use for a given project. Refer to the wire manufacturer's literature for product-specific recommendations.

Beading Wire Diameter (Inches)	Best Used for
.010	Very lightweight beads, such as small pearls and seed beads.
.012–.014	Lightweight beads with very small holes, including crystal beads, seed beads, and pearls.
.015–.019	Lightweight to heavy beads, including beads made from stone and metal.
.020–.021	Medium-weight to heavy beads, especially gemstone beads with uneven hole diameters.
.024–.026	Large and heavy beads, or any beads with larger holes, including trade beads, glass, and stone.
.030–.036	The largest, heaviest beads made of glass, metal, or stone.

POUND TEST STRENGTH

Some beading wire is also labeled with its *pound test strength*. Manufacturers use this measurement to indicate wire strength. It denotes the maximum weight the wire can hold under testing conditions without breaking.

Pound test strength is a good general indicator of how strong is a certain size and type of wire. However, do not take it too literally. Many factors affect the durability of your jewelry, including how much friction is caused by the beads and end findings. Therefore, a necklace strung on "7-pound test" wire would not necessarily hold up under the weight of a 7-pound pendant.

CONTINUED ON NEXT PAGE

How to Attach Crimps to Beading Wire

Using crimps is the best way to finish beading wire. As described in Chapter 1, there are three main types of crimps: crimp beads, crimp tubes, and crimp ends. You can attach crimp beads and crimp ends using chain nose pliers, and you can use either chain nose pliers or crimping pliers to attach crimp tubes.

ATTACH CRIMP BEADS OR CRIMP TUBES USING CHAIN NOSE PLIERS

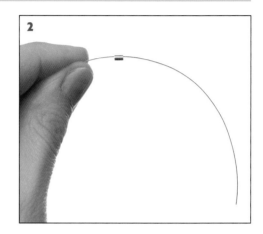

1 Beginning with a length of beading wire about 6 inches longer than the desired jewelry length, string a crimp bead or tube onto one end.

2 Position the crimp about 3 inches from the end of the beading wire.

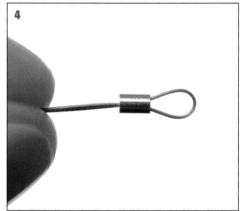

3 Holding the crimp in place with one hand, use the other hand to pull the end of the beading wire back into and through the crimp.

4 Continue holding the crimp in place, and gently pull the beading wire end until you have created a small loop.

Note: Be sure that this loop is large enough to loosely hold a jump ring.

5 Use chain nose pliers to squeeze the crimp flat. The crimp should now be secured over both strands of beading wire.

6 Using small wire cutters or nippers, trim the tail of extra beading wire close to the crimp.

The crimp is now in place, as shown here (a).

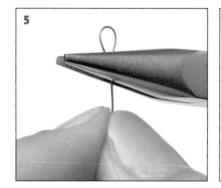

7 After stringing on all of the beads in your design, string on the second crimp and position it close to the last bead.

8 Repeat Step 3 to begin making a loop.

9 When the loop starts to become small and the beading wire more difficult to pull through using your fingers, use chain nose pliers to gently hold the crimp close to the last bead, while you continue pulling the wire to complete the loop.

10 Repeat Steps 5–6.

11 Attach a clasp part to each end of the strand using jump rings.

The completed strand is shown here.

CONTINUED ON NEXT PAGE

TIP

Learn How to Open and Close Jump Rings

You will probably use jump rings in most of your jewelry creations. It's important to learn how to open and close them properly to ensure that they are not weakened and will remain closed during wear.

To open a jump ring, hold it in front of you using two pairs of chain nose pliers, with the ring opening facing upward. Gently twist one end of the ring toward you and the other end away from you. To close the ring, twist the ends back in the opposite direction, and wiggle them together until the ring is completely closed.

Never pull or push the ends of a jump ring with a side-to-side motion. This can weaken the metal and deform the ring's shape.

ATTACH CRIMP TUBES USING CRIMPING PLIERS

If you don't like the look of flattened crimp beads or tubes, you can use specialty crimping pliers—instead of chain nose pliers—to make a crimp tube appear more rounded.

1 When you're ready to close the crimp tube, place it inside the V-shaped indentation in the pliers.

2 Use your fingers to position both beading wire strands so that each strand is up against one side of the tube, on either side of the "V" in the indentation.

3 Gently squeeze down the pliers.

4 Turn the beading wire sideways so that the "V" shape you just created is pointed to the side.

5 Place the crimp into the rounded indentation in the pliers, and squeeze them closed over the crimp.

The final rounded crimp is shown here (a).

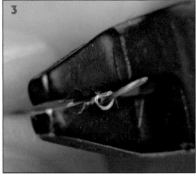

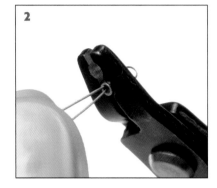

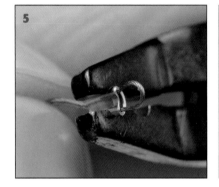

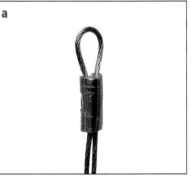

FAQ

How do I know which size of crimp to use?

Crimp beads are available in different diameters, and crimp tubes come in different diameters and lengths. Both measurements typically range from 1–3mm.

Interestingly, many artisans disagree on which crimps are the best to use. For example, some believe that long crimp tubes are more secure than short ones, while others don't like the look of long tubes and insist that short tubes work well if attached properly.

You may need to experiment to see which styles and sizes you like best. In the meantime, ask the manufacturer or supplier of your beading wire which sizes they recommend for the beading wires they offer. The most popular beading wire makers have Web sites with this information, and the best jewelry supply companies provide similar information in their catalogs or on their own Web sites. Refer to the Appendix for a list of suppliers who may be of help.

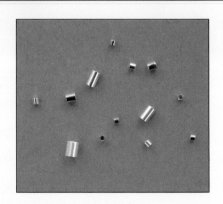

ATTACH CRIMP ENDS

Crimp ends have pre-attached rings or clasp parts. You crimp them directly to the ends of your beading wire.

① Insert the first wire end into the opening in the crimp end.

② Use chain nose pliers to squeeze down on the collapsible part of the crimp (usually the middle area).

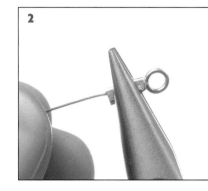

③ After stringing on all of your beads, use the tips of one pair of chain nose pliers to hold the beading wire just after the last bead.

④ Trim the end of the beading wire short, so that it will fit inside the crimp end as far as possible.

⑤ Insert the beading wire end into the crimp end, and use a second pair of chain nose pliers to squeeze down the crimp.

The final beaded strand with the crimp ends in place is shown here (a).

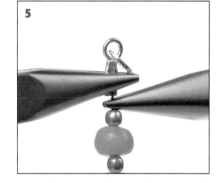

CONTINUED ON NEXT PAGE

TIP

Making Beading-Wire Jewelry Last Longer

Unfortunately, all strung jewelry eventually needs to be restrung. Even steel beading wire weakens and deteriorates over time. As a bead jewelry artisan, your job is to make sure your jewelry lasts as long as possible. The following tips will make that task easier.

1. Always use quality crimps. Less expensive, base-metal crimp beads are more likely to crack and break than sterling-silver crimp beads or higher-quality crimp tubes.

2. Leave space in your design. Do not string beads too tightly. This creates friction, which the beading wire manufacturers say is the number one cause of wire breakage. When you have a finished strand laid out flat, you should be able to see a little beading wire showing through, near the ends. (Keep in mind that this will not be as noticeable when the strand is worn, because it will be curved into a rounded shape.)

3. Use the proper beading wire. Take the time to determine which beading wire flexibility and size rating is best for a given project. Refer to the chart on page 47 for help.

Ways to Hide Crimps

By now, you may have noticed that crimp beads and tubes are not the most attractive elements of your designs. You can improve the appearance of tubes by using crimping pliers, but the best way to deal with the problem is to hide your crimps altogether.

Try using one of these techniques to give your work a more professional appearance.

USE CRIMP COVERS

Crimp covers are special findings that you can secure over crimp tubes. They make crimps look more like beads so that they blend with your design. Most are intended for use with crimp tubes that have been closed with crimping pliers. You use the rounded indentation of the crimping pliers to attach the covers to your crimps.

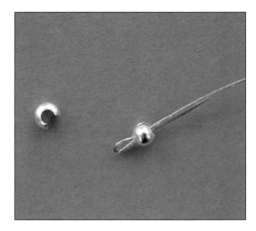

USE BEAD TIPS

Bead tips are most commonly used to cover finishing-knots in cord. You can also use them to cover crimps. Because bead tips have metal "claws" for attaching jump rings and clasps, you won't need to make wire loops after your crimps. Instead, just attach a crimp to the end of your wire, and then cover the crimp with a bead tip. For more information on using bead tips, see "String and Finish Beading Cord," later in this chapter.

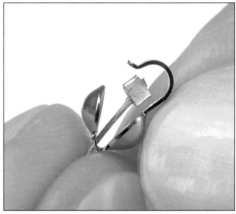

USE BULLET ENDS

Once you have some basic wire-wrap skills, you can use small-diameter bullet ends to hide crimps. Use a head pin to pull the end of the strand into the bullet end, and then use round nose pliers to loop and wrap the end of the pin to hold the strand in place. You will learn to use this technique to make multiple-strand bead jewelry using cone ends in Chapter 4.

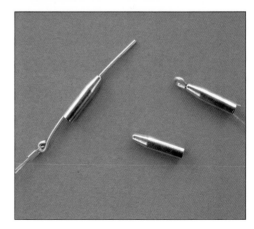

Ways to Cover Beading Wire Loops

The loops at the ends of your beading-wire jewelry probably won't be too unsightly, but they do contrast a little with the look of metal findings. Bullet ends and bead tips provide a workable solution by hiding loops, or eliminating the need for them entirely.

Here are some other possibilities for disguising beading-wire loops in your designs.

USE FRENCH BULLION WIRE

This tiny, coiled wire is most often used for finishing silk cord. Its main purpose is to protect cord from breakage, but bullion can also be used with beading wire to give end loops a metallic look.

To use it, string a short length of bullion onto your beading wire before sliding it back through the crimp to make a loop. For more information on using bullion, see "Use French Bullion Wire on Cord," later in this chapter.

USE WIRE GUARDIANS

Wire Guardians are specialty findings that are designed to protect beading wire loops, while also giving them a more professional appearance. You attach them by stringing them onto your beading wire after a crimp bead, before you string the wire back through the crimp (similar to bullion wire).

You may want to experiment with Wire Guardians to see how you like them. They are not intended to completely cover the beading wire, and you should be careful not to string them too tightly. For best results, always follow the manufacturer's instructions carefully.

FAQ

What are Scrimps?

Scrimps are specialty findings made by the same company that invented Wire Guardians. You can use Scrimps in place of regular crimp beads or crimp tubes.

You attach a Scrimp by stringing it onto your beading wire as you would a crimp bead. Then, you use a screwdriver to fasten a tiny screw in the side of the Scrimp. The screw locks down over the wires inside, holding them in place.

Scrimps can give your jewelry a more professional appearance than traditional crimps. However, they do not cover beading-wire loops. You'll still need to use bullion or Wire Guardians for that purpose.

The best way to finish cord is with knots and end findings. Depending on the type of cord you use, you may or may not need a beading needle. (See the chart on page 45.) Always be sure to use a style of end finding that is appropriate for the type of cord you're using.

Needles Used with Cord

Use a beading needle when your cord is too thin and soft to thread directly through your beads. You can attach a needle by threading it onto the cord, doubling the cord back, and tying the double strands together with a square knot.

If you'd prefer to string your beads on a single strand, you can tie a small double-overhand knot behind the needle to hold it onto the cord. (See "Tie an Overhand Knot" later in this chapter.) Choose a needle with an eye small enough to keep the knot from slipping through, and make sure the knot can pass through your beads. Another option is to leave the cord unknotted, and just be careful not to let the needle fall off while stringing.

Here's a look at the most common needles used with bead-stringing cord.

TWISTED WIRE NEEDLES

Twisted wire needles are made from thin, twisted strands of steel or brass wire. A wire loop at the end forms the eye. This is the kind of needle you find on needle-attached cards of silk cord. You can also purchase them separately.

The wire in twisted wire needles is relatively soft. You can collapse the eyes to fit them through smaller-holed beads.

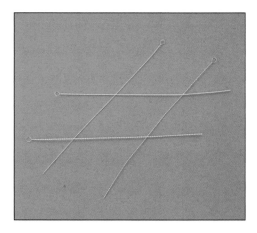

BEADING NEEDLES

Beading needles look like very thin, sharp sewing needles. They are popular for stringing seed beads on very thin cord, like braided nylon, or on beading thread. You will use them for bead weaving in Chapter 5. These needles look like very thin, sharp sewing needles, and their eyes are small enough to pass through tiny bead holes. If you have trouble threading them, try using a special beading-needle threader designed specifically for beading needles and beading thread. They are available at some bead shops and in beading supply catalogs.

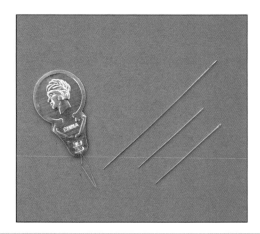

BIG EYE NEEDLES

Big eye needles look like long, flexible sewing needles that are slit length-wise down the middle. Instead of threading your stringing material through a regular eye, you string it through the slit.

You can use these needles to thread suede cord through beads with larger holes, or to string beads on ribbon.

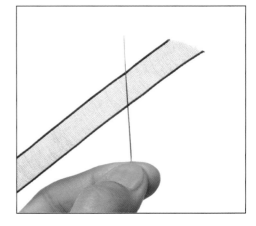

MAKE A FAUX NEEDLE

Sometimes you don't need a real needle on your cord, just a way to stiffen the end and keep it from unraveling as you bead. Try dipping the end of the cord in clear nail polish or instant bond glue and allowing it to dry. This creates a kind of faux needle, which you can simply trim off when you finish stringing.

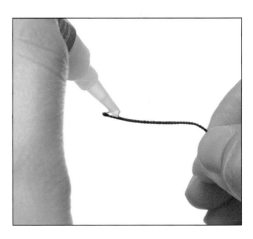

CONTINUED ON NEXT PAGE

Knots Used with Cord

The most common knots you'll use on cord are the *overhand knot*, the *double-overhand knot,* and the *square knot.* (These knots are also used with beading thread; see "String and Finish Beading Thread" later in this chapter.)

TIE AN OVERHAND KNOT

You can use a single overhand knot to knot between two beads.

1 Pull the end of your cord back up and over itself to form a loop.

2 Thread the cord end through the loop.

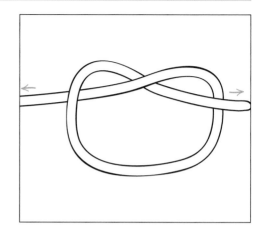

3 Pull the cord end to tighten the knot. The photo on the right shows a close-up of the overhand knot you just created.

Note: *You will learn how to properly place overhand knots between beads in Chapter 4.*

TIE A DOUBLE-OVERHAND KNOT

A double-overhand knot is simply one overhand knot tied on top of another. You can use it to finish single cord ends.

1 Make an overhand knot.

2 Repeat this procedure, slowly pulling a second overhand knot into position over, or just next to, the first knot.

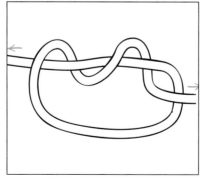

TIE A SQUARE KNOT

Use a square knot to tie together two cord ends, or to tie a cord back onto itself after making a loop.

1 Beginning with one strand in each hand, wrap the left strand around the right strand. The strands will look twisted around each other.

2 Now wrap the right strand over and around the left strand, creating a second twist.

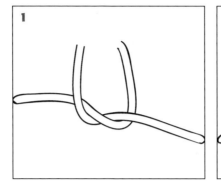

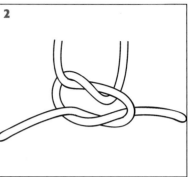

3 Pull down the second twist snugly onto the first twist.

4 Pull the two strand ends to tighten the knot.

CONTINUED ON NEXT PAGE

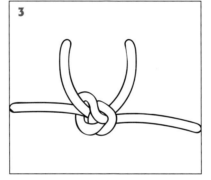

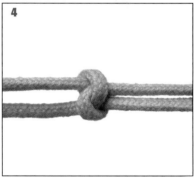

FAQ

How is a square knot different from a double-overhand knot?

The most important difference between these knots is the number of strands involved.

You use a double-overhand knot when you're knotting a single strand. You make a square knot when you're fastening two strands together.

As you probably noticed, the procedures for making the two knots are also a little different. The double-overhand knot loops back around itself. With the square knot, one strand wraps around the other.

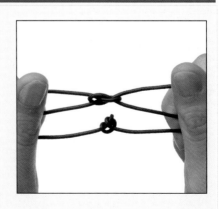

Ways to Keep Beads from Falling Off of Cord Before Finishing

Usually, you finish one end of beading cord, string on all of your beads, and then finish the other end. However, there are times when you will want to string your beads before you finish the ends.

For example, if you make a long necklace with no clasp, you may want to string all of the beads first, and then tie the ends together with a single square knot. Alternatively, you may want to string several beaded strands and tie them all together at the ends. You'll see how this method works for multiple-strand necklaces and tassels in Chapter 4.

When you use one of these techniques, you will need a way to keep beads from falling off of the cord while you work. Here are the most common methods

USE MASKING TAPE

Fold a piece of masking or drafting tape around the first cord end. Make sure you leave enough of an extra "tail" between the tape and the end of the cord to knot the strand later. To remove the tape, simply peel it apart. Alternatively, you can tape the first cord end directly to your work surface.

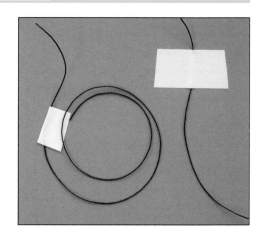

USE BEAD STOPPERS

Bead Stoppers are specially designed little coils of stainless steel wire. You squeeze the looped ends with your fingers to open the coil, slip the cord inside, and then release the ends to clamp the cord.

USE ALLIGATOR CLIPS

You can also use small, metal alligator clips to clamp cord. They are especially useful for larger-diameter cord.

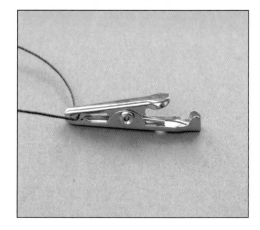

USE BEAD TIPS ON CORD

Bead tips look like little clamshells that close over a knot. They have an open end loop, or "claw," which you can attach to a jump ring and clasp.

1 Thread your cord into the hole at the base of the bead tip, with the clamshell opening facing the end of the cord.

2 Tie a double-overhand knot between the end of the cord and the bead tip.

3 Trim off the end of the cord close to the knot.

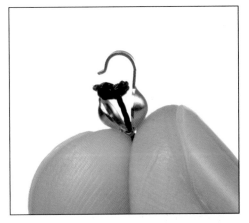

4 Slide the bead tip up over the knot.

5 Apply a drop of E6000 glue to the knot, inside the bead tip.

6 Use flat nose pliers to close the clamshell over the knot, with the knot contained inside.

7 After stringing on all of your beads, repeat Steps 1–6 to finish the other end of the cord.

> **Note:** If necessary, use a beading awl to position the second knot inside the second bead tip. For more information on using a beading awl with knots, see Chapter 4.

8 Use chain nose pliers to open each claw, and slip in a jump ring that you've already attached to a clasp finding.

9 Close down each claw using chain nose pliers.

The bead tips with the clasps attached are shown here (a).

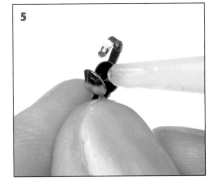

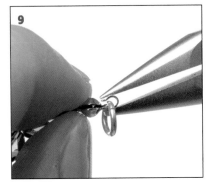

CONTINUED ON NEXT PAGE

USE FRENCH BULLION WIRE ON CORD

French bullion wire can protect your end loops from damage, while giving them a more professional appearance.

1 String on a bead with a hole large enough for the cord to pass through twice.

2 Use sharp side cutters to cut a length of bullion about ½ inch long.

3 String the bullion onto the cord, next to the bead.

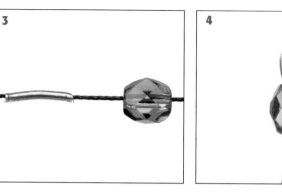

4 Thread the cord back into the bead to create a loop in the bullion, leaving a cord tail of several inches at the end.

5 Tie a square knot at the base of the bullion loop.

6 If desired, apply a tiny drop of E6000 glue to the knot.

7 String on the beads for your design, and repeat Steps 1–4 to apply bullion to the other end of the cord.

8 To conceal the cord tails at each knot, use a twisted wire beading needle to thread them back into the beaded strand.

9 Attach clasp findings to each bullion loop using jump rings.

The bullion loop with clasps attached are shown here (a).

USE COIL ENDS

You can use coil ends to finish larger-diameter cord, like satin rattail and leather. Choose a size that fits snugly over your cord.

1 After trimming your cord to the desired length, slide a coil end onto the end until the tip of the cord is flush with the top coil of the coil end.

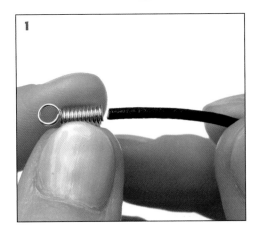

2 Use chain nose pliers to squeeze down the first coil of the coil end.

3 Turn the cord and squeeze evenly all the way around the first coil until it is securely attached to the cord.

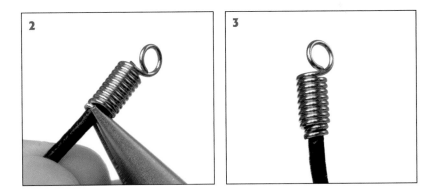

4 String the beads for your design.

5 Repeat Steps 1–4 to finish the other end.

Note: For added security, you can add a drop of E6000 glue near the end of the cord before attaching the coil end.

The coil ends with clasps attached is shown here.

CONTINUED ON NEXT PAGE

USE END CAPS

End caps work like coil ends but have a more formal look. Unlike coil ends, you must use glue to attach them.

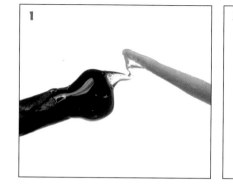

1 After trimming your cord to the desired length, apply a drop of E6000 glue to the last few millimeters of the cord end.

2 Slide an end cap over the end of the cord, as far as it will go.

3 Quickly wipe away any excess glue with a paper towel.

4 Gently string on the beads for your design, being careful not to dislodge the end cap.

Note: If the end cap moves, wait until the glue sets before stringing your beads.

5 Repeat Steps 1–2 to attach the other end cap.

6 Allow the glue to set for 24 hours.

7 Attach clasp findings to both end caps using jump rings.

The end caps with the clasp attached are shown here.

TIP

How can I make a simple pendant necklace?

You can make a simple cord necklace without using any beads at all. Slide a pendant with a pre-attached bail over larger-diameter cord made of leather, suede, or rubber. Finish the ends with coil ends, end caps, or fold-over crimps.

USE FOLD-OVER CRIMP ENDS

You can use fold-over crimp ends to finish soft or flat cord, like satin or suede. They also work for folded-over ends of ribbon (see the Tip below).

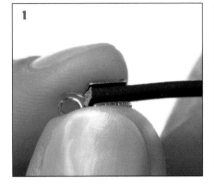

① After trimming your cord to the desired length, lay the very end of the cord inside the fold-over crimp, with the little "wings" of the crimp facing up.

   Note: *Fold-over crimp ends tend to hold pretty well on their own, but for added security you can add a drop of glue to the inside back of the crimp end before placing the cord inside.*

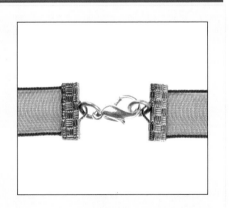

② Using chain nose or flat nose pliers, slowly squeeze down one wing of the crimp end, so that it clamps down securely onto the cord.

③ Repeat this process for the second wing, squeezing it down over the first.

④ String on all of the beads for your design.

⑤ Repeat Steps 1–4 to finish the other cord end.

⑥ Attach clasp findings to each crimp-end loop using jump rings to complete the cord ends.

CONTINUED ON NEXT PAGE

TIP

Finishing Ribbon

You can use ribbon as a stringing material instead of cord to hold a pendant (see the Briolette Pendant Ribbon Necklace project on page 251 in Chapter 11) or to string large-holed beads. As mentioned in Chapter 1, the most popular types of ribbon for jewelry are made of organza or satin. You can cut both of these materials easily with sharp scissors, and you can knot them using the same knots you use with cord.

The best findings to use for finishing ribbon are fold-over crimp ends and clamp ends. If you use a crimp end that is narrower than the ribbon, fold-over the very end of the ribbon before inserting it into the crimp end. If you use a clamp end, select one that is just slightly wider than the ribbon you use. Simply insert the end of the ribbon into the clamp end, and squeeze the clamp end closed using chain nose pliers. As with crimp ends, you can use a small amount of E6000 glue to help keep clamp ends secure.

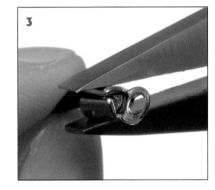

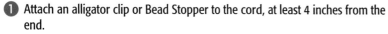
FINISH STRETCH CORD

Knotting is the best way to finish stretch cord. You can hide the knot by covering it with a larger-holed bead.

1 Attach an alligator clip or Bead Stopper to the cord, at least 4 inches from the end.

2 String the beads for your design, leaving at least 4 inches at the other end of the strand.

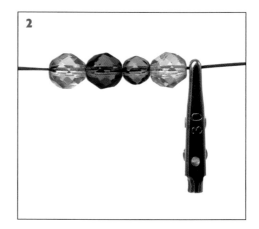

3 String on one last bead with a hole just large enough to cover a knot in the cord.

4 Holding both ends of the cord together, carefully remove the alligator clip or Bead Stopper.

5 Tie a square knot.

6 Apply a small drop of E6000 glue to the knot.

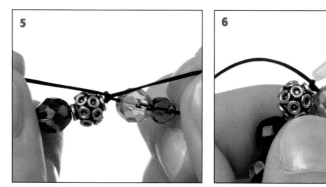

7 Slide the larger-holed bead over the knot.

8 Use a paper towel to wipe away any extra glue.

9 Allow the glue to set for 24 hours.

10 Use sharp scissors to trim off the extra tails of cord.

FAQ

How can I keep stretch cord jewelry from breaking?

Stretch cord usually wears and breaks sooner than other types of stringing material. The more the material is stretched, the faster it weakens.

Always apply these rules to make your stretch jewelry as durable as possible:

1. Don't string beads too tightly. Leave some wiggle room in your designs to reduce stress on the cord.
2. Size your jewelry so that it's not worn too snugly. The tighter stretch cord jewelry fits, the more stress it will endure when it's taken on and off.
3. Avoid using heavy or sharp-edged beads. The edges of bead holes can slice through stretch cord.
4. Use the largest-diameter stretch cord that will fit through your beads.
5. Avoid using crimp beads on stretch cord. Crimps have sharp edges that can cut through the cord over time.

Although beading thread is usually used for beaded lace and bead weaving (see Chapters 4 and 5), you can also use it to string simple strands of small, lightweight beads.

You can finish these designs with bead tips or French bullion wire, or with the bead-and-loop or button-and-loop clasps you'll learn to make in Chapter 4.

For information about thread and needle sizes, see Chapter 5.

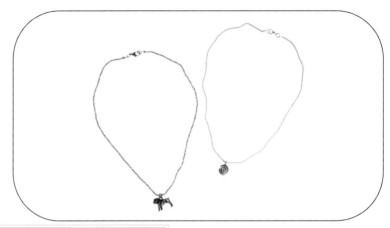

Ways to String and Finish a Simple Beading Thread Design

USE BEAD TIPS ON BEADING THREAD

You can attach bead tips to thread in a way similar to when you attach them to cord by closing the bead tips over knots. However, this method is more difficult with thread because thread is very thin. To keep the bead tips from slipping off, you will need to use much smaller bead tips or make multiple knots on top of one another. Here is an easier method that uses seed beads in place of knots.

1 Apply thread conditioner to a length of beading thread that is twice the desired jewelry length, plus about 20 inches.

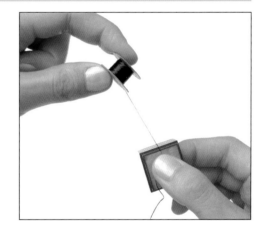

2 String on a beading needle, and position it halfway along the strand.

3 String on one seed bead and then a bead tip with the open clam shell facing the ends of the thread.

4 String on another seed bead.

5 Position the two seed beads and the bead tip about 8 inches from the ends of the thread.

6 String the needle back down through the bead tip and the first seed bead you strung on in Step 3.

7 Tie a square knot just below the first seed bead.

8 String on all the beads for the design.

9 At the other end of the beaded strand, string another bead tip (with the open clamshell facing the needle) and one more seed bead.

10 String the needle back through the bead tip and the very next seed bead in the strand, and tie a double overhand knot.

CONTINUED ON NEXT PAGE

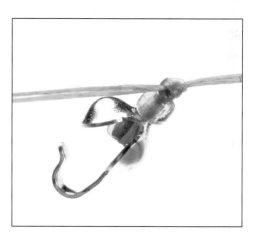

⑪ String the needle back through the next 2 inches of beads in the strand and bring it out again.

⑫ Trim off the needle and thread close to the strand.

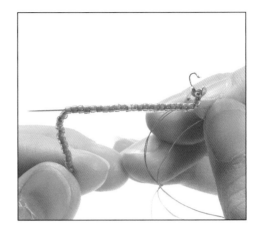

⑬ Go back to the first end of the strand and thread the needle onto one of the thread tails, and then string back through the strand and trim it off, as you did in Steps 11–12.

⑭ Repeat Step 13 for the other thread tail.

⑮ Use chain nose pliers to close each bead tip and use jump rings to attach clasp findings.

The bead tips with the clasps attached are shown here.

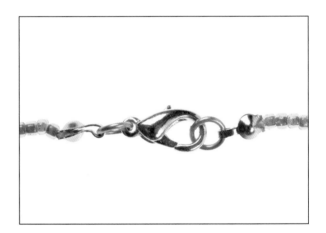

FAQ

How can I keep beads from falling off of beading thread before I finish the ends?

As with cord, there may be times when you want to string all your beads onto beading thread before you finish either of the ends. Although you can use the same techniques for holding beads onto thread as you can for cord (see page 58 earlier in this chapter), these methods do not always work as well with thread because of its small diameter. Moreover, tape and clamps are especially prone to slip off of beading thread that has been treated with slippery thread conditioner.

A better way to keep beads on unfinished thread is to use a *stop bead*. A stop bead is typically a seed bead, and it's the very first bead you string onto the thread, but it does not become part of your design. After you string on the stop bead, thread back through it once or twice, pulling the thread taut to hold the stop bead in place. As you string the beads for your design, the stop bead should keep them from falling off. When you're ready to finish your design, use the needle to loosen the thread around the stop bead and remove it from the strand. You will use stop beads often when you practice the tasks in Chapter 5, "Bead Weaving."

USE FRENCH BULLION WIRE ON BEADING THREAD

You can also use French bullion wire on thread in a way similar to when you use it on cord.

1 Prepare your thread by completing Steps 1–2 of "Use Bead Tips on Beading Thread."

2 Complete all of the steps for "Use French Bullion Wire on Cord," earlier in this chapter, using the beading thread in place of cord and the beading needle in place of the big eye needle.

The ends are now complete, as shown here.

FAQ

Why do my bead tips only have half a clamshell?

Traditionally, there was a difference between a "bead tip" and a "clamshell" end. Original bead tips did not close completely over knots. Instead, they simply held onto an end knot and provided a claw for attaching findings.

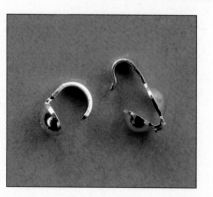

Today, most artisans use full-clamshell style bead-tip findings, and the terms "bead tip" and "clamshell" are used interchangeably.

The old style of bead tip is still available, but you'll find that clamshells give your jewelry a more professional look.

String and Finish Memory Wire

You can finish memory wire jewelry without using any end findings at all.

For best results, design multiple-coil bracelets to have at least three coils. Necklaces and anklets typically have just one coil. Remember that larger beads may make memory wire jewelry uncomfortable to wear. Keep in mind that you should only cut memory wire with heavy, household, or specialty memory-wire cutters; it will damage your regular side cutters.

Ways to Finish Memory Wire

FINISH MEMORY WIRE BY LOOPING

1. After cutting the desired number of loops of memory wire from the coil, firmly grasp one end of the wire with round nose pliers.

2. Roll the pliers away from you to create a loop.

3. Use flat nose pliers to wiggle the loop closed, as if you were closing a jump ring.

4. String on all of the beads for your design, leaving about ¾ inch of bare wire at the other end.

5. Holding the wire up so that no beads fall off, position the round nose pliers at the end of the wire as you did in Step 1 and create a loop.

6. Use flat nose pliers to close the loop, as you did in Step 3.

7. If you want, you can attach a bead drop or charm to one or both end loops, either directly or using a jump ring. (To learn how to make bead and wire drops, see Chapter 6.)

The completed coil bracelet is shown here (a).

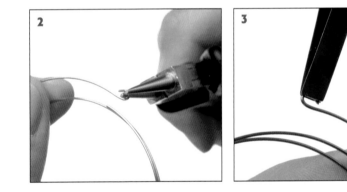

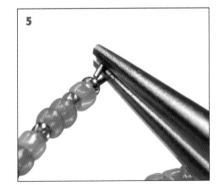

USE MEMORY WIRE END CAPS

For a more professional look, try finishing your memory wire jewelry with end caps instead of loops. Some even have built-in loops for attaching drops or charms.

1 After cutting the desired number of loops of memory wire from the coil, dip one end into E6000 glue.

2 Slide the end into the hole in a memory wire end cap as far as it will go.

3 Set the project aside for 24 hours, to allow the glue to fully set.

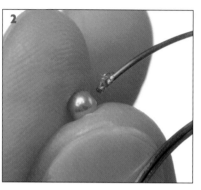

4 Apply a tiny drop of glue to the end cap where it connects with the memory wire.

5 String on all of the beads for your design, leaving a little extra bare wire at the end to attach the other end cap.

6 Holding the wire up to keep the beads from falling off, clamp a small alligator clip to the wire, up against the beads.

7 Perform Steps 1–2 on the other end of the wire.

8 Carefully remove the alligator clip.

9 Repeat Step 4.

10 Slide the last bead in the design up against the memory cap, so that it sticks in the glue.

11 Set the project aside for another 24 hours to allow the glue to fully set.

The completed memory wire bracelets with end caps is shown here (a).

4

More Advanced Bead Stringing Techniques

Now you have the skills needed to create simple beaded necklaces, bracelets, and anklets using your choice of popular stringing materials. In this chapter, you'll learn how to build on those fundamentals to complete more elaborate designs.

String Multiple Strands

You can add drama and elegance to jewelry by combining more than one strand of beads in a single design. Here are two popular ways to accomplish this. Choose the method that best suits your design and how you would like the jewelry to lie when worn.

Necklace designed by Lori "Trixxie" Juergens

Use a Multiple Strand Clasp

The easiest way to create jewelry with more than one strand is to use a *multiple strand clasp*. These clasps are designed with multiple connection points, usually in the form of attached rings.

1 Complete all of your beaded strands, and finish them with jump rings. (See Chapter 3 to review bead stringing and finishing.)

2 Lay out the strands parallel to one another on your work surface in the order that you would like them to be in your jewelry.

3 Position the clasp parts at either end.

4 One by one, attach each strand to matching connection points on both clasp ends using jump rings.

The completed clasp, with all of the strands attached, is shown here (a).

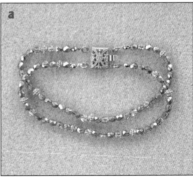

chapter 7

Use End Cones for Multiple Strands

An *end cone* is a cone-shaped metal component with a small hole at one end and a much larger hole at the other end. You can gather strands together and hide their ends inside an end cone.

The way you gather the strands depends on the type of stringing material you use.

GATHERING STRANDS WITH END FINDINGS

When you finish strands with findings, you can usually use the findings or the loops they create to gather the strands together.

1 Select an eye pin with a loop large enough to hold one end of all of your beaded strands together.

2 Open the "eye" of the eye pin by twisting it gently to the side using chain nose pliers, as if you were opening a jump ring.

3 Slip one end of each beaded strand onto the eye pin loop, through the cable loop if you're using cable and crimps, or through the ring on the end piece if you're using cord findings.

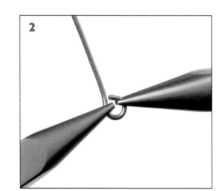

Note: *If the beads near the ends of the strands are too large for the strands to bunch closely together at the eye pin, try attaching the strands to the eye pin with small jump rings instead of attaching them directly. This may help the strands to fit more deeply inside the cone.*

4 Carefully close the eye pin using chain nose pliers as if you were closing a jump ring.

5 Hold up the eye pin and shake it a little to make sure that the strands are securely attached.

6 Repeat these steps to finish the other end of the design.

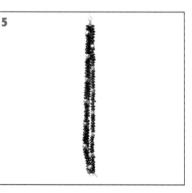

CONTINUED ON NEXT PAGE

GATHERING STRANDS WITHOUT END FINDINGS

You can gather multiple strands of beaded thread or small-diameter cord (like silk) without using end findings.

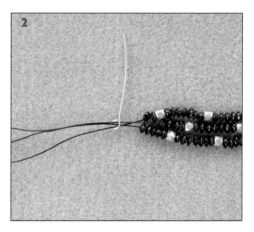

1 As you string the beads, leave tails of about 8 inches of thread or cord at the strand ends after the finishing knots.

2 String an eye pin onto the tails.

3 Holding the tails together, tie an overhand knot around the eye pin (a) as close to the beads as possible (b).

4 Apply a drop or two of clear nail polish or glue to the completed knot.

5 Use scissors to trim down the tails so that they will fit inside the cone.

ATTACHING END CONES

1 Thread the eye pin through the end cone, pulling the gathered strands into the cone as far as they will go. If you have chosen the proper size of end cone, then the ends of the strands should now be hidden inside.

2 Holding the base of the eye pin wire with chain nose pliers, use side cutters to trim the eye pin (if needed) to about ¼ inch from the top of the end cone.

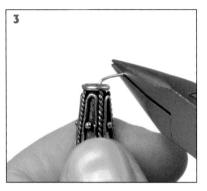

3 Use the chain nose pliers to bend the eye pin toward you.

4 Grasp the end of the wire with round nose pliers.

5 Slowly roll the pliers away from you to create a loop.

Note: *If the new loop doesn't close all the way, use chain nose pliers to wiggle the end back and forth to close it, as you would to close a jump ring.*

6 Finish by attaching a clasp with a jump ring.

As shown here, the clasp is attached to the end cone (a).

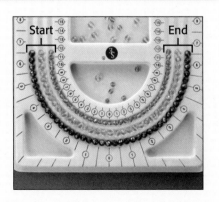

FAQ

How can I make a graduated strand necklace?

If you're creating your own necklace design, you might like the strands to be *graduated* in length. With graduated strands, the topmost strand is the shortest, and each strand below it is a little bit longer than the one above.

To accomplish this, use a bead board with multiple, curved bead channels to lay out your design. Start with the shortest strand, laying it out to the desired length. Then lay out each subsequent strand, being sure to start and end each strand at the same marks on the board.

Knot Between Beads

You can give beaded jewelry a softer feel, and better protect the beads, by placing knots between some or all of the beads in a strand. Pearls are traditionally strung this way to keep their soft surfaces from scratching against one another, but you can knot between beads that are made of just about any material. Soft cord, like silk, is the best stringing material for knotting.

Here are the two most common between-bead knotting methods.

Knot with a Darning Needle or Awl

1 Finish or tape one end of an unbeaded strand that measures at least five times longer than you would need if you were beading without knots.

2 String on the first bead, and position it up against the finished end or tape.

Note: *If you used French bullion wire to finish the strand, this will actually be the second bead on the strand. You will have already knotted behind the first bead during the finishing process.*

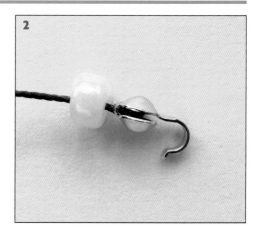

3 Make a very loose overhand knot near the bead.

4 Insert a darning needle or awl into the open part of the knot.

5 Close the knot loosely over it.

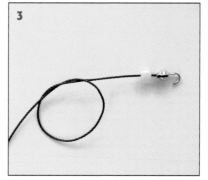

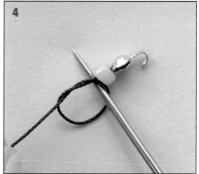

6 Holding the unfinished end of the string in one hand, use your other hand to slowly pull the knot up against the first bead with the needle or awl.

7 Remove the needle or awl, but do not pull the knot tight just yet.

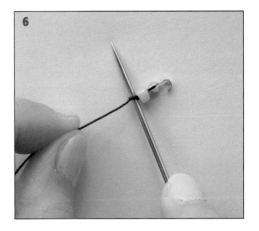

8 While still holding the unfinished end of string in one hand, use the other hand to place the tips of tweezers or knotting pliers against the knot you just made, and use them to position the knot as close to the bead as possible. The knot should tighten down during this step.

The completed knot is shown here.

9 Continue stringing on beads and securing knots to the desired length.

10 Finish the other end of the strand.

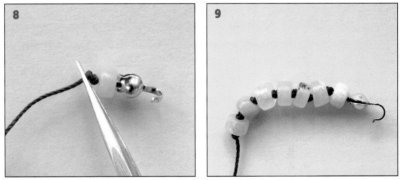

CONTINUED ON NEXT PAGE

TIP

The "Tin Cup" Necklace

In a *tin cup necklace,* beads are held in place by knots and separated by unbeaded portions of stringing material. These necklaces are typically strung on silk cord, and the beads are usually pearls spaced evenly along the strand.

To make one, you need a guide to help you knot at consistent intervals between beads. Cut a strip of paper board to the length you'd like the intervals to be, and fold it in half lengthwise. After securing a bead with a knot, place the folded paper over the string, and secure it with a paper clip or alligator clamp. Create the next knot against the end of the guide, and remove the guide when the knot is complete.

Use a Specialty Knotting Tool

Specialty knotting tools combine the action of a needle and tweezers in one unit. With a little practice, they can speed up your knotting.

1. Hold the finished or taped end of the strand in one hand and use it to wrap the string around the index and middle finger of your other hand.

2. Wrap the string up over your index finger again and cross over the first wrap, so that the finished end of the string is pointing slightly toward the base of your fingers.

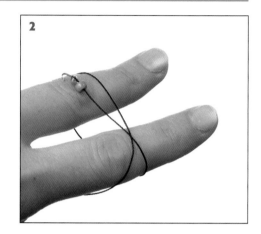

3. Drop the finished end down through the loop you created between your fingers, making sure that it goes through in a direction moving toward your fingertips.

4. While still holding the looped string between your fingers, insert the awl device of the knotting tool into the loop, behind the top string, with the bend in the awl facing away from you.

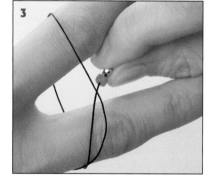

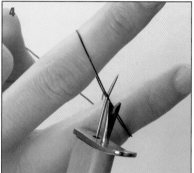

5. Place your index finger on the side of the awl, above the string, to keep the string from sliding off.

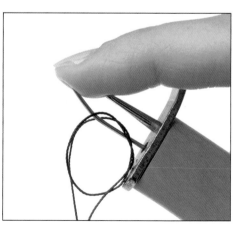

6 Remove the fingers of your other hand from the loop, and use them to grab the string behind the loop.

7 Position the knotting tool perpendicular to your abdomen, and pull the strand slowly upward toward your chin until the loop creates a knot and is positioned close to the bead.

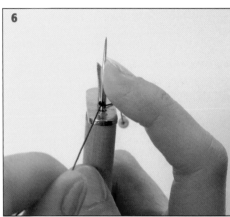

8 Rotate the knotting tool so that the bend in the awl is facing toward you.

9 Gently position the strand inside the fork-shaped device on the tool.

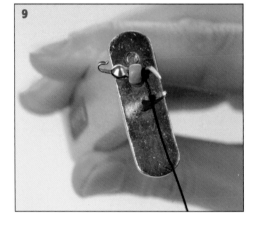

10 Holding the strand taught, remove your index finger from the side of the awl device. Use your thumb to push up on the metal lever while pulling the knotting tool away from you until the completed knot slips off the end of the awl device.

The completed knot is shown here (a).

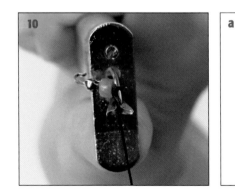

Create Beaded Lace, Drops, Fringe, and Tassels

These ornate jewelry embellishments are inspired by traditional fabric adornments. You can string them using seed beads on beading thread, or regular beads on soft, small-diameter cord or beading wire. You'll string through some beads more than once, so if you use a needle, be sure that it can pass through your beads with extra room to spare.

Mastering the techniques in this section will prepare you for the more complex *bead weaving* in Chapter 5.

BEADED LACE

Here are two basic patterns that you can expand on as you become more skilled. Feel free to experiment by altering the numbers of beads used in each step.

Chain Lace Using One Strand

This pattern has even-sized loops on the top and bottom, making it useful for bracelets.

1 Beginning with a finished or taped unbeaded strand, string on 13 beads.

2 Insert the needle back up through the third bead, in the opposite direction that you strung through it the first time, and pull the thread taught to form a loop.

3 String on seven more beads.

4 String back through the 11th bead that you originally strung on, as you did with the third bead in Step 2.

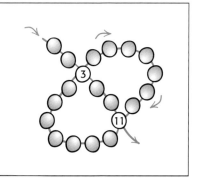

5 String on seven more beads.

6 String back through the 19th bead that you originally strung on.

7 Continue this pattern until you get to the desired length.

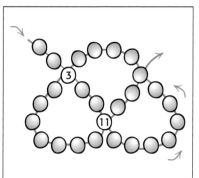

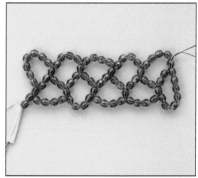

Chain Lace Using Two Strands

In this pattern, loops drop down from a straight upper strand, which is a nice design for necklaces.

1 Finish or tape together the same ends of two unbeaded strands.

2 String beads loosely along the entire upper strand, leaving some extra space between beads, and tape the other end.

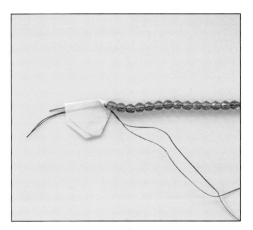

3 Thread the lower strand through the first three beads of the upper strand, and out again.

4 String on seven more beads.

5 String back into the third bead, in the same direction you strung it the first time, and all the way through the next three beads on the upper strand, then out again.

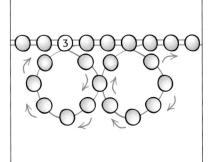
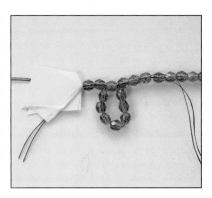

6 String on five more beads.

7 String up through the second bead on the previous loop, and out again.

8 String on one more bead.

9 String back into the upper strand as you did in Step 5, passing through a total of four beads.

10 String on another five beads.

11 Continue this pattern to the desired length.

CONTINUED ON NEXT PAGE

BEADED DROPS

You can make simple beaded strands or lace-pattern loops more decorative by adding beaded drops. For the best results, select a drop bead that is larger than the rest of the beads along the loop or strand.

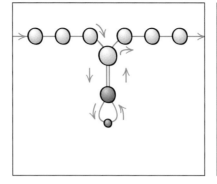

1. At the location where you'd like to place a beaded drop, string on a larger-size bead, a smaller bead, and a seed bead.

2. String back up through the smaller bead and the larger bead and the bead directly before it.

3. Continue stringing on beads as required for your pattern.

SIMPLE BEADED FRINGE

Beaded fringe is made up of many long drops strung near one another along a strand. The easiest method for making fringe involves using two strands of stringing material.

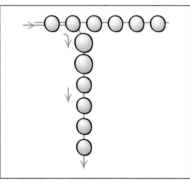

1. Beginning with a loosely beaded strand taped at both ends, string a second, unbeaded strand into the beads at one end, and bring it out again where you'd like to begin making fringe.

2. String on the beads that you've chosen to make the fringe to the desired length.

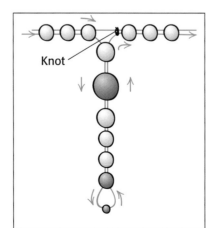

Knot

3. After stringing on the last fringe bead, string back up into the bead just before it, and all the way back up the entire fringe piece.

4. Pull the fringe taut but not too tight, allowing the fringe to drape softly without exposing bare areas of thread or cord.

5. Keeping the fringe piece in that position, tie an overhand knot around the top beaded strand to keep the fringe piece in place.

6 Thread into the first beaded strand to the point where you'd like to create the next fringe (at least one bead away from the previous fringe).

7 Repeat Steps 2–6 until you have the desired number of fringes.

8 Complete the second strand by stringing it through the remaining beads on the top strand.

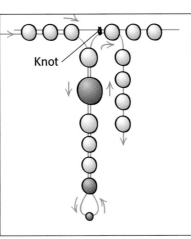

Knot

BEADED TASSELS

There are many different methods for making beaded tassels. This section covers two of the most popular, which share a common technique for making the tassel fringe.

Tassel Fringe

1 Tape a strand of thread or cord about 8 inches from one end.

2 Attach a needle to the other end, and string on all of the beads that you've chosen to make the first piece of tassel fringe to the desired length.

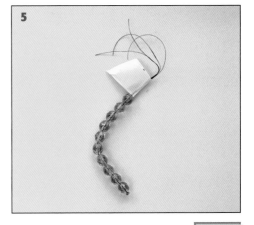

2

4

←Tape

3 String back up into the bead just before the last bead you strung on in Step 2, and all the way back up the entire fringe piece.

4 Add the strand to the tape at the top of the fringe piece.

5 Trim the strand, leaving a 5- or 6-inch tail after the tape.

6 Repeat Steps 1–5 until you have completed the desired number of fringe pieces for your tassel.

5

CONTINUED ON NEXT PAGE

End Cone or End Cap Tassel Top

You can thread this style of tassel onto a necklace or bracelet using the eye of its eye pin or a jump ring.

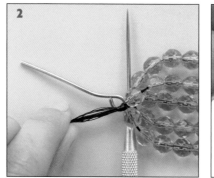

1 Remove the tape from all fringe pieces, and thread the tails through the eye of an eye pin.

Note: *If this proves difficult, open the head pin loop with chain nose pliers and twist the fringe tails together before placing them inside.*

2 Use the tails to tie a secure overhand knot around the eye as close to the beads as possible.

3 After applying a drop of clear nail polish or glue to the completed knot, trim the tails down to ¼ inch in length or shorter.

4 Thread the eye pin through an end cone or end cap as far as it will go.

5 Use round nose pliers to create a loop to hold the eye pin in place. (See "Attaching End Cones" on page 77.)

6 Attach a jump ring to the loop for hanging, if desired.

The completed tassel is shown here (a).

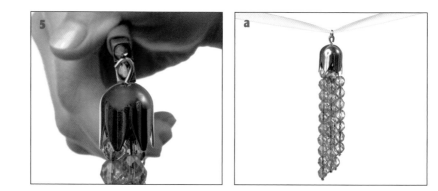

TIP

Designing Effective Tassels

Tassels can have a lot of fringe pieces, or just a few. Here are some basic design tips to help your tassels look their best:

- Experiment with different lengths and numbers of fringe pieces during the design process. String some temporary pieces, gather the tails together, and hold them up to see how they drape before finalizing your plan.

- Make sure your fringe pieces are heavy enough to drape softly from the tassel top. If most of your beads are lightweight, try adding a heavier focal bead at the bottom of each fringe piece.

- For necklaces, tassels with slightly varying lengths of fringe tend to look more dramatic than tassels with fringe of equal length.

- Make sure your design has balance. If your tassel is thick with a lot of fringe, your necklace should probably have more than one strand.

Focal Bead Tassel Top

This tassel is typically strung directly into a necklace through a focal bead. The bead's hole must be large enough to contain the knot at the top of the fringe *and* double the number of strands the necklace will have.

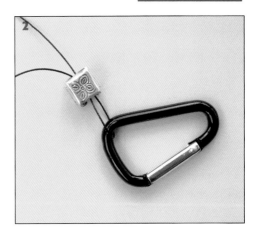

1 String the focal bead onto an unbeaded strand long enough to bead the desired length of necklace.

2 At the center point of the necklace, wrap the strand through a small carabiner or shower curtain ring, and thread it back up through the focal bead in the opposite direction.

Note: Use a carabiner only if the loops it creates will fit inside your focal bead. If you're using a shorter focal bead, you may need to use a thin shower curtain ring so that the loops will be smaller. See Chapter 1 for examples of carabiners and shower curtain rings used as jewelry making supplies.

3 Repeat Steps 1–2 for the desired number of necklace strands.

4 Remove the carabiner or curtain ring, leaving a loop of strands at the bottom of the focal bead.

5 Remove the tape from the fringe pieces, and thread them all through the loop.

6 Tie the fringe tails securely around the loop with an overhand knot, as close to the fringe beads as possible.

7 After adding a drop or two of clear nail polish or instant bond glue to the knot, trim the ends.

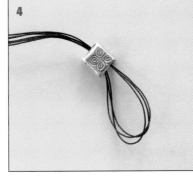

8 Gently pull the necklace strands up through the focal bead, pulling the fringe knot inside the bead, until the upper fringe beads touch the focal bead.

9 String beads onto the strands on each side of the necklace, and finish as usual.

The finished tassel with the beaded necklace strand is shown here.

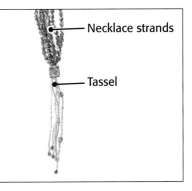

Necklace strands

Tassel

Use Beads or Buttons in Place of Findings

You can save money and customize the look of some of your jewelry by using beaded components or buttons in place of pre-made findings.

Beaded Faux Pendant Bail

Hang drilled pendants from your beaded necklaces with this easy technique.

It requires one bead large enough to cover two strands of your stringing material knotted together.

1 Using a strand long enough to bead your necklace plus a few inches, string on one medium-size bead and enough smaller beads to create a half loop to the pendant hole.

2 String through the pendant hole, and string on another set of the same number of smaller beads.

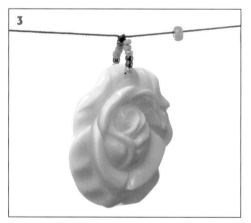

Medium bead

Pendant hole

3 Moving the medium-size bead back a little so that it is out of the way, tie the two strands above the pendant together using a square knot, as close to the smaller beads as possible.

4 String back up through the medium-size bead in the opposite direction that you did the first time.

5 Push the medium-size bead down over the knot.

6 Continue beading both sides of the necklace, and finish as usual.

Simple Bead-and-Loop Clasp

This fun clasp works like a toggle.

1 Prepare a strand about 15 inches longer than you would need for a bracelet or necklace with pre-made findings.

2 If you're using cable, string on a crimp bead.

3 String on a bead of your choice that is larger than a seed bead, with a hole large enough to be threaded through twice.

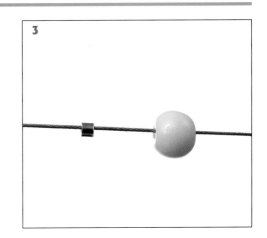

4 Select a medium- to large-size bead for the clasp, but do not string it on yet.

5 String on enough seed beads to make a continuous loop of beads around the clasp bead.

6 Add or remove beads until you can insert the clasp bead comfortably through the loop, without it fitting too tightly or too loosely.

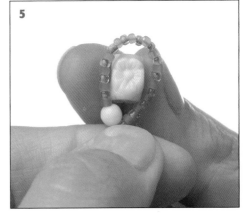

7 String back down through the first bead and the crimp (if you're using one), in the opposite direction that you strung through them the first time.

8 Crimp or tie a square knot to close the loop, as close to the larger bead as possible.

9 Continue stringing on beads in the pattern of your choice.

Finished bead-and-loop clasps are shown here.

CONTINUED ON NEXT PAGE

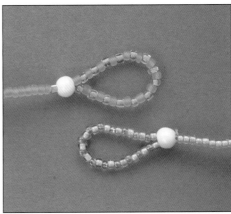

⑩ When you're ready to finish the other end of the strand, string on another crimp bead (if you're using one) and another larger bead to form the base of the loop.

⑪ String on a length of seed beads a little longer than the width of the clasp bead.

⑫ String on the clasp bead and one more seed bead.

⑬ String back down into the clasp bead and through the seed beads, larger bead, and crimp (if you're using one).

⑭ Crimp or tie another square knot, and finish as usual.

Two finished bracelets, one knotted and one crimped, are shown here.

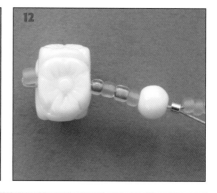

FAQ

How can I make a built-in clasp with leather or another thick stringing material?

Some cording, like leather, is too thick to pass through seed beads, or through many larger beads, more than once. Fortunately, this material tends to knot well. The knots are large enough to take the place of some or all of the clasp beads.

To make a bead-and-loop clasp with thick cord, begin by making the loop. Fold over the end of an extra-long strand of cord, and tie a secure overhand knot in the doubled strand. Make the bead toggle at the other end by tying an overhand knot, stringing on the clasp bead, and then tying a second overhand knot.

If the cord is thick enough, you can even use a knot in place of a bead for the clasp. Simply tie a secure overhand knot on the second end of the cord to fit inside the loop you made on the first end. (This type of knot-and-loop closure is used for the Four-Strand Braided Leather Bracelet project in Chapter 11.)

With either method, finish by adding a tiny drop of E6000 glue to each knot, if desired, and trim off the extra cord ends.

Button-and-Loop Clasp

This clasp works just like the bead version, but uses a button as the toggle.

1. Perform Steps 1–3 from "Simple Bead-and-Loop Clasp" on page 89.

2. Select a medium-size, two-hole button for the clasp, but do not string it on yet.

3. String on enough seed beads to make a continuous loop of beads around the button.

4. Add or remove beads until you can insert the button comfortably through the loop, without it fitting too tightly or too loosely.

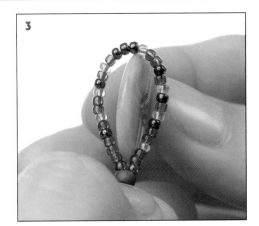

5. When you're ready to finish the button-end of the strand, string on a series of seed beads a little longer than the width of the button.

6. Pass through one hole in the button, add a few more seed beads, and thread down through the other hole.

7. String on another series of the same number of seed beads.

8. Thread back down through the larger bead and the crimp (if you're using cable).

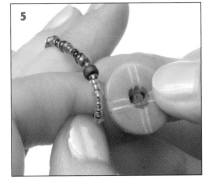

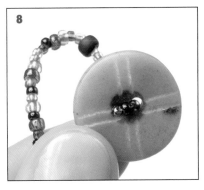

9. Crimp or tie another square knot to close the loop, and finish as usual.

A completed bracelet with a button-and-loop clasp is shown here.

5

Bead Weaving

Using a needle and thread, you can weave small beads into beaded fabric. This process is called *bead weaving*. There are several popular bead weaving stitches used for making jewelry. Before you explore them, you'll learn how to begin and end a thread within a design, and how to add a new piece of thread when an old thread runs out. Once you become comfortable with the basic stitches in this chapter, you can start creating your own jewelry using patterns.

Bead Weaving Patterns

Before you begin learning stitches, it's helpful to look at some bead weaving pattern grids to see how the beads are arranged for each type of stitch. When you're ready to weave a design, you can use a pre-made pattern from a book or from the Internet, or you can create your own.

Patterns are laid out on special graph paper. The type of graph that you'll use depends on the type of stitch. Here are examples of graphs used for some of the basic stitches that you'll learn in this chapter: the peyote stitch, the square stitch, and the brick stitch.

Because each box in the grid represents one bead in the design, these graphs give you a preview of how the beads are arranged for each stitch. With the peyote and brick stitches, the beads in each row are offset, like the bricks in a wall. By contrast, the beads line up evenly with the square stitch.

Now take a look at the more detailed graph used for the right-angle weave. In this graph, beads are rounded to distinguish them from empty spaces in the design.

Blank pattern grids are available for download on the Internet (some recommended sources are provided on page 285 in the Appendix). After printing out a pattern grid, you can use colored pencils to indicate the approximate color of each bead in your design. Take your completed patterns with you when you shop for beads.

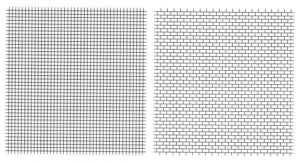

Square stitch grid   Peyote and brick stitch grid

As you progress into more intricate designs, you may want to create patterns online using bead design software. Many of these allow you to scan pictures, even photographs, and convert them into bead-weaving patterns that you can print with a color printer.

Keep in mind that the dimensions of a pattern grid often do not match the size of the completed project. This is because beads tend to vary in length and width depending on their manufacturer, style, and when they were made (size standards change over time). To determine how large a project will be with your beads, try weaving a small sample of beaded fabric before you begin. Use a ruler to determine how many beads you have per inch both vertically and horizontally. By counting the number of rows and columns in the pattern, you can then estimate the length and width of the project.

Right angle weave grid

When you create a design using a pre-made bead weaving pattern, the pattern typically indicates which bead types, sizes, and colors work best for the project. Some patterns even provide thread size recommendations.

But if your pattern is less helpful, or you're creating a design from scratch, you'll need to choose the proper beads, thread, and needle on your own. The best place to begin is by selecting your beads.

SELECTING BEAD TYPE

Most quality seed beads are manufactured in the Czech Republic or Japan. Less expensive seed beads from other countries are available at craft stores, but they're not recommended for bead weaving because of their uneven size.

Czech and Japanese Seed Beads

Czech beads and Japanese beads have a slightly different shape and look. Czech seed beads are oval and rounded in shape, and Japanese seed beads are slightly more squared or angular. Although you can use either type for any bead-weaving stitch, Czech beads are typically recommended for looser stitches like the right-angle weave, and Japanese beads for tighter weaves like the brick stitch, square stitch, and peyote stitch.

Cylinder Beads

Instead of seed beads, you may opt for a similar style of bead called *cylinder beads*. Most cylinder beads (often sold as Delicas or Toho Treasures) are manufactured in Japan, but they are different from Japanese seed beads. Instead of being rounded or "seed-shaped," they are short, precisely cut tubes with extra-large holes. Cylinder beads give any bead-weaving stitch a smoother, more even appearance.

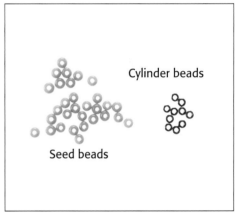
Cylinder beads
Seed beads

SELECTING YOUR BEAD SIZE

The sizes of seed beads and cylinder beads are denoted by numbers called *aught sizes*, which are often written to look like fractions.

The most versatile size for seed beads is 11/0, pronounced "eleven aught" or simply "number eleven". Other seed-bead sizes range between about 6/0 (larger, also called *pony beads*) and 15/0 (very small). For simplicity, just keep in mind that the larger the number, the smaller the bead.

Cylinder beads are available in a much more limited range of sizes than seed beads. The most common cylinder-bead size is 11/0, but you can also find them in size 8/0.

Which bead size you choose depends largely on how you'd like your design to look and feel. Smaller beads have a more condensed, delicately woven appearance than larger beads. Other considerations are how many beads you want in your design, and how proficient you are with bead weaving. Projects using smaller beads will require a larger number of beads and may take more time to complete than projects using larger beads. Smaller beads are also harder to work with than larger beads, and you may have more difficulty threading through them multiple times.

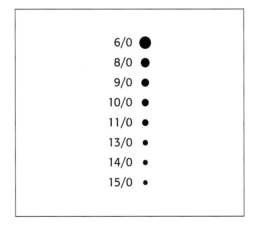
6/0 ●
8/0 ●
9/0 ●
10/0 ●
11/0 ●
13/0 ·
14/0 ·
15/0 ·

CONTINUED ON NEXT PAGE

SELECTING BEADING THREAD

Beading thread is available in a range of sizes or thicknesses. The thicker a thread is, the stronger it tends to be. Most beading thread sizes are denoted by letters, with the very thinnest sizes described by zeros. Here is a typical range of available sizes.

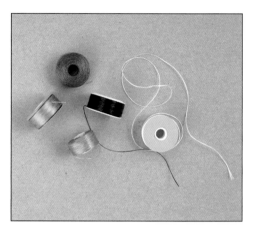

Beading Thread Sizes								
Thinner	→	→	→	→	→	→	→	→	*Thicker*
00	0	A	AA	B	C	D	E	EE	F

For bead weaving, you will typically use threads sized 00 to D. You should try to use the thickest thread possible for your project. This is both for strength and to ensure that the beads lie properly in your design. Thickness is always limited by how many times you need to string your thread through a single bead and by the sizes of the holes in your beads.

After you select the type and size of beads to use, try to determine the maximum number of times you'll need to thread through any bead in your design. All stitches require you to pass through some beads twice, and most require at least three passes. You'll need to factor in any thread ends that will need to be woven-in, and whether you'll be attaching fringe or findings using additional thread.

Use this number as the basis for determining which thread to use. For example, if you need to pass through some beads four times, test to make sure that the thread you choose can do this without breaking a bead.

You can use the chart on the next page to narrow your options of thread sizes to try. Then, take the time to experiment before you begin weaving your project.

SELECTING A NEEDLE FOR BEADING THREAD

You always need to use a beading needle for bead weaving. Beading needles are available in a range of sizes, typically beginning with #16 (the thinnest) through about #10 (the thickest). These sizes approximate the aught sizes used for seed beads, but they do not match exactly. You will need to experiment with needle size as you did with thread size, before you begin your project. Always check to make sure that the eye of your needle is not so large that it will break a bead, especially when you make multiple passes.

Beading needles are also available in varying lengths from about 1¼ inches long to about 3 inches long. (Three-inch needles are usually only used for weaving very wide pieces of beaded fabric on a loom.) As a beginner, you will probably find that a needle about 2 inches long is easiest to work with.

COMMON RECOMMENDATIONS

Over time, you will develop some favorite types and sizes of beads, thread, and needles. You'll also learn which combinations work best for the types of bead weaving projects you prefer. In the meantime, refer to this chart for some general guidelines.

Needle and Thread Size Recommendations			
	Bead Size	*Needle Size*	*Thread Size*
Larger	8/0	#10	E, F, or FF
	9/0	#10	D, E, or F
	10/0	#10	B or D
	11/0	#10	A or B
	12/0	#11	A or B
	13/0	#12	A or 0
	14/0	#13	A or 0
Smaller	15/0	#13 or #15	0, 00, or 000

TIP

Bead Size Versus Hole Size

You have probably guessed that your beads' hole size—not the beads' overall size—is what affects the size of thread and needle that you can use for a project. Unfortunately, not all beads of the same size have the same size holes. For example, Japanese seed beads may have slightly larger holes than the same size Czech seed beads. Delicas have very large holes, and so you'll be able to use larger thread and needles with them than with seed beads. (They also have thinner sides, so be careful not to use a needle so large that it may break them.)

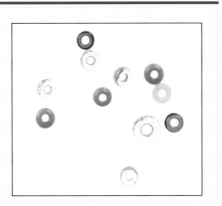

In general, recently manufactured beads have larger holes than their earlier counterparts. If you come across some nifty antique seed beads, be aware that you may be limited to thinner thread and a smaller needle than that to which you are accustomed.

Work with Beading Thread for Bead Weaving

This section covers the fundamentals of working with beading thread for bead weaving. You will use these techniques for all of your bead weaving projects, regardless of the type of stitch you choose.

Begin a Strand of Beading Thread: Double-Strand Weaving

One way to string beads for bead weaving is to use a double strand of thread. With this method, you will not need to worry about your needle falling off.

1. Begin with a length of beading thread no more than about 1 yard in length.

2. Rub a piece of beeswax or a thread conditioner along the entire length of the thread.

   Note: If your thread is pre-conditioned, you may skip Step 2.

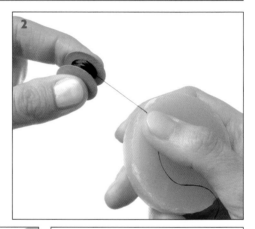

3. String the thread through the eye of a beading needle.

4. Position the needle at the half-way point along the thread.

5. Bring the thread ends together.

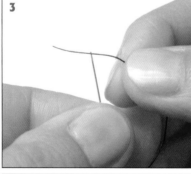

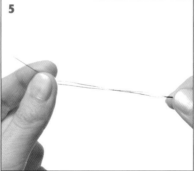

6. String on a stop bead (see page 58 in Chapter 3), and position it about 6 inches from the ends of the strands.

7. String back through the stop bead once or twice to hold it in place.

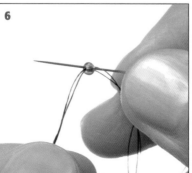

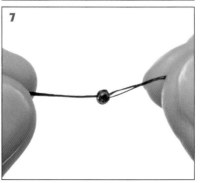

Begin a Strand of Beading Thread: Single-Strand Weaving

You will probably find that a double strand of thread is too thick to string through some beads multiple times, or that it limits the size of thread you can use for a project. Double strands also make it more difficult to correct mistakes in stitching (because you can't remove the needle from the thread to undo stitches), and they can tangle easily.

For these reasons, it's a good idea to learn how to weave beads using a single strand of thread.

1 Begin with a length of conditioned beading thread no more than about 2 feet in length.

2 String on a beading needle.

3 Position the needle just a few inches from the end of the thread.

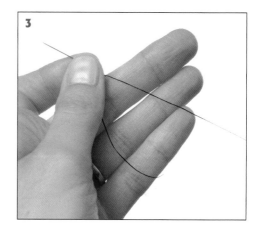

4 Fold-over the thread tail, and hold both strands between your fingers at the bottom of the needle.

Note: You will need to hold the thread like this while you weave your project to keep the needle from falling off. If it does fall off, simply thread it back on.

5 String on a stop bead, and secure it near the other end of the thread as usual.

The completed task is shown here.

CONTINUED ON NEXT PAGE

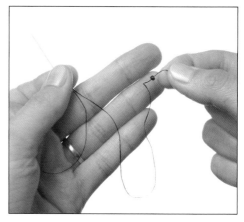

TIP

Alternatives to Using a Stop Bead

If you have trouble attaching a stop bead, you can try using a Bead Stopper or tape to secure your thread instead, although these methods do not work as well with thread as they do with cord. (See Chapter 3 for a review of these techniques.)

For less time-consuming projects, you can try simply winding the ends of the thread around your finger a few times, and use a finger in place of a stop bead. Whichever method you use, make sure it holds the beads securely enough to help you maintain proper tension as you work.

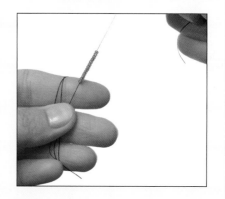

End a Thread by Weaving-In

Apply this technique, called *weaving-in*, when you finish your design, or in mid-design when you've used all but about 8–10 inches of your thread.

1 Tie an overhand knot over and around the nearest thread between two beads.

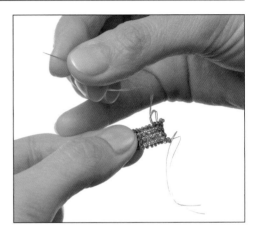

2 Weave the thread back through the previous few beads in the design.

3 Tie an overhand knot over and around the thread between two other beads.

4 Repeat Steps 2–3, working backward along the row.

5 Weave the thread through a few more beads in the design and out again.

6 Use sharp scissors to trim off the remaining thread and needle.

Add a New Thread

Use this technique when you need to begin a new thread mid-design.

① After preparing the new thread without a stop bead, pass the needle into the design about nine beads away from where you need to begin weaving again, but in a different place than you wove-in the end of the old thread.

② Go through a few beads, leaving a tail of about 6 inches of thread at the beginning.

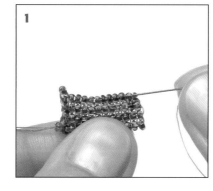
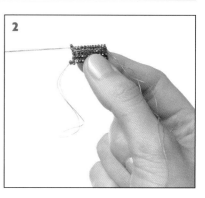

③ Tie an overhand knot over and around the thread between beads, as you did when you were finishing the old thread.

④ Repeat Steps 2–3 as you work your way closer to where you need to begin weaving again.

⑤ When you reach the proper place, continue weaving where you left off.

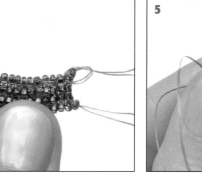

⑥ Before you finish your project, go back and use sharp scissors to trim off the extra thread tail.

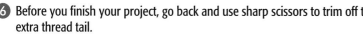
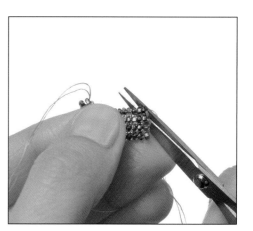

Weave the Basic Off-Loom Stitches

You can weave many interesting bead stitches without a loom simply by holding your work in your hands as you "sew" beads together.

With the exception of the daisy chain (which has only one row), work each design one row at a time. Stitch on beads from left to right, or right to left, whichever is more comfortable. At the end of each row, turn your work around so that you can work the next row in the same comfortable direction.

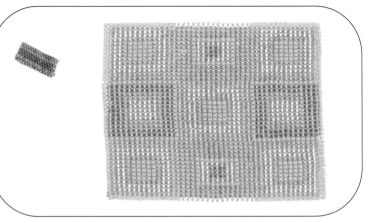

Daisy Chain

The *daisy chain* is a simple stitch that creates a narrow band of woven beads. Try using it for children's jewelry or eyeglass leashes.

1. After securing a stop bead to a conditioned strand of thread, string on the first six beads of your design.

2. Thread back into the first bead in the same direction that you did the first time.

3. Add one new bead.

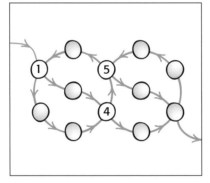

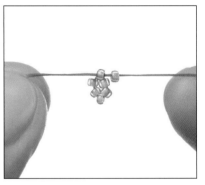

4. In the opposite direction than you did the first time, thread down and through the fourth bead.

5. String on four more beads.

6. String back into the fifth bead that you strung on in Step 1.

7. Add one new bead as you did in Step 3.

8. Continue this pattern to the desired length.

A completed length of daisy chain is shown here (a).

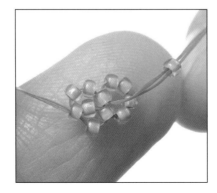

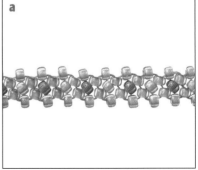

Even-Count Flat Peyote Stitch

The even-count flat peyote stitch is one of the easiest stitches to master. Keep in mind that the first two rows are the most difficult to weave, but you will be able to stitch subsequent rows more quickly.

1. After preparing your thread, string on an even number of beads to equal the width that you'd like your finished design to be.

2. String on one more bead.

3. String back through the second to last bead that you strung on in Step 1, in the opposite direction.

4. Turn your work around.

5. String on another bead.

6. String back through the fourth from the last bead that you strung on in Step 1 (Bead 3 in the diagram).

7. Continue adding a new bead and stringing through a lower bead until you arrive back at the beginning of the first row, stringing back through the first bead that you strung on in Step 1.

8. Turn your work around again.

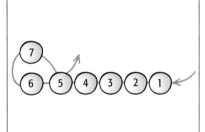

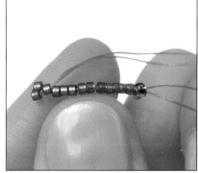

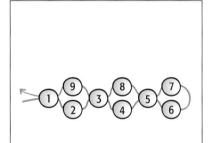

9. String on a new bead (Bead 10 in the diagram).

10. String back through the first bead in the second row (Bead 9 in the diagram).

11. Continue this pattern to complete this and future rows, stitching each row in the opposite direction to the prior row.

   A completed length of even-count flat peyote stitch weaving is shown here (a).

CONTINUED ON NEXT PAGE

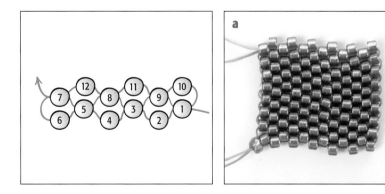

Square Stitch

In the square stitch, the beads are aligned in straight rows and columns. You can change the shape of your design by making some rows longer or shorter than others through *increasing* and *decreasing*.

BASIC SQUARE STITCH

1 After preparing your thread, string on enough beads to create the first row.

2 String on one more bead. This will be the first bead of the second row.

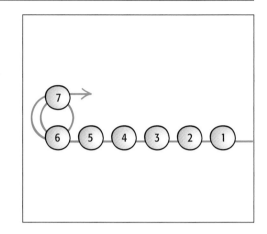

3 Thread back through the last bead that you strung on in Step 1, going in the same direction.

4 Thread back into the bead from Step 2.

5 This bead should now be on top of the first bead in the first row.

6 Continue adding one bead at a time, stitching them as you did the first bead in Steps 3–4, until you reach the end of the row.

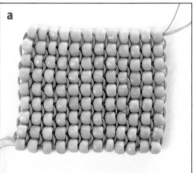

7 Turn your work, and begin stitching back in the other direction.

8 Continue stitching rows to the desired length.

A completed section of square stitch weaving is shown here (a).

TIP

Thread Tension

One of the most important skills that you'll learn is how to maintain the proper *thread tension* as you work.

As you weave each bead or group of beads, you need to gently pull the thread taut while positioning the beads up against one another. If you pull too tightly, your final design will be pinched or uneven. If you don't pull tightly enough, your beads will be loose and too much thread will show through.

The best way to learn to control tension is through a lot of practice. Don't expect your first few projects to be perfect; your skills will naturally improve over time.

SQUARE STITCH INCREASE

Use this technique to make a row longer than the previous row.

1 At the end of the row that you want to lengthen, thread on *two* beads, instead of one. Essentially, you are adding one more bead to this row before stringing on the first bead of the next row.

2 Thread back down through the first bead that you added in Step 1, and out again.

3 Thread back through the second bead from Step 1.

4 Continue performing square stitches as usual.

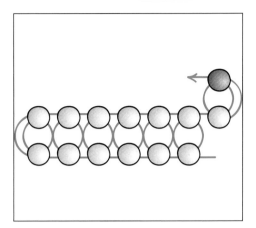

SQUARE STITCH DECREASE

Use this technique to make a row shorter than the previous row.

1 At the end of the row *before* the row you'd like to make shorter, thread back down and through the last two beads in the previous row.

2 Thread up into and through the second to last bead in the upper row, coming out between the second-to-last bead and the last bead.

3 String on one new bead to begin the shorter row. You have effectively moved the thread back by one bead in the row.

4 Continue square stitching as usual, ending the row one bead short of the row beneath it if you'd like it to be equally short on the other side.

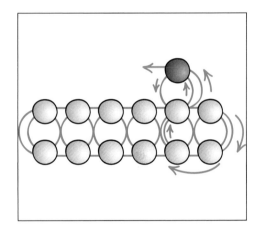

CONTINUED ON NEXT PAGE

FAQ

What should I do when my thread becomes tangled?

The longer your thread is, the more likely it is to twist and tangle. You can reduce tangling by conditioning your thread before you start weaving, and reconditioning it from time to time while you work.

When a tangle begins to occur, immediately stop stitching. Let go of the needle and allow it to dangle down as you hold your work up over your work table. (If your thread is very long, you may need to stand up to allow the needle to dangle freely.) Run your fingers along the length of the thread to remove any tangles or twists, and then pick up the needle and continue stitching.

Weave the Basic Off-Loom Stitches *(continued)*

Brick Stitch

Like the peyote stitch, rows of beads in the brick stitch are offset, like the bricks in a wall. But brick stitch rows naturally decrease in length as you work, allowing you to create a triangle-shaped piece of fabric, if you wish. To create even-width fabric, you need to adjust the length of each row with an increase. Begin the brick stitch with a single row of beads called the *ladder*.

WEAVE A LADDER

1 After preparing your thread, string on two beads.

2 Hold the beads side-by-side with your fingers so that the thread between them is in a "U" shape at the bottom.

3 Thread down into the first bead and up through the second bead again.

4 String on a third bead.

5 Thread down into the second bead and up through the third bead again.

6 Continue this pattern until you have reached the desired width of the design, finishing with an odd-numbered bead.

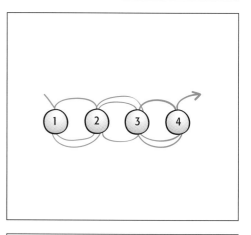

7 To stabilize the ladder row, weave back through each bead—top to bottom, then bottom to top—until you arrive back at the beginning of the row.

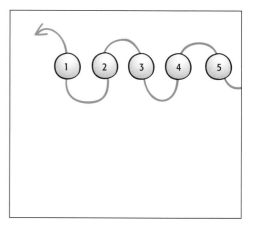

ADD BRICK ROWS

1 After creating your ladder row, string on two new beads.

2 Pass your needle under the bridge of thread between the second and third beads in the ladder row, and up again.

3 Thread back up through the second bead that you strung on in Step 1 and back down through the first bead.

4 Thread back up through the second bead again.

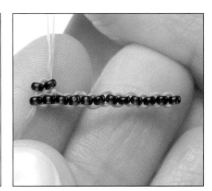

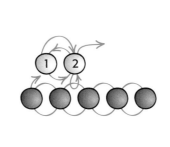

5 String on one new bead.

6 Pass your needle under the bridge of thread between the next two beads in the ladder row, and up again.

7 Thread back up through the bead that you added in Step 5.

8 Repeat Steps 5–7 until you reach the end of the row.

9 Turn your work around to begin stitching the next row, repeating Steps 1–8. As you continue stitching rows, each will be shorter than the previous row unless you perform an increase (a).

CONTINUED ON NEXT PAGE

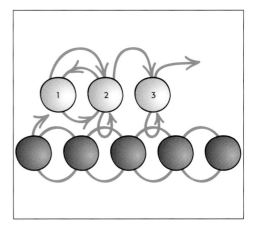

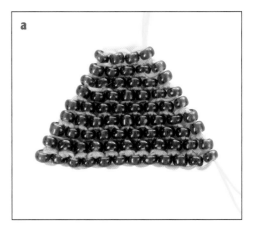

a

BRICK STITCH INCREASE AT BEGINNING OF ROW

Use this method at the beginning of each brick stitch row that you would like to be the *same* length as the prior row.

1 At the beginning of the new row, string on two new beads, as usual.

2 Instead of passing your needle between the second and third beads in the previous row, pass it beneath the bridge of thread between the *first* and *second* beads in that row.

3 Continue brick stitching the remainder of the row as usual.

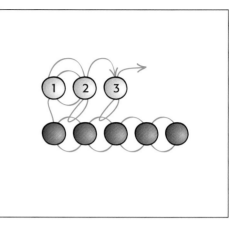

BRICK STITCH MID-ROW INCREASE

Sometimes you may want to make a row longer than the row before it. Perform an increase at the beginning of the row, and then perform one or more increases in the middle of the row.

1 Begin a new row by first creating an increase.

2 String on a new bead (bead 3).

3 Pass your needle under the bridge of thread between the next two beads in the previous row, and up again.

4 String on another bead (bead 4).

5 Pass your needle back down under the *same* bridge of thread that you passed under in Step 3. This will increase the current row's length by one additional bead.

6 If you'd like the row to be even longer, continue brick stitching the row by adding more increases.

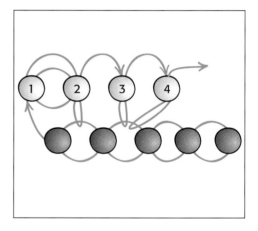

EXTRA BRICK STITCH ROW DECREASE

Use this technique if you'd like a row to be at least two beads shorter than the previous row. (Remember, the rows decrease by one bead naturally unless you perform an increase.)

1 Begin a new row without creating an increase.

2 String on a new bead.

3 *Skip* the very next bridge of thread in the previous row, and instead pass your needle under the following bridge of thread.

4 Continue brick stitching the row.

> **Note:** If you'd rather decrease by one bead at the end of a row, skip these steps and simply stop stitching one bead short at the row's end.

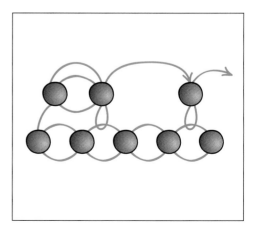

Single-Needle Right-Angle Weave

The traditional right-angle weave is stitched using two beading needles, and it can be difficult to master. The more common weave used today by American beaders requires just one needle. It uses a figure-eight technique to create a kind of beaded net.

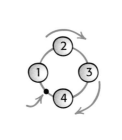

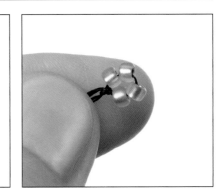

RIGHT-ANGLE WEAVE FIRST ROW

1. After preparing your thread *without* a stop bead, string on four beads.

2. Bring the thread back around and tie a square knot at the base of the first bead.

3. You now have a tiny loop of four beads.

4. Thread into the first bead again, going in the same direction.

5. Thread through the next two beads and out again.

6. String on three more beads.

7. Thread back down into the third bead that you strung on in Step 1 from top to bottom.

8. Thread back through the first two beads that you strung on in Step 5 and out again.

9. String on three more beads.

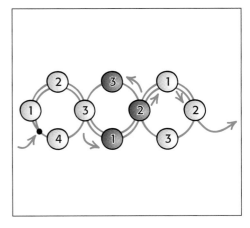

10. Thread back up into the second bead that you strung on in Step 5.

11. Thread through the next two beads and out again.

12. Continue adding groups of three beads until you have a row of the desired length with the thread pointing up.

    Note: *You'll see that the thread alternates from pointing up to pointing down with each stitch. The last stitch in any row should be the type that leaves the thread pointing up.*

CONTINUED ON NEXT PAGE

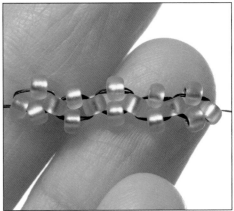

RIGHT-ANGLE WEAVE SUBSEQUENT ROWS

1 To begin the next row, thread back into the last upper bead in the row.

2 String on three more beads.

3 Thread back down into the last upper bead in the previous row, and back through the three beads you strung on in Step 2.

4 Thread down into the last upper bead in the previous row again, then back through the first bead from Step 2 one more time. (Notice that you just created another figure eight; this one is pointing up and down instead of side to side.)

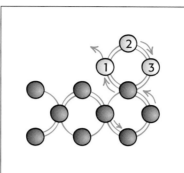

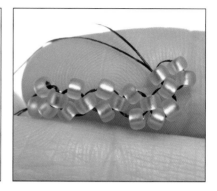

5 Turn your work around.

6 String on two more beads (beads 4 and 5).

7 Thread down through the next upper bead of the previous row and back up through the first bead from Step 2.

8 Thread back into the two beads from Step 6.

9 Thread down through the next upper bead of the previous row and out again.

10 String on two more beads.

11 Continue creating figure-eight loops to the end of the row.

12 Continue stitching rows back and forth to the desired length.

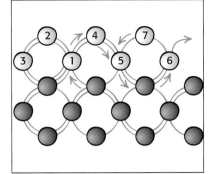
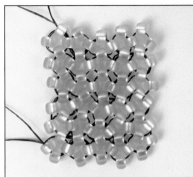

FAQ

What other stitches are used in off-loom bead weaving?

This chapter covered some of the most common bead-weaving stitches, but there are others that you can learn as your skills develop. For example, there is a *flat odd count peyote stitch*, in which you weave rows of odd numbers of beads rather than even numbers of beads. Both the even count and the odd count peyote stitches can alternatively be worked in the *round* to create seamless tubes of beaded fabric.

The *herringbone stitch* is also used in bead weaving. It involves stitching beads at angles to mimic the look of "herringbone" fabric. *Netting* is another type of bead weaving stitch. It results in a lacey, open weave that is popular for adorning vases and holiday ornaments.

For tips on finding ways to learn these and other new techniques, see Find Advanced Help and Training in Chapter 12.

Weave on a Loom

If you'd like to weave a long strip of beaded fabric with the beads aligned like the square stitch, try using a loom.

You can probably stitch faster with a loom than off-loom, but you need to take some extra time to *warp* the loom before you begin. You will also find that the length and width of your beaded fabric is limited by the length and width of the loom you use, so you always need to select a loom that will accommodate your project.

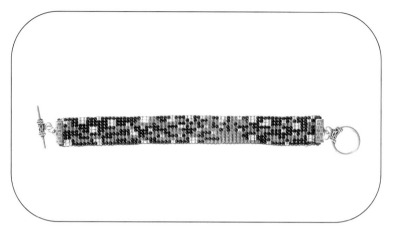

Warp the Loom

The warping and weaving tasks in this section are for a standard, economical loom that uses wooden dowels at the ends. It's a good idea to read the instructions provided with your own loom to confirm whether it operates in the same manner.

When you warp a loom, you attach the ends of a number of long threads to each end. You will weave your beads into these *warp threads* to create the fabric.

1. Position the dowels on each end of the loom so that they are pointing outward to the sides.

2. Using thread directly off the spool, tie the end in a square knot around one of the screws.

3. Pull the thread up over the dowel and over the spring at the location where you'd like your rows to begin or end.

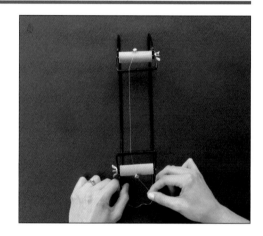

4. Position the thread across the loom and into the spring on the other side.

5. Wrap the thread around the screw on the dowel on that end and back up again.

6. Pull the thread back over the loom, positioning it in the next coil of the spring.

7. Back on the other side of the loom, wrap the thread around the screw again.

8. Continue until you have the same number of warp threads as beads that will be in each row—*plus one thread*.

9. To finish, tie the last warp thread around the screw with another square knot.

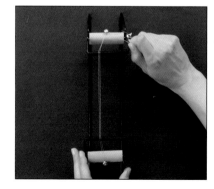

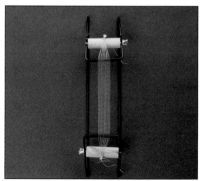

The completed warped loom is shown here (a).

Loom Weaving

After you warp the loom, you're ready to begin weaving your pattern.

1 Begin with an extra-long length of conditioned thread (up to 8 or 10 feet) with a beading needle threaded onto one end.

2 String on all of the beads for the first row of the pattern, positioning them about 12 inches from the end of the thread.

3 With the loom positioned vertically in front of you, use the fingers of your non-dominant hand to hold the beads on the thread under the warp threads. The needle-end of the thread should be pointing toward your dominant hand.

4 Bring the beads up to the warp threads with your non-dominant hand, and use your dominant hand to position each bead between two warp threads. Every bead should now be between exactly two warp threads.

Note: If you have difficulty with this step, try tying the beaded thread to the first warp thread before positioning the beads.

5 While continuing to hold the beads in place between the warp threads, use your dominant hand to thread the needle back through each bead in the row *above* the warp threads, and pull the thread taut. The beads are now woven into place.

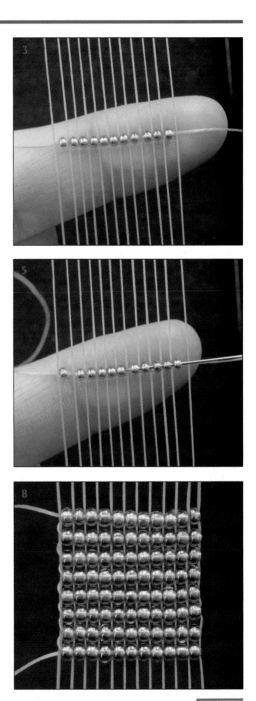

6 String on all of the beads for the next row, and position them as you did in Steps 3–4.

7 Thread back through the beads in the other direction, weaving the second row.

8 Continue weaving rows, back and forth to the desired length.

CONTINUED ON NEXT PAGE

Create a Selvage

When you have finished weaving all of the beads for your design, you can help to hold them in place by creating a *selvage* at each end. A selvage is a length of woven thread that does not contain beads. After you remove your design from the loom, you can hide the selvage by gluing it to the back of the beaded fabric.

1 After weaving your final row of beads, weave your needle under and over each warp thread to create a woven, unbeaded row.

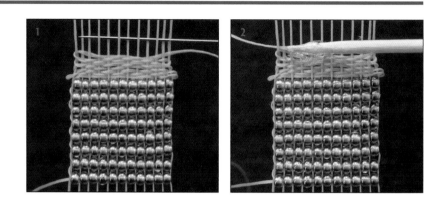

2 Create several more rows like this until you have about ¼ inch of woven thread at the end of your design.

3 Spread a thin layer of E6000 glue along the last few rows of thread.

4 Carefully remove your needle, and thread it onto the 12-inch tail of thread that you created earlier on the other end of the loom.

5 Weave another ¼ inch of threaded rows on this end of the design, and secure the last few rows with E6000 glue.

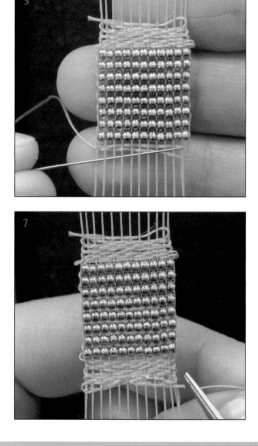

6 Put your work aside and allow the glue to set.

7 Using scissors, trim off the extra tails of thread at each end.

8 Remove your design from the loom by cutting through all of the warp threads on each end—about ⅛ inch from the selvage.

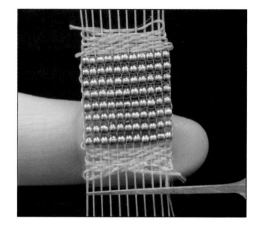

9 Fold-over the selvage at each end and glue it to the back (a) to complete the design (b).

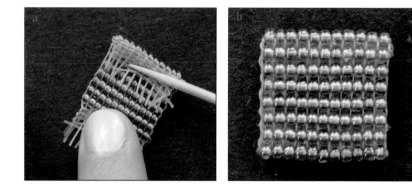

FAQ

What else can I do with the warp-thread tails if I don't want a selvage?

A downside of loom weaving is that you'll have many tails of thread sticking out of your design when you finish. If you don't want to have a selvage glued to one side of your beaded fabric, you can try weaving-in each warp-thread tail individually. For this to work, you will need to leave the warp threads at least 5 or 6 inches long at each end. This may limit the length of the beaded portion of your design, since the loom will need to accommodate the design and the extra-long warp threads. Also, this may not be appropriate for wider designs with a lot of warp threads, as they might not all fit through the beads.

Common Finishing Techniques

You're only limited by your imagination when it comes to finishing woven bead jewelry. You can weave-in or glue on pre-made findings, or you can weave your own beaded clasps. Try using the basic finishing techniques from Chapters 3 and 4 by adapting them to the size and shape of your design. You can learn more complicated finishing techniques if you decide to become an advanced beader.

Examples of Finishing Techniques

WEAVING-IN TO ATTACH END FINDINGS

With many designs, you can use the thread tails to create loops for attaching findings. Try stringing them with French bullion wire (see Chapter 3) or beading them to protect the thread. Weave the ends back into the design as you normally do when you have finished beading. You can use jump rings to add a clasp or attach the clasp directly by enclosing its rings within the loops as you make them.

If you don't have enough thread tail left to create the end loops, you can make them with new pieces of thread that you weave into the design instead.

GLUING TO ATTACH CLAMP ENDS

You can attach clamp ends to many woven bead designs in a manner similar to how you attach them to ribbon (see "Finishing Ribbon" on page 63 in Chapter 3). Prepare the ends of your design by weaving-in and trimming any remaining thread tails. Apply a bit of E6000 glue to each end. (Optionally, you can cover the ends with strips of fabric or ribbon to give the clamp something to hold on to.) Insert each end of the design into an end clamp, and use flat nose pliers to gently close the clamps down over your work, being careful not to damage any beads inside.

This technique works best for wide bands of beaded fabric, including loom work, and with large clamp ends that can accommodate the thickness of the beads. It's especially attractive for bracelets.

BEADED CLASPS

As you may recall from Chapter 3, you can build clasps directly into some of your jewelry. Bead clasps and button clasps work well for many woven designs, because you can use the same or matching beads for your clasp as for your design.

If you decide to progress into advanced beadwork, you can experiment with more complicated clasp designs, such as bead toggles and bead-and-loop clasps featuring larger beads that are covered with seed beads.

USING FABRIC

With some designs, you can attach a fabric backing to your beadwork. This works especially well for loom work with selvages, but you can also use it with square-stitched designs.

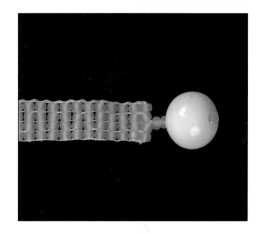

Using a heavy fabric, like suede or ultrasuede, you sew it onto your beadwork by stitching through the outer beads, or across the threads between the outer beads, as you go. Alternatively, you can cover a base-metal jewelry form or blank, such as a cuff bracelet, with your design on one side and fabric on the other.

These are more advanced techniques that are beyond the scope of this book, but you may want to consider them for later.

6

Basic Wirework

You can make all kinds of jewelry and jewelry components by cutting, bending, and hammering metal wire. You do not need to solder or glue any parts because the wire holds its shape with tension. Start out by learning to make some of the key components that you would otherwise purchase pre-made. Then, try making your own beaded links, hook clasps, and chains. For a review of basic wirework tools and supplies, see Chapter 1.

Jewelry making wire is available in many different varieties and sizes. The wire you select for a project depends on how well practiced you are with wirework, how you'd like the jewelry to look, and how much money you want to spend on supplies.

Wire Metal

The most popular metals for jewelry wirework are the base metals copper, nickel, and brass and the precious metals silver and gold. (See Chapter 1 for more information about base metals and precious metals.)

COPPER WIRE

Copper is one of the best metals to work with because it's easy to bend into nicely rounded curves. It has a feel similar to sterling silver, but is much less expensive. This makes it a great metal to use for practice. You can also use it to make *prototypes*, or experimental mock-ups, of new designs.

A potential downside of copper is that it *tarnishes*, or takes on a dark surface color, very easily. It may also develop a scaly green coating when it's exposed to excess moisture. In sufficient quantities, this coating, called *vertigris*, can be toxic. For this reason, some people prefer not to wear copper jewelry.

At minimum, some people find that copper temporarily stains their skin if they wear it for long periods of time.

NICKEL-SILVER WIRE

Nickel silver is a base metal that is silver-colored but does not contain any precious silver; it is an alloy, or mixture, of copper, zinc, and nickel. It is much less expensive than silver, but is slightly more expensive than copper.

Nickel silver has a somewhat dull-gray hue. Although it is a soft metal, it does not bend quite as smoothly as copper and sterling silver. Keep in mind that many people are allergic to nickel, which can create redness or even a rash on their skin. For this reason, you may want to avoid it for jewelry that will be worn closely against the skin.

BRASS WIRE

Brass is an alloy of copper and zinc. It ranges in color from bright yellow to reddish-gold (often referred to as *red brass*). Brass wire tends to be less expensive than nickel silver, and similar in cost to copper.

Like pure copper, brass is prone to tarnishing. Some people like the look of darkened brass because it gives jewelry a more "antique" look.

Brass wire is more difficult to work with than copper, nickel, silver, or gold. Although it is a soft metal, it is stiffer than the others and resists bending as smoothly.

STERLING-SILVER WIRE

Sterling silver is an alloy of pure silver and copper. In wire form, it is soft and very easy to manipulate. Because sterling silver is a favorite jewelry metal, it's naturally one of the most common metals used in jewelry wirework. Unfortunately, it's also relatively expensive.

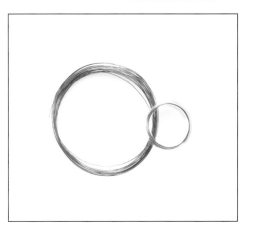

As you probably know, sterling silver is also prone to tarnishing. You can reduce tarnish by wearing sterling-silver jewelry often because the oils in your skin help to protect it from the air. To fight tarnish when your sterling-silver wire or jewelry is in storage, store it with *anti-tarnish paper* or *anti-tarnish fabric*. These materials are specially treated with chemicals that reduce the formation of tarnish. They are available through many jewelry supply catalogs and at jewelry stores. When silver does begin to tarnish, you can clean it with a silver polishing cloth or foaming silver cream. There are some special varieties of sterling silver that resist tarnishing, but they are generally more expensive than regular sterling silver.

Some designers use chemicals to purposely tarnish their jewelry to give it an antique look. This jewelry is often referred to as *oxidized sterling silver*. Oxidation is an advanced technique that is beyond the scope of this book, but if you like this style of jewelry, you may want to try it in the future.

GOLD AND GOLD-FILLED WIRE

You're probably familiar with gold. In addition to being a gorgeous metal for jewelry, it resists corrosion better than most metals, and it typically does not tarnish. Gold is normally alloyed with other metals to make it stronger. The amount of gold in a given piece of metal is denoted by its *karat*.

Karat gold is extremely expensive, and as a beginning wireworker, it's pretty safe to say you won't be using gold wire. A popular alternative that you may want to try is gold-filled wire, which is made up of an inner core of base metal covered with a relatively thick layer of real gold. Although gold-filled wire is usually more costly than sterling-silver wire, it's much less expensive than gold.

SILVER- AND GOLD-PLATED WIRE

Plated wire is usually solid copper wire that has been washed with a very thin coating of silver or gold. Although it is very affordable and has a nice look when it's brand new, it is not recommended for elaborate wirework. This is because the thin coating can scratch or rub off very easily. Try to use it sparingly or only as practice wire.

CONTINUED ON NEXT PAGE

Wire Size

WIRE GAUGE

Wire size is denoted by a number called *gauge:* the larger the number, the thinner the wire; and the smaller the number, the thicker the wire. The following chart provides the approximate diameters of the most popular American wire gauges (also called AWG) for jewelry making and suggested uses for each.

Note: *The AWG is the standard for wire sold in the United States. If you purchase wire in another country, be sure to ask your supplier whether they size their wire differently.*

Wire Gauge	Actual Size	Diameter in Millimeters	Diameter in Inches	Use for
12		2.05	.81	Solid cuff bracelets or bangles
14		1.63	.064	Wrapped bangles, heavy finger rings, heavy hook clasps
16		1.29	.051	Hook clasps, larger jump rings, heavy bead links for beads with large holes
18		1.02	.040	Jump rings, head and eye pins, simple bead links, heavier ear wires
19		.912	.036	Same uses as 18 gauge
20		.812	.032	Smaller jump rings, head and eye pins, smaller simple bead links, heavier wrapped bead links, lightweight hook clasps, ear wires
21		.723	.028	Head and eye pins, heavier wrapped bead links, ear wires
22		.644	.025	Head and eye pins, wrapped bead links, ear wires
24		.511	.020	Standard wrapped bead links
26		.405	.016	Small or fine wrapped bead links
28 and smaller		.321	.013	Wire crochet and weaving (advanced)

FAQ

Can I use "craft wire" for jewelry making?

Craft and hobby stores often sell inexpensive base-metal wire for crafting that doesn't fit perfectly into any of the categories in this section. Before purchasing it, check the packaging to see which metal or metals it contains. Steel and aluminum wires are not good for jewelry work, because they are difficult to bend and may be subject to corrosion.

In contrast, some craft wire is made of solid copper with a coating of color on its surface. Because it's made of copper, this wire is very easy to bend. However, you will need to be extra careful not to scratch the color coating with pliers, and you should avoid hammering it, which can remove entire areas of color.

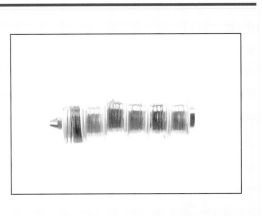

CONTINUED ON NEXT PAGE

MEASURING WIRE GAUGE

As you can tell by the chart on the previous page, there are small size differences between one gauge and the next. When you purchase wire, the gauge should be indicated on the spool or package. However, you will often find stray pieces of wire, of various gauges, strewn across your work area. It may be difficult to tell the exact gauge of a piece of wire by looking at it, and so it's a good idea to invest in a disc-shaped measuring device called a *wire gauge plate*.

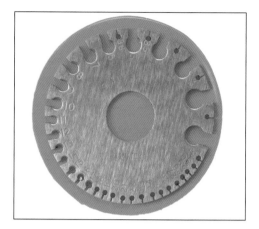

To use a wire gauge plate, insert the wire that you want to measure into a slot along the edge of the gauge. (Do *not* pass it through the round hole.) Move the wire from slot to slot until you find the one that most snugly fits it. The number stamped near that slot is the gauge, or approximate gauge, of your wire.

Once you've determined the gauge of a piece of wire, you should mark it for future reference. Fold a small piece of masking tape around one end, and mark it with the gauge using a permanent marker.

TIP

Determine How Much Wire You Need

The lengths of wire that you need to create various wire components depend on the size of your pliers, the gauge of wire you use, and your personal taste. The lengths suggested in the tasks in this chapter are estimates. Through experimentation, you'll learn which precise lengths are right for you, depending on what you're making and how you would like it to look.

It's a good idea to keep a journal of your favorite wire components to record the gauge of wire you use, the length of wire required, and any tips or notes you'd like to remember later.

Before you get started, take the time to assemble some basic safety equipment and prepare your work area for wirework. You can find basic protective equipment at the local hardware store. Take the following measures in combination with the general safety tips at the end of Chapter 1.

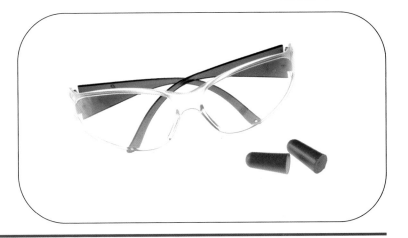

EYE PROTECTION

When you trim wire with wire cutters, little pieces of wire will fly out across your work area or even across the room. Because you won't want any of these pieces of wire flying into your eyes, be sure to wear safety glasses as often as possible when you work. Also, always be extra careful when other people or pets are in the room.

You should also wear safety glasses when you hammer wire. Although it's rare for pieces of wire to fly up during hammering, a piece of your hammer or bench block could shatter and become airborne. Again, although this shouldn't happen very often, if at all, don't take the risk.

EAR PROTECTION

Basic wirework doesn't require the use of noisy mechanical tools or equipment. However, you'll probably find that hammering on a bench block can be uncomfortable for your eardrums. Keep some earplugs or earmuff-style ear protectors near your hammer and bench block, and wear them whenever you need to make more than one or two taps on a wire.

FIRST AID KIT

Although it's unlikely that you will seriously hurt yourself when working with wire, you may experience an occasional finger prick or scratch. Keep a small first aid kit with disinfectant and bandages nearby, just in case.

STORAGE

As you become more involved with wirework, you'll begin to find pieces of wire—short and long—throughout and near your work area. Try to pick these up and store them, so they don't prick a foot or become unsafe toys for pets or children. Plastic storage boxes marked with the type of metal wire that they contain are useful for collecting scraps. You can rummage through them for usable pieces when you need to make smaller components like single jump rings or head pins.

Make Jump Rings, Eye Pins, and Head Pins

You can save money and add a more customized look to your jewelry by making your own jump rings, eye pins, and head pins.

Keep in mind that the wire lengths recommended in these tasks are estimates. You need to experiment to discover which precise lengths work best for you.

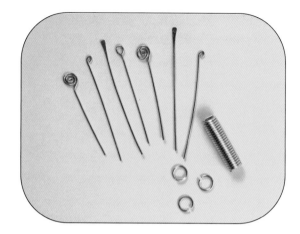

Make a Single Jump Ring

Use this technique when you only need to make a few jump rings at a time. Begin by making a wire coil, and then cut each coil to create a ring.

MAKE A SHORT WIRE COIL WITH PLIERS

1. Grasp the end of the wire with round nose pliers at the point along the nose that matches what you'd like the inside diameter or your jump rings to be.

2. Holding the base of the wire with your fingers, rotate your wrist away from you to roll the wire into a loop.

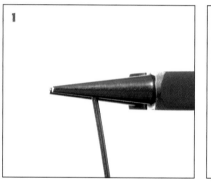

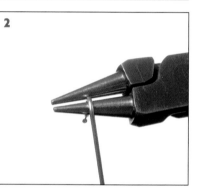

3. Remove the pliers and re-insert them into the new loop in its original position.

4. Begin rolling the wire away from you again while using the thumb and index finger of your other hand to position the new loop *below* the first loop on the pliers.

5. Position this new loop up against the first loop to make a wire coil.

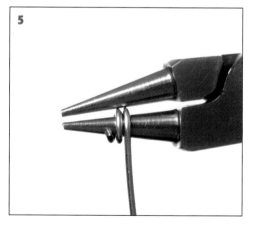

6 Continue using your thumb to guide the wire while using the pliers to make repeated coils at the same place on the nose of the pliers. The coils will move toward the tips of the pliers as you create them.

7 Stop when you have created at least one more coil than the number of jump rings you need.

CUT JUMP RINGS WITH SIDE CUTTERS

1 Use side cutters to trim off the tip of the first coil.

Note: *To create a flush cut, be sure that the flat side of the cutters is facing away from the end of the wire.*

2 Turn the pliers around so that their flat side is facing the opposite direction, and use the cutter tips to cut through the coil just above your first cut. Your first jump ring should fall off the coil.

3 Trim off the next tip of wire with the flat side of the cutters facing away from the tip.

4 Continue cutting all of your rings from the coil, turning your pliers each time to ensure a flush cut.

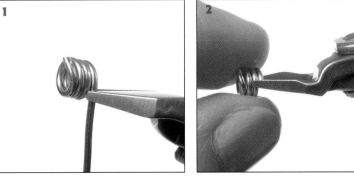

CONTINUED ON NEXT PAGE

TIP

Creating Consistently Sized Rings and Loops

The noses of round nose pliers are graduated in diameter; they're smallest at the tips and thickest at the base. This allows you to choose how large of a ring or loop you'd like to make. You can grasp the wire closer to the tips for a smaller loop or closer to the base for a larger one.

To help you make consistently sized loops for a given project, try marking the point you're using on the pliers with a permanent marker. (These markers are not really "permanent" on metal; the mark will wear off.)

As an alternative, affix a small piece of masking tape to the nose of the pliers, with one edge of the tape marking the spot.

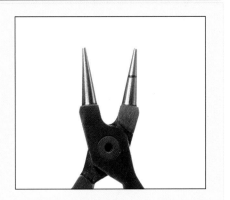

Make Multiple Jump Rings

You can make more jump rings in less time by using a mandrel and a jeweler's saw. (For more information on mandrels and saws, see Chapter 1.)

MAKE A WIRE COIL ON A MANDREL

1 Hold a piece of wire perpendicular to the mandrel with about an inch of wire remaining on one side.

2 Use your thumb to hold the wire securely against the mandrel, and hold the other end of the wire with your other hand.

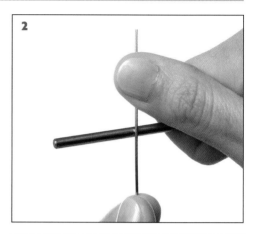

3 Rotate your wrist to turn the mandrel slowly and begin making the first coil, positioning your thumb gently against the 1-inch tail of wire for leverage.

4 Continue turning the mandrel to make coils, using your other hand to position each new coil up against the previous coil.

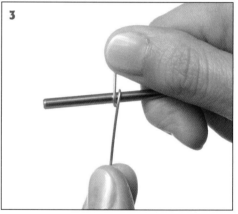

5 Complete at least one more coil than the number of jump rings you'd like to make, up to a maximum of about 1 inch of coil.

6 Slowly pull the coil off of the mandrel, being careful not to open any spaces between coils.

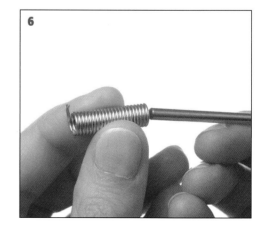

CUT JUMP RINGS WITH A SAW

Cutting jump rings with a saw takes a little practice. Experiment with holding both the coil and saw at slightly different angles to see which angle works best for you.

1 Hold the coil securely between your fingers and against a bench pin or other secure block of wood. (For more information on bench pins, refer to Chapter 1.)

2 Run the saw backwards along the first coil a few times to create a small groove.

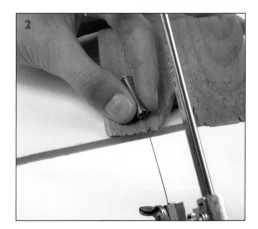

3 Keeping the blade in that groove, slowly saw into the first and second coils.

4 Continue sawing slowly, in a straight line, until you have cut through the entire coil.

Note: The last few coils may start to fall over when you reach them. If that happens, hold them securely with your fingers to complete your cut. The jump rings will fall off as you cut them.

CONTINUED ON NEXT PAGE

TIP

Setting Up a Jeweler's Saw

A jeweler's saw is composed of an adjustable metal frame and a handle. To attach a blade, loosen all three bolts in the frame. Support the saw between your chest and bench pin or table, and position the blade in both ends of the frame. (The blade's teeth should be facing you and pointing downward.) Tighten the bolt at both ends of the blade. Pull the ends of the frame away from each other as far as they will go, and then tighten the last bolt on the back of the frame.

To prepare the blade for cutting, run it across a piece of beeswax or blade lubricant. This will protect the blade and make cutting a little easier.

Saw blades are available in a variety of sizes. Use a size 2 blade for 16- or 18-gauge jump rings, and a size 1 blade for 20-gauge jump rings.

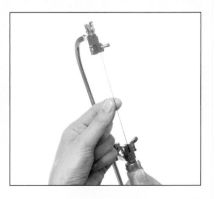

Hammer Jump Rings

You can stiffen jump rings and give them a more finished looked by gently hammering them.

1 Place a jump ring on a clean bench block.

2 Use a chasing hammer to tap the jump ring, with the hammer angled slightly down toward the side of the jump ring that is opposite its opening.

Note: *By hammering at this angle, you create a ring that is slightly more flattened on one side than the other. This is beneficial because it stiffens the jump ring without flattening down the opening, leaving it easy to open and close.*

FAQ

How can I create larger numbers of jump rings more quickly?

If you plan to do larger-scale production work or projects that use many jump rings, you may want to invest in special equipment for making jump rings. Popular versions include built-in steel mandrels and special jigs for cutting. With motorized versions, you typically need to use a professional-grade flexible motor-shaft tool to cut the rings properly.

Make Eye Pins

① Use side cutters to cut a length of wire for each eye pin that you'd like to make. It should be approximately ⅜ inch longer than you'd like the straight part of each finished pin to be.

② Trim the tips with side cutters, as needed, so that both ends of each wire have straight, flush cuts.

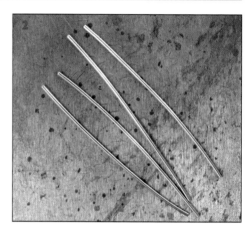

③ To make the eye of each pin, hold one end of the wire with round nose pliers, and rotate your wrist to roll the wire away from you.

④ Return the pliers to their starting position.

⑤ Roll the wire away from you again to complete the eye.

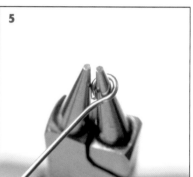

⑥ Return the pliers to their starting position, and use them to hold the wire securely.

⑦ Place the tip of your thumb just below the base of the eye loop, and rotate your wrist slightly back toward you to center the eye on the pin.

The completed eye pin is shown here (a).

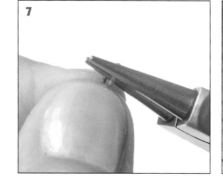
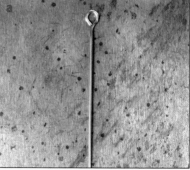

CONTINUED ON NEXT PAGE

Simple Wire Head Pins

Manufacturers use special machinery to create head pins with little nail heads on the ends. You can create simpler head pins that work just as well.

1. Prepare each length of wire as you did for Steps 1–2 of "Make Eye Pins" on the previous page.

2. Use the very tips of round nose pliers to create a tiny loop at one end of each wire.

3. Use chain nose pliers to squeeze down each loop so that the wire is folded back against itself.

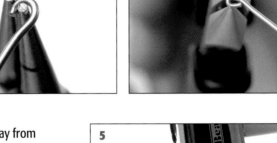

4. Place one pin on your bench block with the folded end facing away from you.

5. Use a chasing hammer to tap the folded end of the pin with a motion that is moving away from you. The face of the hammer should be angled slightly downward. This will flatten the pin's head more at its tip than at its base.

6. Repeat Steps 4–5 for each length of wire that you prepared in Step 1.

   The completed head pins are shown here.

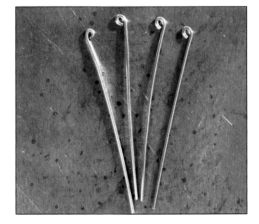

Paddle Head Pins

Paddle head pins are easy to make and have a more artistic look than simple head pins.

1. Prepare each length of wire for your pins as you did for Steps 1–2 of "Make Eye Pins" on page 131.

2. Place one wire on your bench block, with the end that will be the head pointing away from you.

3. Holding your chasing hammer at a slight downward angle, hammer the end with a motion that is moving away from you and toward the end of the pin.

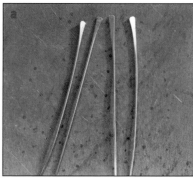

4. Continue hammering until you have created a small paddle at the end of the wire.

5. Use a needle file to smooth the paddle edges.

6. Repeat Steps 2–5 for each length of wire that you prepared in Step 1.

The completed paddle head pins are shown here (a).

CONTINUED ON NEXT PAGE

FAQ

How can I avoid scratching and marring wire with my pliers?

You may not always be able to avoid scratching your wire, but you can take measures to reduce the occurrence and severity of scratches.

An easy way is to cover the jaws of your pliers with a layer or two of masking tape. It will need to be replaced from time to time, and more often when you're working with larger-gauge wire.

Another option is to use a special tool-liquid product designed to coat the jaws of your pliers with a layer of soft plastic. You can purchase these products from the larger jewelry supply retailers. Typically, you need to dip your pliers into the liquid, and then hang them up to dry.

If you don't want to bother with either of these methods, practice using a gentle grip with your pliers. You will probably experience fewer scratches and less marring on your work over time.

Spiral Head Pins

These head pins have hammered spirals at the ends.

1. Prepare a length of wire for each pin that you'd like to make, as you did in Steps 1–2 of "Make Eye Pins" on page 131; however, this time, make each wire about ¾ inch longer than you'd like the straight part of each pin to be.

2. To begin the first pin, use the tips of round nose pliers to create a tiny loop at the end.

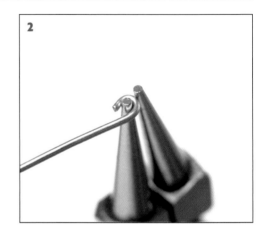

3. Use chain nose pliers or flat nose pliers to flatten down this loop (as you did for Step 3 under "Simple Wire Head Pins" on page 132).

4. With the loop or fold facing away from you and your thumb against the wire at the base of the loop, use flat nose pliers to hold the looped or folded tip flat.

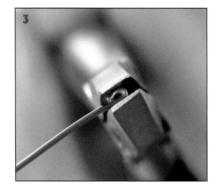

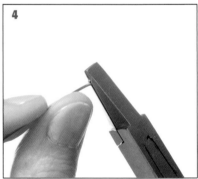

5. Rotate the handle of your pliers away from you while pressing the wire against your thumb to begin a flat spiral.

6. Return the flat nose pliers to their starting position on the new spiral.

7. Repeat Steps 5–6 until you have completed two full coils of spiral.

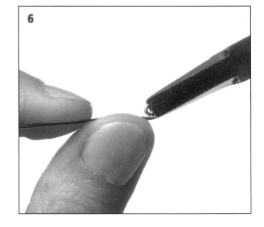

8 Use the flat nose pliers to grasp the wire at the base of the spiral, exactly as shown.

9 Use your index finger to bend the spiral slightly toward you to center it on the pin.

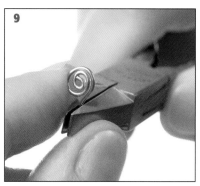

10 Repeat Steps 2–9 to complete each head pin.

The completed spiral head pins are shown here.

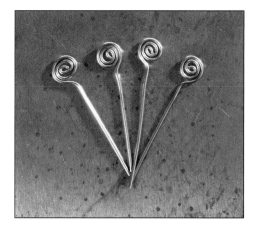

TIP

Using Nylon Jaw Pliers to Straighten Wire

As you work, your wire may become bent or kinked. The easiest way to straighten it is by using nylon jaw pliers. Holding the wire securely at one end with your fingers or chain nose pliers, grasp the wire between the jaws of the nylon pliers, and pull them along the entire length of the wire. Repeat this process until the wire is straight enough to work with.

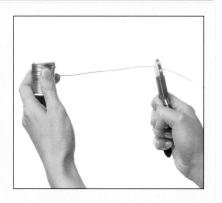

Create Wire-and-Bead Drops and Links

You can use wire and bead drops to embellish almost any type of jewelry. By connecting wire and bead links, you can create entire necklaces, bracelets, and anklets.

As always, keep in mind that the recommended wire lengths in these tasks are estimates. You'll need to experiment to find which precise lengths work best for you.

Bead Drops

SIMPLE WIRE-AND-BEAD DROPS

1 Begin with a head pin in which the straight part is about ¼ inch longer than your bead.

2 Place the bead on the head pin.

3 Holding the pin in place, bend the wire tail back toward you and against the bead as shown.

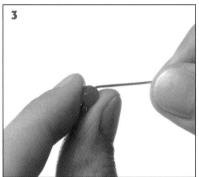

4 Grasp the end of the wire with round nose pliers, and rotate your wrist away from you to create a loop.

5 If necessary, return the pliers to their starting position, and roll the wire again to complete the entire loop.

Note: If you use an eye pin instead of a head pin for your drop, you can add a charm or another drop to the bottom by attaching it to the eye loop.

The completed drop is shown here (a).

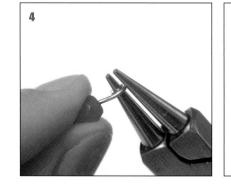
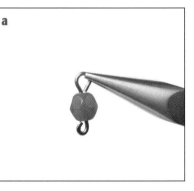

WRAPPED WIRE-AND-BEAD DROPS

If you wrap the wire at the base of your loop, it cannot be pulled open accidentally.

1. Begin with a head pin whose straight part is at least 2 inches longer than your bead.

2. Place the bead onto the head pin.

3. Use round nose pliers to grasp the wire up against the bead as shown.

4. Bend the rest of the wire back toward you as you did in Step 3 of "Simple Wire and Bead Drops" on the previous page.

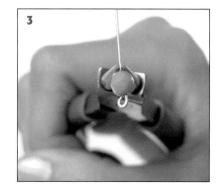
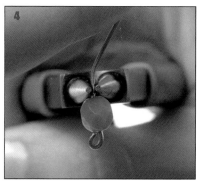

5. Reposition the round nose pliers so that they grasp the wire just above the bend that you made in Step 4.

6. Bend the rest of the wire tail away from you, over the nose of the pliers, and all the way around the pliers to form a loop.

7. Remove the round nose pliers.

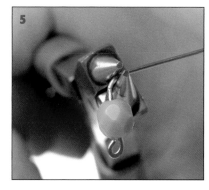

8. Turn the wire over so that the tail is pointing upward.

9. Use chain nose or flat nose pliers to gently hold the loop closed and flat.

10. Using the round nose pliers in your other hand, grasp the wire tail, and wrap it all the way around the base of the wire just below the loop. You should be wrapping in a direction that is moving away from you.

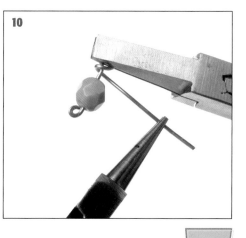

CONTINUED ON NEXT PAGE

⑪ Reposition the round nose pliers at their starting position, and continue making wraps down the base of the wire until it is completely covered with wraps.

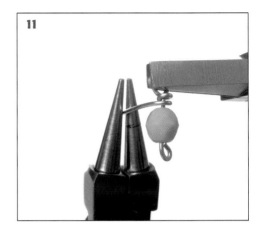

⑫ Use side cutters to trim the extra wire tail flush against the wraps.

⑬ If necessary, squeeze the end of the wire flat with chain nose pliers.

The completed drop is shown below.

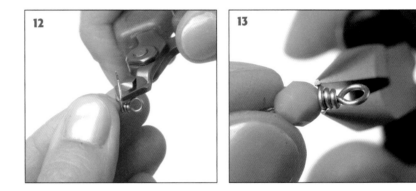

Bead Links

SIMPLE BEAD LINKS

To make a simple bead link, combine the techniques that you used to make an eye pin and a wire and bead drop.

1️⃣ Begin with a flush-cut length of wire that is about ½ inch longer than your bead.

2️⃣ Use round nose pliers to create a loop at one end as if you were making an eye pin.

3️⃣ Place the bead onto the wire and position it against the new loop.

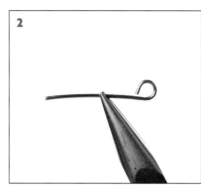

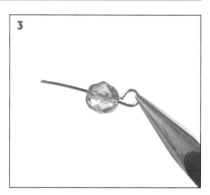

4️⃣ Holding the bead in place, perform Steps 3–5 of "Simple Wire and Bead Drops" on page 136 to complete the link.

Note: Links tend to look best if the loops face opposite directions.

The completed simple bead link is shown here.

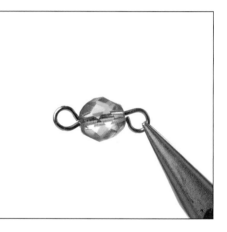

WRAPPED BEAD LINKS

Like wrapped bead drops, wrapped bead links cannot be pulled open accidentally.

1️⃣ Begin with a flush-cut length of wire at least 4 inches longer than your bead.

2️⃣ Grasp the wire with round nose pliers about 1 inch from one end, with the short end facing upward.

3️⃣ Bend the short end of wire toward you.

4️⃣ Reposition the round nose pliers so that they are grasping the wire just above the bend you made in Step 3.

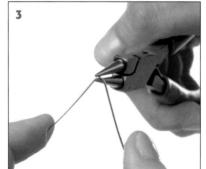

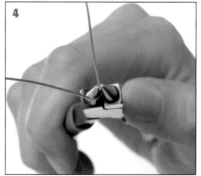

CONTINUED ON NEXT PAGE

5 Use your fingers to bend the wire over and around the pliers to create a complete loop.

6 Remove the round nose pliers, and reposition the wire so that the short tail is pointing upward.

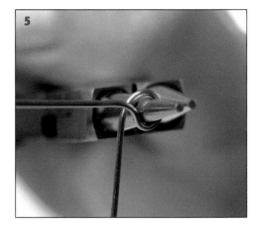

7 Perform Steps 9–10 of "Wrapped Wire-and-Bead Drops" on page 137 to begin making your wrap.

8 Continue wrapping until you have two or three full wraps around the wire.

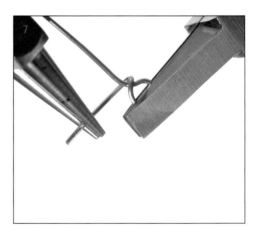

9 Use side cutters to trim off the extra wire, flush with the wraps.

10 If needed, squeeze down the end with chain nose pliers.

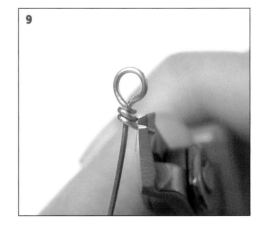

⑪ Place the bead on the wire, and position it up against the first wrapped loop.

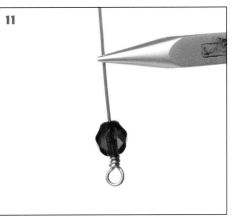

⑫ Perform Steps 3–13 of "Wrapped Wire-and-Bead Drops" on page 137 to complete the second wrapped loop.

The completed wrapped bead link is shown here.

Make Wire Hook Clasps

You can make your own clasps by forming hooks and eyes with wire. Begin with the basic styles, and then experiment to invent your own signature designs.

As always, keep in mind that the recommended wire lengths in these tasks are estimates. You need to experiment to determine which precise lengths work best for you.

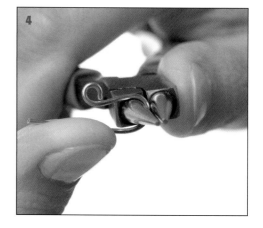

Simple Hook Clasp

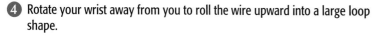

① Begin with a flush-cut piece of wire that is about 2 inches in length.

② Using the tip of the round nose pliers, roll one end of the wire into a small loop.

③ Grasp the wire about ⅛ inch away from the base of the small loop, using the largest part of the round nose pliers.

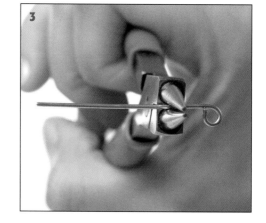

④ Rotate your wrist away from you to roll the wire upward into a large loop shape.

5 Turn the piece around and use the tip of the round nose pliers to grasp the other end of the wire.

6 Roll that end away from you to create a smaller loop.

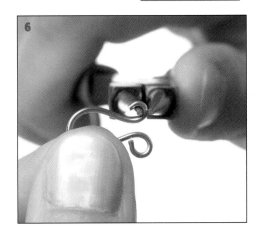

7 Place the hook on a bench block with the large hook-loop facing away from you.

8 Hammering away from you, slightly flatten the top curved portion of the hook.

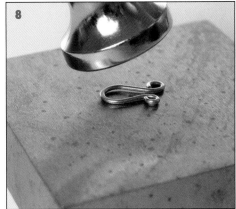

9 Use your fingers to wiggle the hook so that it is just slightly open, if it's not already.

10 If needed, use flat nose pliers to wiggle the small loop at the other end closed.

The completed simple hook clasp is shown here.

CONTINUED ON NEXT PAGE

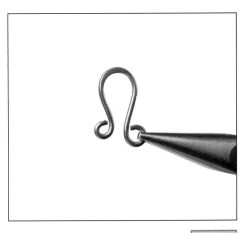

"S" Hook Clasp

As its name implies, an "S" hook is shaped like the letter S.

1 Begin with a flush-cut piece of wire that is about 2½ inches in length.

2 Use round nose pliers to create a small loop at one end.

3 Turn the wire over, and create a small loop at the other end, facing the opposite direction.

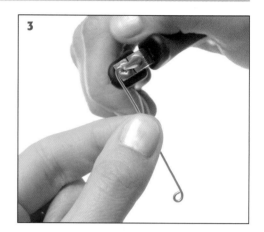

4 Grasp the wire with the largest part of the round nose pliers about ⅛ inch from the base of the loop. The loop should be facing toward you.

5 Rotate the pliers away from you to create a complete large loop. The small loop should touch the center of the wire.

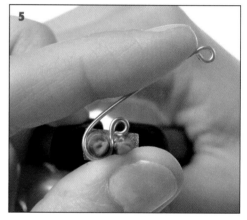

6 Turn the piece around and repeat Steps 4–5 to create a matching large loop on the other end, facing the opposite direction.

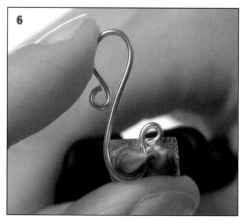

7 Place the hook on a bench block.

8 Hammering away from you, slightly flatten the top curved portion of one of the large loops.

9 Turn the piece around on the bench block, and hammer the other end.

10 Use your fingers or flat nose pliers to wiggle one loop open a little.

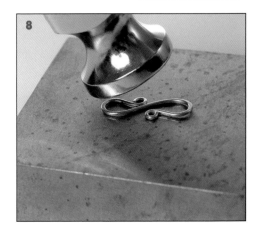

11 Wiggle the other loop completed closed, if it isn't already.

The finished "S" hook clasp is shown here.

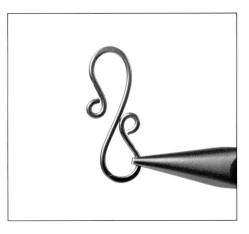

CONTINUED ON NEXT PAGE

Spiral Hook Clasp

1 Using wire directly from the roll and flush-cut at the end, use round nose pliers to create a small loop.

2 Grasp the loop with flat nose pliers, and place your thumb against the wire at the base of the loop.

3 To begin a flat spiral, rotate the handle of your pliers away from you while pressing the wire against your thumb.

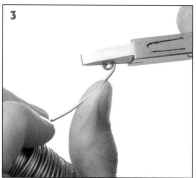

4 Continue this process to create two or three flat spirals.

5 Grasp the wire at the base of the spiral with the tips of the round nose pliers.

6 Without removing the round nose pliers, use your fingers to complete an additional half-flat spiral.

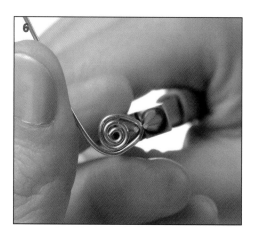

7 Use side cutters to flush-cut the wire about 1¼ inches away from the flat spiral.

8 With the flat spiral facing toward you, grasp the tip of the wire with the round nose pliers.

9 Roll the pliers away from you to create a small loop.

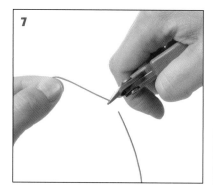

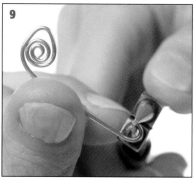

⑩ Turn the piece around so that the flat spiral is facing toward you.

⑪ Grasp the wire just beneath the loop you made in Step 9, using the largest part of the round nose pliers.

⑫ Roll the round nose pliers away from you to create the large hook loop.

⑬ Use your fingers to wiggle the hook slightly open and into alignment with the flat-spiraled base of the hook.

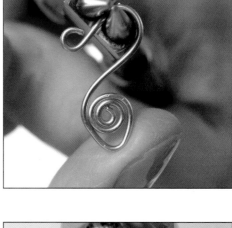

⑭ Place the piece on a bench block with the hook loop pointing away from you.

⑮ Hammering away from you, slightly flatten the top of the hook.

⑯ Turn the piece around on the bench block, and hammer away from you to slightly flatten the bottom of the flat spiral.

The completed spiral hook clasp is shown below.

CONTINUED ON NEXT PAGE

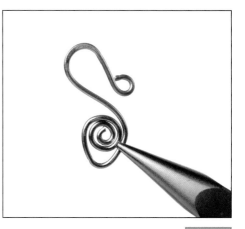

Simple Clasp Eyes

The part of a clasp where your hook attaches is called the *clasp eye*. It can simply be a large jump ring, but a figure-eight style is easier to use and even easier to make.

1. Beginning with a flush-cut length of wire about 1¼ inches long, use the largest part of your round nose pliers to create a large loop at one end.

2. Turn the piece around, and create a smaller loop at the other end that faces in the opposite direction to the first loop.

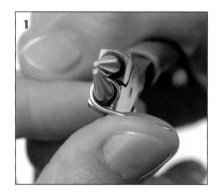

3. Place the clasp eye on a bench block with the large loop pointing away from you.

4. Hammering away from you, slightly flatten the top of the large loop.

5. Turn the piece around on the bench block and repeat Step 4 on the smaller loop.

6. Use flat nose pliers to wiggle both loops closed as needed.

The completed simple clasp eye is shown here, with a hook attached.

Wrapped Clasp Eyes

① Beginning with a flush-cut length of wire about 5 inches long, grasp the wire with the largest part of your round nose pliers about 1½ inches from one end.

② Bend the shorter (1½-inch) end of the wire away from you over the pliers to create a full loop.

③ Remove the round nose pliers, and grasp the loop with flat nose pliers.

④ Use the round nose pliers to wrap the tail two or three times below the loop.

⑤ Trim off the excess wire.

⑥ Turn the piece around, and grasp the wrap with the round nose pliers.

⑦ Bend the unlooped end of the wire toward you, creating a bend next to the wrap.

⑧ Use the round nose pliers to grasp the wire just above the bend.

⑨ Use your fingers to bend the wire away from you and over the round nose pliers. This will create another loop that is smaller than the first.

⑩ Holding the loop with flat nose pliers, use the round nose pliers to wrap the remaining wire end around the first wrap two or three times.

⑪ Trim off the excess wire tail, and file the end with a needle file, if necessary.

The finished wrapped eye clasp is shown here, with a hook attached (a).

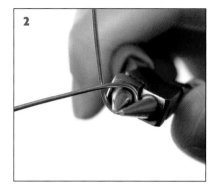

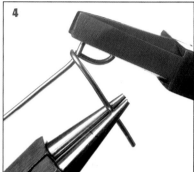

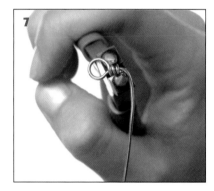

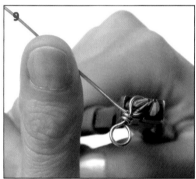

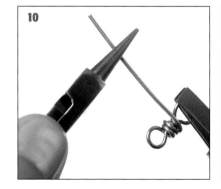

Assemble Some Basic Wire Chains

You can create chains by linking together certain components that you create with wire.

As before, keep in mind that the recommended wire lengths in these tasks are estimates. You'll need to experiment to find out which precise lengths work best for you.

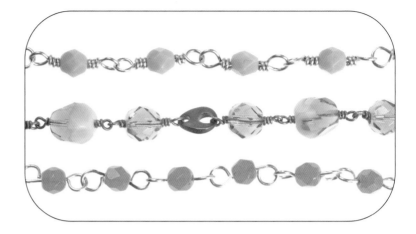

Bead Link Chains

You can turn your wire and bead links into chains simply by connecting them with jump rings. Alternatively, you can connect them directly to one another with their loops.

CONNECTING SIMPLE BEAD LINKS

1 Open one loop on a simple bead link by using chain nose pliers to twist the open half to the side.

2 Insert the closed loop of another bead link into the open loop on the first.

3 Use the chain nose pliers to bend the open loop back into its closed position.

Some connected simple bead links are shown here.

CONNECTING WRAPPED BEAD LINKS

Because wrapped links do not open, you need to connect them as you make them.

1️⃣ Complete Steps 1–11 of "Wrapped Bead Links" on page 139. You now have a link with the first side looped and wrapped, and the bead is in place.

2️⃣ Grasp the wire tail at the end of the bead using round nose pliers, with the tail pointing upward.

3️⃣ Bend the wire tail back toward you.

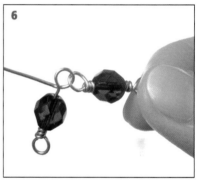

4️⃣ Reposition the round nose pliers to grasp the wire just above the bend that you made in Step 3.

5️⃣ Use your fingers to wrap the wire tail away from you and over the pliers to create a full loop.

6️⃣ Remove the pliers and slip the completed loop of another bead link over the wire tail and into the loop.

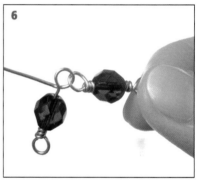

7️⃣ Grasp the unfinished loop with chain nose pliers, being careful not to mar the other loop that is now inside.

8️⃣ Use the round nose pliers to wrap the wire tail around the base of the wire.

9️⃣ Complete this wrap as usual.

Some connected wrapped-bead links are shown here (a).

CONTINUED ON NEXT PAGE

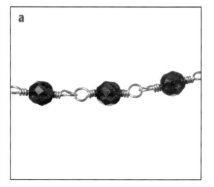

Simple Chain Without Beads

Sometimes you may want a chain that contains no beads, or a chain with beaded links that are separated by unbeaded links. Here are three simple approaches.

"S" CHAIN

This chain is made up of closed "S" hooks that are linked together with jump rings.

1 Make some "S" hooks, and use your fingers or flat nose pliers to close their loops on both ends.

2 Link them together with double sets of jump rings.

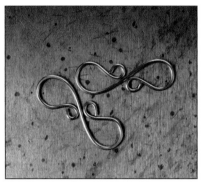

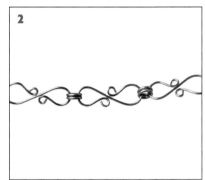

DOUBLE WRAPPED LOOP CHAIN

To make this chain, you connect a series of two-loop connectors that look a lot like wrapped clasp eyes.

1 Make several wrapped clasp eyes, but make all of the loops the same size.

2 Link them together with double sets of jump rings.

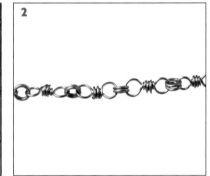

DOUBLE JUMP RING CHAIN

This basic chain is made entirely of jump rings. It serves as an introduction to the more advanced Byzantine chain that you will learn in Chapter 7.

1 Begin with two closed jump rings.

② Use chain nose pliers to pass an open jump ring through both closed jump rings.

③ Close the open jump ring.

④ Pass another jump ring through the first two closed rings, and close it. You now have two links of chain.

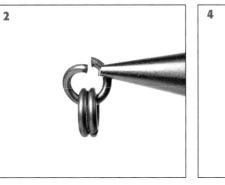

⑤ Continue adding sets of two jump rings to the desired length.

A completed length of double jump ring chain is shown here.

chapter 7

More Advanced Wirework Techniques

Once you are comfortable working with wire, you can expand on your basic skills to create more distinctive designs. In this chapter, you'll learn simple versions of some of the most popular techniques used by wire-jewelry artists and designers. Don't be afraid to experiment by altering the examples to suit your taste. Over time, you'll develop your own unique preferences and personal style. Because many of these tasks require practice, be sure to use inexpensive wire when you first attempt them.

Make a Wrapped Briolette Drop

Briolettes are drop-shaped beads that have elegant, triangular facets. They're commonly used as focal beads and centerpieces and are some of the most popular beads to wrap with wire. Here is the standard technique for creating a wrapped briolette drop.

How to Make a Wrapped Briolette Drop

1. Using 24-gauge wire directly from the spool or coil, insert the end of the wire through the hole in the briolette until a tail of at least ½ inch of wire protrudes from the other side.

2. While holding the briolette in place, bend the wire on the spool-end of the briolette toward the top of the briolette.

3. On the other side of the briolette, bend the wire tail in the same manner. The wire is now crossed just above the top of the briolette.

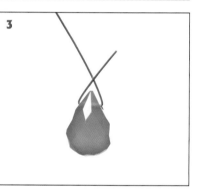

4. Using flat nose pliers, grasp the shorter wire, just above the very top of the briolette.

5. Bend the wire directly upward.

6. Turn the briolette around and repeat Steps 4–5 with the wire on the other side.

   The wire should now look like this (a).

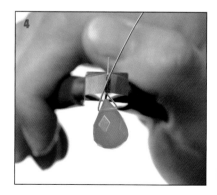

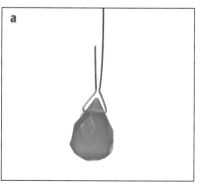

7 Using sharp-tipped side cutters, carefully trim the wire tail about ⅛ inch above the bend that you made in the shorter wire.

8 With the tips of chain nose pliers, grasp the two wires, side-by-side.

9 Align the upper edge of the pliers with the end of the short wire.

10 Use your other hand to bend the spool end of the wire downward to one side.

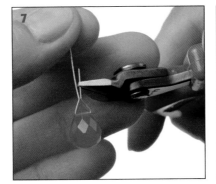
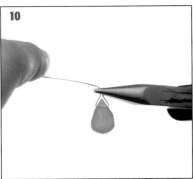

11 Grasp the spool end of the wire with round nose pliers just above the bend that you made in Step 10.

12 Using your other hand, wrap the wire around the nose of the pliers to create a loop.

13 While still holding the loop with the round nose pliers, wrap the spool end of the wire around both wires below the loop.

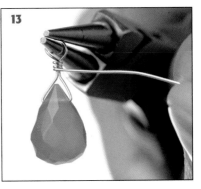

14 Continue wrapping until you reach the bends in the wires.

15 Trim the wire with side cutters.

16 If necessary, use chain nose pliers to flatten down the end of the wire.

The completed briolette drop is shown here.

Use Double Wire

You can use two pieces, or layers, of wire instead of one to add bulk and interest to jewelry and components. Here are two popular techniques for doubling-up on wire to create detail and greater three-dimensionality.

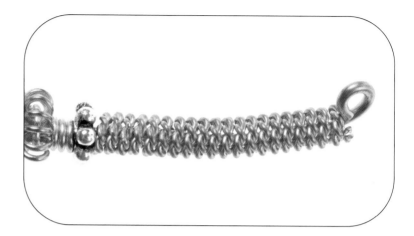

Double-Twisted Wire

Try making some components (like jump rings and connectors) with two strands of wire twisted together. Use an inexpensive hand drill and some hooks to create this *double-twisted wire*.

1 Beginning with a length of 20-gauge wire about 3 feet long, insert the wire into an eye hook that is securely attached to your workbench or another heavy, stable object.

2 Center the eye hook along the wire, and pull both ends of the wire together.

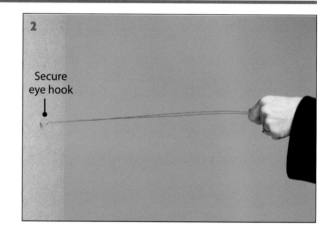

Secure eye hook

3 Hold the wire securely with your fingers an inch or two from the ends, and use chain nose pliers to twist the ends together several times.

4 Insert a small hook (like a cup hook) into the chuck of a hand drill, and tighten the chuck securely over the screw-end of the hook.

5 Slide the twisted end of the wire over the hook in the drill.

6 Gently pull the wire taut between the eye hook and the drill hook.

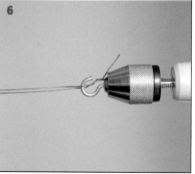

⑦ Slowly turn the crank on the hand drill to begin twisting the two strands of wire together.

⑧ As the wire becomes shorter, walk toward the eye hook, keeping the wire taut as you work.

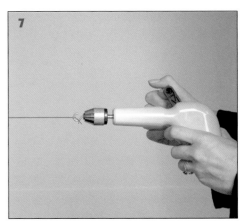

⑨ Continue twisting until you have the desired density of twists along the wire.

⑩ Trim both ends of the twisted wire with side cutters to prepare it for use.

CONTINUED ON NEXT PAGE

FAQ

Are there other ways to twist wire besides using a hand drill?

Absolutely. One of the most basic methods is to use a pencil or pen to hold the wire, instead of a hook and hand drill. Simply insert the pencil or pen behind the twisted-together wire ends, and use both hands to turn it again and again to twist the wire. This technique is much more time-consuming than using a hand drill, but it works.

Some jewelry making suppliers also sell a specialized tool for twisting wire. It looks like a large, strange pair of pliers. You lock the ends of your wire into its jaws, and then pull a lever at the other end of the tool to cause it to spin. This tool may speed up your wire twisting, but it's a little awkward and uncomfortable to use. Try one before purchasing it to see whether it's right for you.

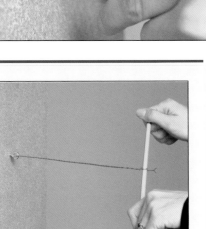

Double-Wrapped Wire Beads

You can make these chunky beads by wrapping wire around wire. Learn this basic method, and then experiment with different lengths of wire and different mandrel sizes. (For a review of mandrels, see page 21 in Chapter 1.)

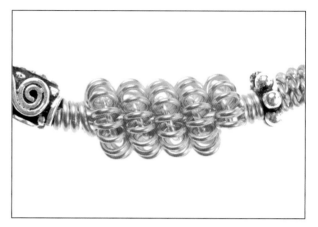

1. Following the directions for making a wire coil on a mandrel (page 128 in Chapter 6), use a small mandrel and 20-gauge wire to create a wire coil 2–3 inches long.

2. After removing the coil from the mandrel and trimming the ends, insert a 7- to 8-inch length of 18-gauge wire all the way through the coil.

3. Position the coil at the center of the 18-gauge wire.

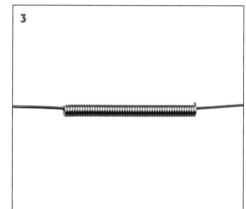

4. Keeping the coil in this position, press one end of the coil firmly against the mandrel.

5. Slowly turn the mandrel while pressing the coil against it to create a new coil moving in the opposite direction. In effect, you are wrapping the 18-gauge wire around the mandrel and taking the 20-gauge coil along with it.

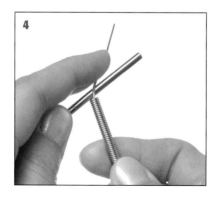

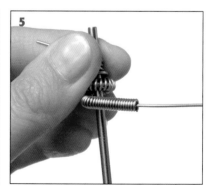

6 Continue coiling until you reach the end of the 18-gauge wire.

7 Turn the mandrel around and coil the other end of 18-gauge wire around the mandrel.

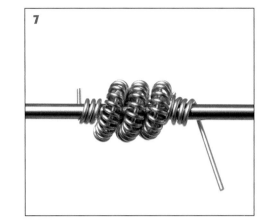

8 Slide the wire off of the mandrel and trim the ends, making blunt cuts.

The completed bead is shown here. You now have a bead that can be strung onto cord or wire.

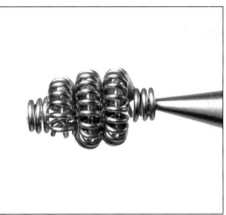

TIP

Specialty Wire Coiling Tools

If you have trouble neatly coiling a long length of wire on a regular mandrel, try using a specialty wire-coiling tool instead. There are several styles of coiling tools to choose from. Most include a mandrel attachment with a handle or crank for easy turning, and a notch or other mechanism for securing your wire. Some are even designed to help you make double-wrapped beads faster and easier than you can using the traditional method.

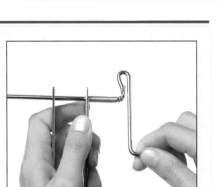

You can create elaborate pendants and cuff bracelets by wrapping beaded wire onto wirework frames. Begin by shaping a frame using heavy-gauge wire, and then fill it with wrapped-in beads on small-gauge wire. Experiment with different shapes and sizes of frames and beads for variety.

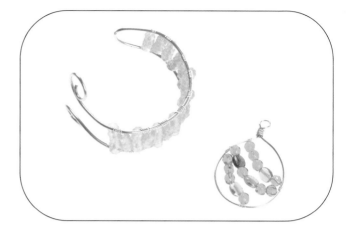

Round Framework Pendant

MAKING THE FRAME

A pendant frame can be just about any shape, but round frames are the easiest to construct. Notice that you wrap the top using the same method that is used to wrap a briolette.

① Beginning with 16-gauge wire directly from the spool or coil, wrap the first several inches of wire around a round mandrel that is as large as you would like the inside of your pendant frame to be.

② Double over the ends of the wire, leaving about 1 inch of wire tail.

③ Hold the wire on the mandrel with one hand, and use your other hand to grasp the base of the wire tail with flat nose pliers.

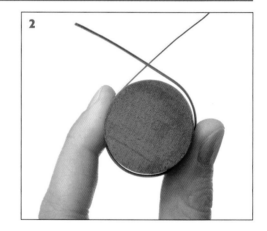

④ Use the flat nose pliers to bend the wire tail upward at a 90-degree angle.

⑤ Use the pliers to grasp the base of the wire coming around the other side of the mandrel.

⑥ Bend this wire upward at a 90-degree angle directly next to the bend that you made in Step 4.

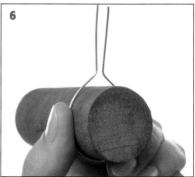

⑦ Remove the frame from the mandrel.

⑧ Using heavy, sharp-tipped side cutters, flush-cut the short wire about ⅛ inch above the top of the circle.

⑨ Grasp the base of the two wires, just above the wire circle, with chain nose pliers.

⑩ Align the upper edge of the pliers with the end of the short wire that you cut in Step 8.

⑪ Use your other hand to bend the spool end of the wire downward to one side.

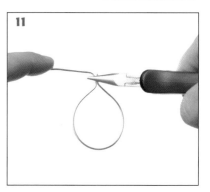

⑫ Grasp the spool end of the wire with round nose pliers, just above the bend that you made in Step 11.

⑬ Using your other hand, wrap the wire around the nose of the pliers to create a loop.

⑭ While still holding the loop with the round nose pliers, slowly wrap the spool end of the wire snugly around both wires below the loop.

⑮ Continue wrapping until you reach the base of the wires at the top of the circle.

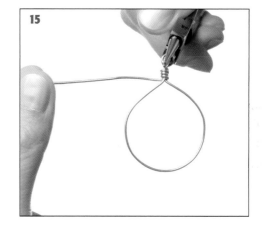

⑯ Make a flush-cut to trim off the wire.

⑰ If needed, use chain nose pliers to neaten the coils and flatten down the wire end.

Note: *If your frame has lost its circular shape, slip it back over the mandrel as far as it will go to reshape it.*

The completed frame is shown here.

CONTINUED ON NEXT PAGE

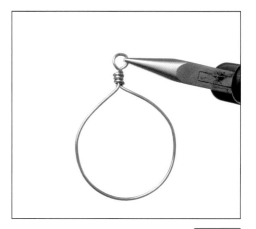

WRAPPING-IN BEADS

You can fill your pendant frame with any beads that will fit inside it. Rows of beads can be aligned closely together, or they can zigzag loosely across the frame.

1 Beginning with 3 feet of 24-gauge wire, use chain nose pliers to fold-over about 4 inches of wire at one end.

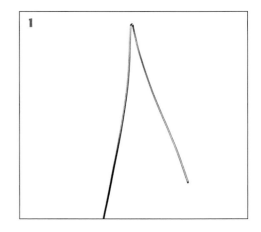

2 Position the wire horizontally over what will be the front of the pendant.

3 Slide one side of the pendant frame all the way into the fold in the 24-gauge wire.

4 Position the wire close to the top of the frame.

5 Using the fingers of one hand, hold the long end of the 24-gauge wire against the opposite side of the frame.

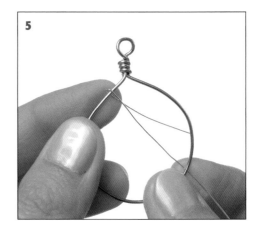

6 With your other hand, use chain nose pliers to bring the short end of the wire up through the frame.

7 Securely wrap the short end of the wire around the side of the frame.

⑧ Continue wrapping around the side of the frame until you have made five or six wraps. You will have a tail of extra wire remaining after this step. For now, leave it in place to use for leverage.

Note: If the rest of your 24-gauge wire is bent, use nylon jaw pliers now to straighten it. You can stop and straighten the wire after you wrap each row of beads into the frame.

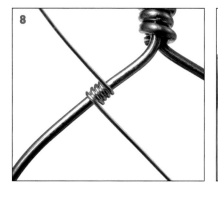

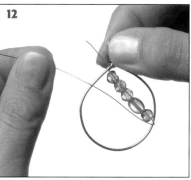

⑨ String enough beads onto the 24-gauge wire to make up the first row.

⑩ Slide the beads up against the side of the frame.

⑪ Position the other end of the wire down through the frame and under its other side.

⑫ Keeping the wire taut, bring it up and around the frame.

⑬ Wrap the wire around the frame five or six times in a downward direction.

⑭ String on the next row of beads.

⑮ Bring the wire over and around the opposite side of the frame and create five or six more wraps.

⑯ Continue adding rows of beads until you reach the bottom of the frame.

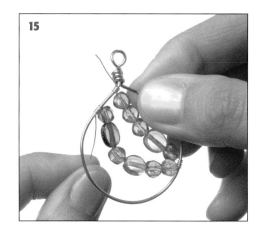

⑰ After securing the last rows of beads with five or six wraps around the frame, use side cutters to trim the wire flush with the frame at both the top and bottom.

⑱ If needed, flatten down both ends of the wire using chain nose pliers.

The completed pendant is shown here.

CONTINUED ON NEXT PAGE

Framework Cuff Bracelet

MAKING THE FRAME

Try this basic method for making a simple cuff bracelet frame. You can customize the design by changing the frame's width and shape.

1 Beginning with 14-gauge wire directly from the spool or coil, with the end blunt-cut, place the first 8 inches of wire along a ruler.

2 With a permanent marker, mark the wire 7 inches from the end.

Note: *You can remove the mark later using nail polish remover or by lightly filing it off with a needle file.*

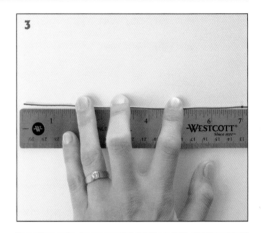

3 Use the marker as a mandrel by holding the wire crosswise against it. The ink mark should be centered above the marker.

4 Bend both sides of the wire down over the marker.

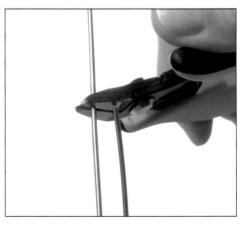

5 Using side cutters, blunt-cut the spool end of the wire so that both wire ends are the same length. The wire now has a long "U" shape.

Note: *You can straighten the frame at this point by holding the wire at the base of the "U" and pulling both ends of the wire through nylon jaw pliers.*

6 Place the frame over a bracelet mandrel or a mandrel substitute, such as a jar or flashlight handle. An eyeglass case is used in the example.

7 Bend down both ends of the frame over the mandrel to form the frame into a curve.

8 After removing the wire from the mandrel, hold the frame with the bottom of the "U" closest to you, and grasp the end of the upper wire with round nose pliers.

9 Roll the pliers away from you to create a loose spiral.

10 Turn the frame over and repeat Steps 8–9 to form a loose spiral on the other wire end.

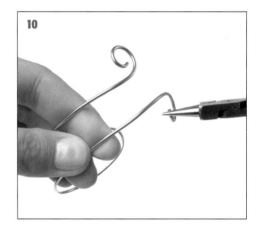

11 Manipulate the wire with your fingers as needed to bring it into an oval cuff-bracelet shape.

Note: You can make the cuff a little larger by gently pulling the ends away from each other, or smaller by bending them closer together.

The completed cuff bracelet frame is shown here.

CONTINUED ON NEXT PAGE

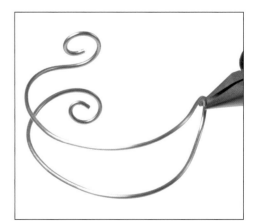

WRAPPING-IN BEADS

Fill your bracelet with beads using essentially the same technique that you use for a pendant frame.

1. Beginning with about 3 feet of 24-gauge wire, use chain nose pliers to fold-over 4 inches of wire at one end.

2. Position the wire vertically over the frame near the "U" end of the frame.

3. Slide the top wire of the frame all the way into the fold in the 24-gauge wire.

4. Using the fingers of one hand, hold the long end of the 24-gauge wire against the bottom wire of the frame.

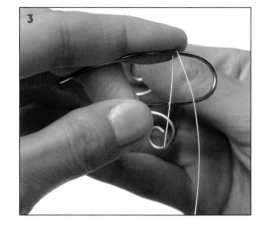

5. With your other hand, use chain nose pliers to bring the shorter wire end up from below the top of the frame and toward the open end of the frame.

6. Use chain nose pliers to wrap the wire around the top of the frame five or six times, moving toward the open end of the frame.

7. String on enough beads to reach the bottom of the frame where you would like the first row of beads to connect.

8. Keeping the beads within the frame, bend the long end of wire over the bottom of the frame.

9. Wrap this wire around the bottom of the frame five or six times.

10. Continue adding beads and wrapping the ends under, then over, the opposite side of the frame until you reach the open end of the frame.

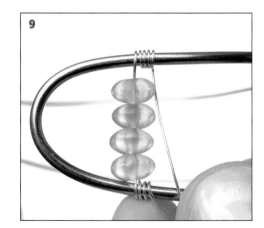

⑪ After stringing on the beads for the final row, wrap the end of the wire five or six times around the frame.

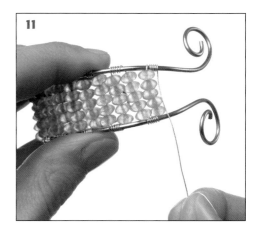

11

⑫ Use side cutters to trim off the excess wire tail at both ends of the frame.

⑬ If needed, use chain nose pliers to flatten the ends against the frame.

Note: If you use up the length of wire at any time before finishing the bracelet, end the wire by wrapping it five or six times around the frame. Begin a new length of 24-gauge wire by wrapping it around the opposite side of the frame.

The completed bracelet is shown here.

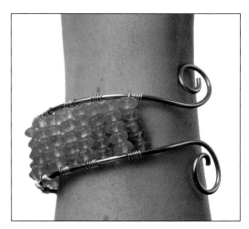

TIP

More Framework Ideas

You can make wire frames in just about any shape. Look around your house for interesting items to use as mandrels. If you're short on time or prefer a more finished appearance, try using pre-made pendant frames. You can often find them at local bead shops or on the Internet. They are usually cast (molded), stamped, or soldered and have a ring or bail at the top for stringing. To get even more creative, look for found objects with general frame-like shapes. See what kind of unusual jewelry designs you can invent by wrapping them with beads.

Create More Wire Clasps

In Chapter 6, you learned how to make basic wire hook clasps. Here are some slightly more complicated clasps that you can use to add variety to your designs. These clasps all work well with simple clasp eyes (see page 148 in Chapter 6). If you'd like to make them larger than the ones shown here, you may want to increase the wire gauge for strength. If you make them smaller, you can use a slightly smaller wire gauge.

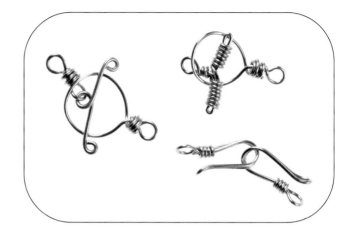

Fold-Over Hook Clasp

This clasp is a wrapped hook made with doubled-over wire.

1 Beginning with a 4¼-inch length of 20-gauge wire, use flat nose pliers to fold over the wire 1¼ inches from one end.

2 Using round nose pliers, grasp the single wire just past the point where the doubled wire ends.

3 Use the pliers to bend the wire away from you at a 90-degree angle.

4 Without removing the round nose pliers, use the fingers of your other hand to pull the wire all the way around the pliers to create a loop.

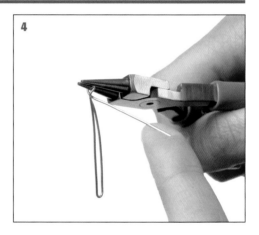

5 Remove the round nose pliers and turn the piece around so that the loop is pointing in the opposite direction.

6 Grasp the loop with chain nose or flat nose pliers.

7 With your other hand, grasp the end of the wire tail with your fingers or round nose pliers.

8 Wrap the wire tail securely around both wires, below the loop, about four times.

9 Trim any excess wire tail and flatten the end against the doubled-wire base, as needed.

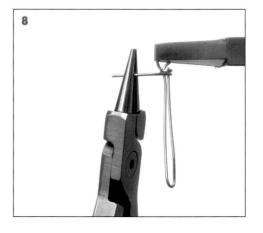

⑩ Grasp the center of the doubled-wire portion of the hook with the largest part of the round nose pliers (the very bottom of the nose).

⑪ Use your fingers to bend the wire over the round nose pliers on both sides.

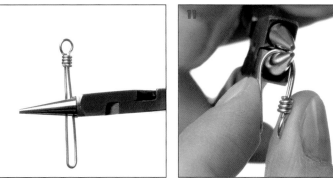

⑫ Grasp the very end of the doubled wire (the tip of the hook) with the round nose pliers.

⑬ Gently bend the tip of the hook outward.

⑭ Use your fingers to bend the wrapped-loop portion of the hook slightly toward the back of the hook.

The completed fold-over hook clasp is shown here (a).

CONTINUED ON NEXT PAGE

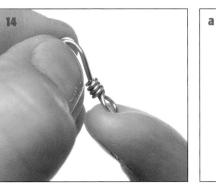

Wire Toggle Clasps

A toggle clasp is composed of a T-bar and a large clasp eye (to review clasp eyes, see page 148 in Chapter 6). For a secure fit, the inside diameter of the clasp eye should be about half the length of the T-bar.

SIMPLE TOGGLE CLASP T-BAR

This T-bar is made of two separate pieces linked together.

1. Beginning with a 1¾-inch length of 18-gauge wire that is blunt-cut on both ends, grasp the very center of the wire with round nose pliers.

2. Use your fingers to bend both sides of the wire upward until they cross over the nose of the pliers.

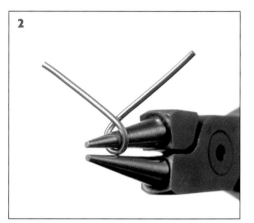

3. Continue bending each wire downward to the side.

4. Check to make sure that the two side wires appear to be the same length.

    Note: If one side is slightly longer than the other, trim it down now. If your loop is more than a little off-center, it's best to start over so that your T-bar will not be too short.

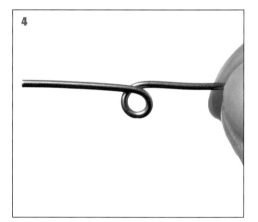

5. Grasp the end of one side of wire with the round nose pliers and create a small, upward-facing loop.

6. Turn the piece around and use the round nose pliers to create a small, downward-facing loop on the other side. Set this piece aside.

7. Using a 5-inch length of 20-gauge wire, grasp the wire with round nose pliers 1¼ inch from one end.

8. Bend the shorter end of wire over the nose of the pliers to create a loop.

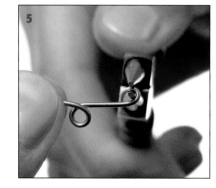

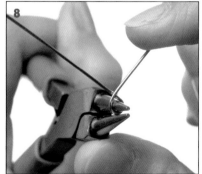

9. Turn the piece around so that the loop is facing the opposite direction.

10. Grasp the loop with flat nose pliers.

11. Use the round nose pliers to wrap the shorter end of the wire around the base of the loop several times.

12. Trim off the excess wire tail and flatten down the end.

13. Holding the wrapped portion of the wire with round nose pliers, bend the long wire end to the side.

    After completing Step 13, the wire should look like this (a).

14. With the round nose pliers, grasp the single wire next to the bend that you just made.

15. Bend the wire over the nose of the pliers to create a loop.

16. Pick up the T-bar that you completed in Step 6, and slide it into the open loop that you created in Step 15.

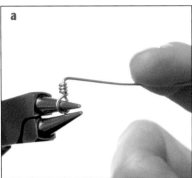

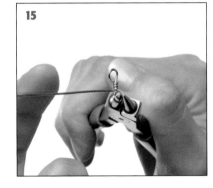

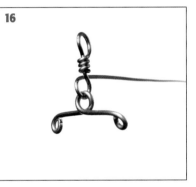

17. Turn the piece around so that the new loop and bar are facing the opposite direction.

18. Grasp the base of the loop with chain nose pliers, being careful not to crush or scratch the bar.

19. Use the fingers of your other hand, or round nose pliers, to wrap the long end of the wire several times over the first wrap.

20. Trim the excess wire tail and flatten the end against the wraps.

    The completed simple toggle clasp is shown here (b).

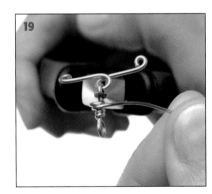

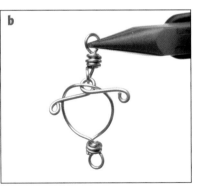

CONTINUED ON NEXT PAGE

WRAPPED TOGGLE CLASP

This toggle is sturdy, even though it's made with smaller, 20-gauge wire. It has a different look than the simple toggle clasp, and you make it in one single piece.

1 Beginning with 8 inches of 20-gauge wire, grasp the center of the wire in round nose pliers.

2 Pull one end of the wire around the nose of the pliers to create a loop.

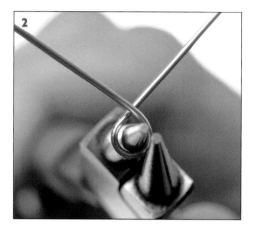

3 Remove the round nose pliers, and turn the wire around so that the loop is facing the opposite direction.

4 Grasp the loop with flat nose pliers, with the two wire ends pointing up and to the side, respectively (in an "L" shape).

5 Using the fingers of your other hand, bend the upper wire down over the lower wire.

6 Bend the other wire out to a 45-degree angle.

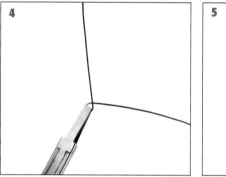

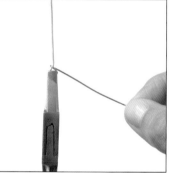

7 Go back to the first wire, and wrap it around the second wire two or three times.

8 With the loop now pointing downward, hold the loop with the fingers of one hand, and use your other hand to bend both wires down to the sides.

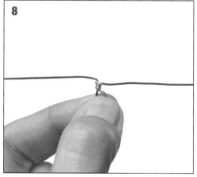

9 Using flat nose pliers, fold over one of the side wires ⅜ inch from the loop.

10 Turn the piece around and repeat Step 9 with the other side wire.

Note: *Make sure that the side wires do not cross over one another.*

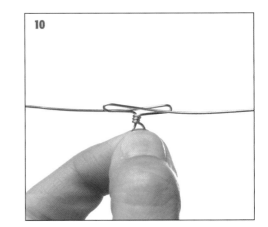

11 Hold one side of the piece firmly between your fingers.

12 Use the fingers of your other hand to bend down the other side wire in front of the bent wire as close to the loop as possible.

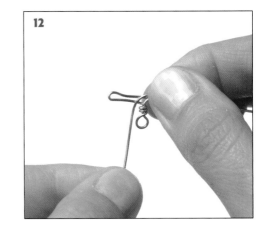

13 Using your fingers or round nose pliers, wrap this wire around the doubled side wire until you are close to the end of the bar.

14 Turn the piece around and repeat Steps 11–13 on the other side.

15 Trim off the excess wire at both ends, and flatten down the wire ends, as needed.

The completed wrapped toggle clasp is shown here (a).

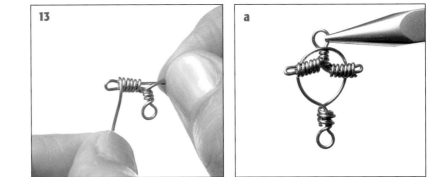

Construct Elaborate Wire Chain

In Chapter 6, you learned how to make some basic wire chains. Now try two slightly more complicated chains made with wire and rings. To make them more ornate, try combining links made from different colored metals or connect chain links with beaded links.

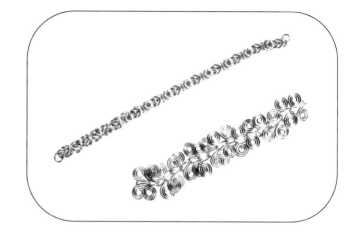

Double Spiral Chain

This showy chain has an ancient Egyptian motif. For efficiency, make the links first and then connect them all together.

MAKING SPIRAL LINKS

1 Beginning with 4 inches of 19-gauge wire that is blunt-cut at both ends, use round nose and flat nose pliers to begin an upward spiral at each end. (For a review of spiraling wire, see Chapter 6.)

2 Work back and forth between the two sides until there is a ½-inch space of wire between two equally sized spirals.

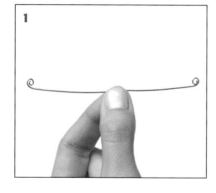

3 Grasp the center of the wire with round pliers, with both spirals facing upward.

4 Use your fingers to bend both of the spirals down below the nose of the pliers.

5 Repeat Steps 1–4 with separate pieces of wire until you have made the desired number of chain links.

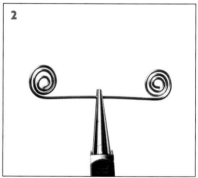

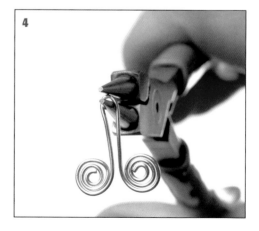

CONNECTING SPIRAL LINKS

1 Pick up one link and use flat nose pliers to fold over its loop, flush with the bottoms of the two spirals. The top of the loop should protrude a little above the two spirals.

2 Pick up a second link and slip its loop through the end of the loop on the first link.

3 Use flat nose pliers to fold-over the loop on the second link, and lock the first loop inside. You should now have two links connected by their loops and facing the same direction. They should be connected loosely enough that the finished chain remains flexible.

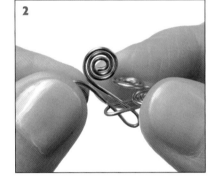

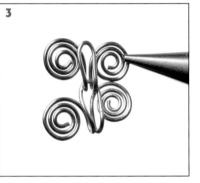

4 Continue attaching links in this manner until you have the desired length of chain.

A completed length of chain is shown here.

CONTINUED ON NEXT PAGE

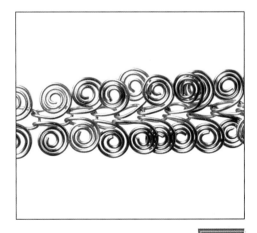

Construct Elaborate Wire Chain *(continued)*

Byzantine Chain

The *Byzantine* is a popular, three-dimensional chain that uses a large number of jump rings. You will use up the jump rings quickly, so consider purchasing some pre-made rings in bulk, or investing in equipment for making jump rings, if you enjoy this technique.

1 Beginning with a supply of 18-gauge, 5.5mm OD (outside diameter) jump rings, place two closed jump rings onto a safety pin.

2 After closing the safety pin, slip an open jump ring through both closed rings, and close it.

3 Repeat Step 2 to add a second closed jump ring to the original two rings.

4 Using the same procedure, add two more jump rings to the two rings that you added in Steps 2–3. You now have a three-link chain of double jump rings.

5 Grip the first two links of the chain (four rings total) with the fingers of one hand.

6 Fold back the last two rings in the chain, so that they fall to opposite sides.

7 Add the two folded-back rings to the rings that you're holding in your fingers.

8 Fold back the next two rings at the end of the chain as far as they will go. This will expose the next set of two rings below (shown in blue).

⑨ While still holding the chain with one hand, use flat nose pliers in your other hand to thread a new open jump ring through the two lower rings that are now exposed (shown in blue in step 8).

⑩ Add a second closed jump ring to those two lower rings.

The chain should look like this (a).

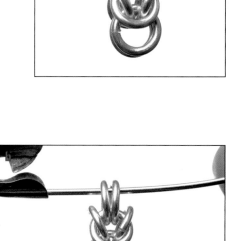

⑪ Attach two more links of two jump rings each to the rings that you added in Step 10.

A chain should now look like this (b).

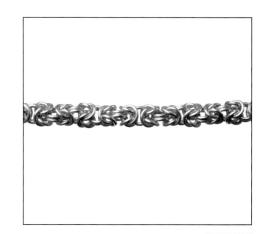

⑫ Fold back the last two rings so that they fall to the sides, as you did in Step 6.

⑬ Fold back the next two rings as far as they will go, exposing the next two rings between them.

⑭ Repeat Steps 9–13 until you have the desired length of chain.

A completed length of Byzantine chain is shown here.

Make a Wire Finger Ring

You can use your wirework skills to create beautiful, stylish rings that don't require solder or molten metal. Begin with a simple all-wire design and then try wrapping a beaded ring. If you like the results, try experimenting with different wraps and embellishments.

Simple Wrapped Ring

1 Beginning with a length of 16-gauge wire that is about 10 inches long, center the wire across a ring mandrel with size markings, aligned with the mark for one-half size larger than you would like the finished ring to be.

2 Holding the wire against the mandrel with the thumb of one hand, use your other hand to bend back both ends of wire behind the mandrel.

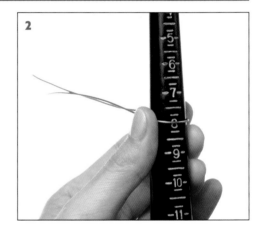

3 Pass both wires around the back of the mandrel, but do not allow them to cross over one another. (They should remain parallel.)

4 While continuing to hold the wire in place on the mandrel, bend the wire back around to the front of the mandrel and cross them past one another there.

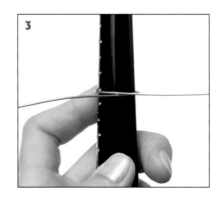

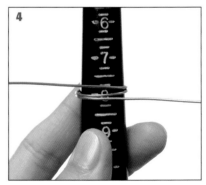

⑤ Bend the upper wire down over the two lower wires.

⑥ Bend the bottom wire up over the upper two wires.

⑦ Remove the wire from the mandrel.

⑧ Using your fingers or pliers, wrap each wire end around the ring two or three times, wrapping outward from the center of the ring.

⑨ Trim off the excess wire and flatten down the ends with chain nose pliers.

The completed wrapped ring is shown here.

CONTINUED ON NEXT PAGE

TIP

Determining Proper Ring Size

A ring mandrel with size markings is useful for making rings of particular sizes, but it's not a fool-proof tool. Notice that you made the simple wrapped ring by wrapping it one-half size larger than its finished size. This is to accommodate the added thickness of the heavy-gauge wire that you wrapped around the band in later steps. (It makes the inside circumference of the ring slightly smaller than it was at first.)

Keep this effect in mind when you design your own rings. Any wire wrapped around the ring's band will decrease its size to some degree. Even some large beads, if they sit low enough in the ring, may change its inside circumference. Keep your sized ring mandrel on hand when you experiment with new designs, and make note of any significant size changes that you experience during the process.

Wrapped Bead Ring

1 Beginning with a length of 20-gauge wire that is about 15 inches long, string on one small- or medium-sized round bead.

2 Center the bead along the wire.

3 Bend up both ends of wire on either side of the bead.

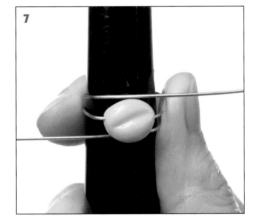

4 Place the bead against a ring mandrel (at the same size mark as you would like the finished ring to measure), with the wire ends positioned toward the back of the mandrel.

Note: *Some ring mandrels have a channel on one side where the bead can rest to help hold it in place.*

5 Cross the wire ends past one another against the back of the mandrel.

6 Bring both wires around to the front of the mandrel.

7 Position the wires so that each wraps slightly under the edge of the bead (between the bead and the mandrel).

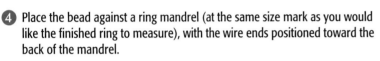

8 Bend the lower wire up against the side of the bead and over the wire that goes through the bead hole.

9 Wrap this wire completely around the bead one time.

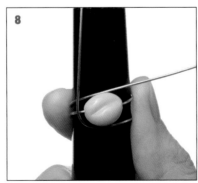

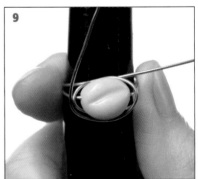

10 Bend the upper wire down against the other side of the bead.

11 Wrap that wire completely around the bead one time.

The two wires should now point in opposite directions at either side of the bead.

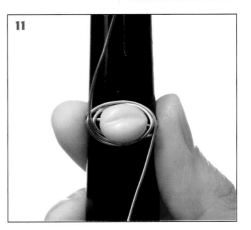

12 Remove the ring from the mandrel.

13 Using your fingers or chain nose pliers, wrap the wire on the left side of the ring down behind the ring band.

14 Wrap this wire securely around the band about three times.

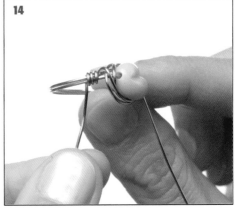

15 Using the same technique, wrap the wire on the right side of the ring around the band on that side.

16 Trim off the extra wire from both sides, and flatten down the wire ends using chain nose pliers.

The completed wrapped bead ring is shown here.

8

Using a Wire Jig

You can use a jig to create wire findings and components that are the same shape and size. Jigs are especially useful for making uniform connectors and ear wires. Most jigs have moveable pegs that you can rearrange to create your own unique designs. By creating jig patterns on paper, you can save your designs to use over again.

Wire jigs are easy to use once you get the hang of them. To begin, arrange some pegs on the jig by placing them into the holes. Next, anchor the end of your wire on the jig, and slowly wrap the wire around each peg in the direction called for by the design. Finally, remove the wire from the jig and trim off the extra wire ends.

ANCHORING

You need to anchor your wire on the jig so that it doesn't slip while you wrap it around the pegs. There are two common ways to do this. Experiment to see which method you like best.

The simplest way to anchor wire is to hold the end down firmly against the surface of the jig with your fingers. You may need to hold the wire in this position while you wrap the entire design using your other hand.

The other way to anchor is to insert the end of the wire into an empty peg hole outside of the design. How well this works may depend on the style of your jig and the depths of its holes.

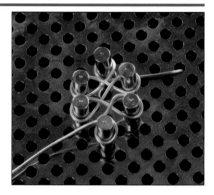

WRAPPING

Once your wire is anchored, you can begin wrapping it around the jig pegs. For best results, go slowly and keep the wire as taut as possible as you move it from one peg to the next. Try to keep the wire as close to the jig surface as possible.

For small designs, or designs where the pegs are very close together, the wire may ride up to the tops of the pegs and try to pop off. If this starts to happen, try pushing the wire down using the eraser end of a pencil or the tips of flat nose pliers.

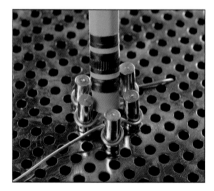

REMOVING

Always lift your design off the jig slowly. Use your fingers to support as much of the wire as possible, so that it doesn't bend or stretch. You'll find that pegs sometimes stick in the wire and get pulled out of the jig when you do this. Simply tap them down again with your fingers, or take them out and replace them after you've removed the design.

You can use connectors as decorative elements or to connect other components directly or with jump rings. Just like beaded links, connectors can be made with simple, open loops or with wrapped loops. For sturdy connectors, use 20-gauge wire for small pieces and 18-gauge wire for larger pieces.

SIMPLE TWO-LOOP CONNECTORS

A two-loop connector looks a lot like the figure-eight clasp eye that is made using round nose pliers in Chapter 6. Experiment to see which technique you like best.

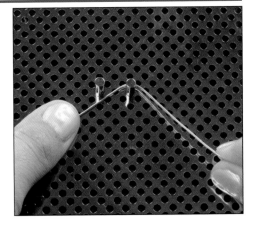

1 Arrange two pegs horizontally on the jig with one empty space between them.

2 Using wire directly from the spool or coil, place the wire diagonally between the two pegs, with the wire end reaching past the bottom peg by about 1 inch.

3 With the fingers of one hand, anchor the wire end against the jig.

4 Using your other hand, wrap the wire over and around one of the pegs.

5 Bring the wire back up between the pegs and around the next peg, in a figure-eight pattern.

6 Position the wire diagonally between the pegs.

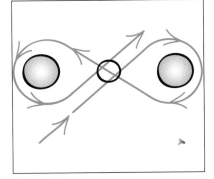

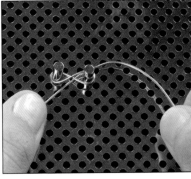

7 After removing the wire from the jig, use side cutters to trim off the ends of the wire at the base of each loop.

8 Use flat nose pliers to wiggle each loop closed.

A completed two loop connector is shown here (a).

CONTINUED ON NEXT PAGE

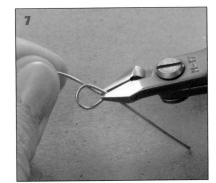

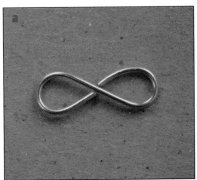

SIMPLE THREE-LOOP CLOVER CONNECTORS

You can use these connectors at the ends of double-strand bracelets and necklaces, or as necklace centerpieces to hold drops.

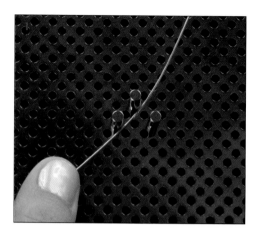

1 Arrange three pegs on the jig in a triangle pattern, leaving one empty space between every two pegs.

2 Using wire directly from the spool or coil, place the wire diagonally between the pegs, with two pegs on one side and one peg on the other.

3 Allow the wire end to reach past the bottom pegs by about 1 inch.

4 With the fingers of one hand, anchor the wire end against the jig.

5 Use your other hand to wrap the wire over and around the top peg.

6 Bring the wire under, around, and over one of the bottom pegs.

7 Wrap the wire underneath, up and over the other bottom peg.

8 Complete the loop by bringing the wire down and out the bottom of the triangle.

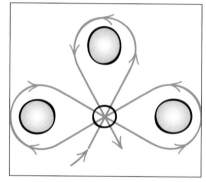
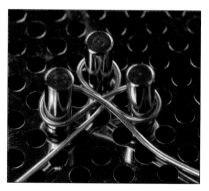

9 After removing the wire from the jig, use side cutters to trim the wire at the base of the top and bottom loops.

10 Use flat nose pliers to wiggle each loop closed.

A completed three-loop clover connector is shown here (a).

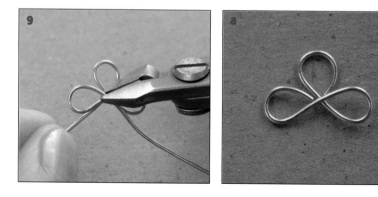

FOUR-LOOP CLOVER CONNECTORS

These connectors are similar to the three-loop version, but they're more versatile because of their extra loop.

1 Arrange four small pegs on the jig in a cross formation, with one empty space in the center.

2 Using wire directly from the spool or coil, place one end of wire diagonally between the pegs, with two pegs on either side.

3 Allow the wire end to reach past the bottom pegs by about 1 inch.

4 With the fingers of one hand, anchor the wire end against the jig.

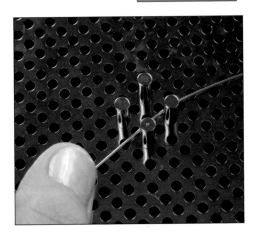

5 Using your other hand, wrap the wire over the top peg.

6 Bring the wire down around the bottom peg in the opposite direction, creating a figure-eight.

7 Cross the wire through the center of the pegs, and wrap it around one of the side pegs.

8 Pull the wire across and around the other side peg in the opposite direction, creating a sideways figure-eight.

9 Position the wire diagonally through the pegs and out again at the top.

10 After removing the wire from the jig, use side cutters to trim both wire ends at the bases of the loops.

11 Use flat nose pliers to wiggle the two open loops closed.

A completed four-loop clover connector is shown here (a).

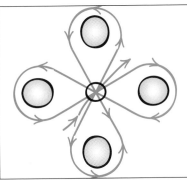

CONTINUED ON NEXT PAGE

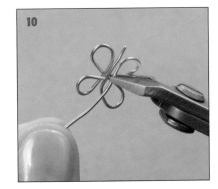

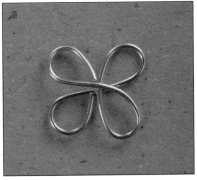

WRAPPED TWO-LOOP CONNECTORS

Wrapped wire connectors are more secure than simple connectors because their loops are wrapped closed.

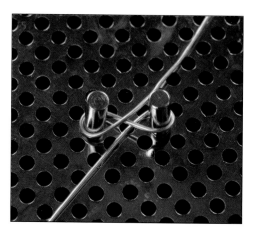

1 Arrange two pegs next to each other on the jig, with one empty space between them.

2 Using wire directly from the spool or coil, place the wire diagonally between the pegs, leaving a tail about 2 inches long at the bottom.

3 Using the fingers of one hand, anchor the wire end against the jig.

4 With your other hand, wrap the wire over and around one of the pegs.

5 Bring the wire back up between the pegs and around the next peg, in a figure-eight pattern.

6 Position the wire diagonally between the pegs.

7 After removing the wire from the jig, trim the wire so that it has about 2 inches of tail on its other end.

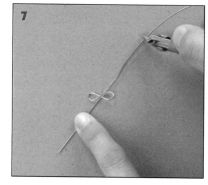

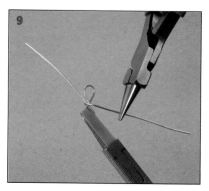

8 Using flat nose pliers, grasp one of the loops close to its base.

9 Wrap the wire tail from that loop, under and around the base of the loop twice, using round nose pliers to grip the wire, if necessary.

10 After trimming off any excess wire tail, flatten the end of the wire against the coil using chain nose pliers.

11 Turn the connector around and grasp the other loop with the flat nose pliers.

12 Wrap the second wire tail over and around the coil that you made with the first tail.

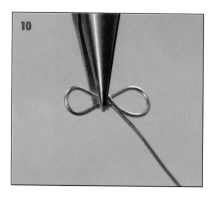

⓭ After trimming any excess wire, flatten the wire end against the coil as you did in Step 10.

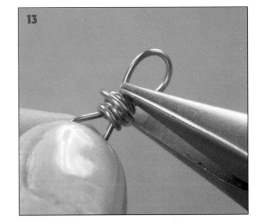

⓮ File the wire end with a needle file to remove any sharp edges.

The completed wrapped wire connector is shown here (a).

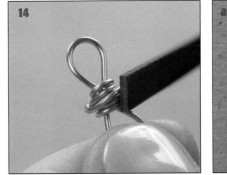 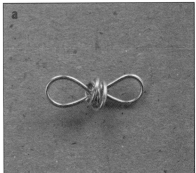

CONTINUED ON NEXT PAGE

TIP

Using Connectors as Spacer Bars

Wire connectors usually lie flat within a design to link components side-by-side. On large-diameter cord, like leather, they can also be used to hold multiple beaded strands next to each other lengthwise.

To do this, simply string on a connector by threading cord through its loops. String on beads or tie knots on either side of the connector to hold it in place.

Make Wire Connectors *(continued)*

WRAPPED THREE-LOOP CONNECTORS

① Arrange three pegs horizontally on the jig, as shown.

② Using wire directly from the spool or coil, place one end of wire diagonally between two of the pegs, leaving a tail about 2 inches long at the bottom.

③ Using one hand, anchor the wire tail against the jig.

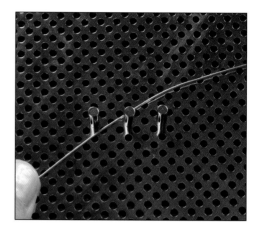

④ With the other hand, wrap the wire over the center peg, and then down again.

⑤ Bring the wire up, around, and over the next peg.

⑥ Position the wire diagonally and down between these two pegs.

⑦ Wrap the wire around the bottom of the center peg, bringing it up diagonally on the other side.

⑧ Wrap the wire over and around the last peg.

⑨ Position the wire diagonally up between these two pegs.

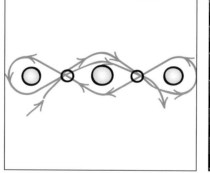

⑩ Wrap the wire over the center peg, leaving it pointing downward on the other side.

⑪ After removing the wire from the jig, trim the wire so that it has about 2 inches of tail on its other end.

⑫ Use flat nose pliers to grasp one of the end loops near its base.

⑬ Wrap the wire tail from this loop over and around the base of the loop two or three times.

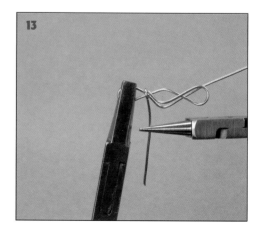

13

14 After trimming any excess wire tail, flatten the wire end against the new coil using chain nose pliers.

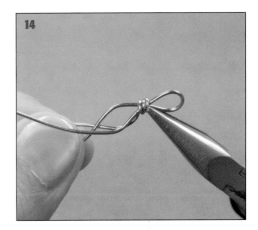

15 Turn the connector around, and grasp the other end-loop with the flat nose pliers.

16 Repeat Steps 12–13 to complete this wrap.

The completed three-loop wrapped connector is shown here (a).

CONTINUED ON NEXT PAGE

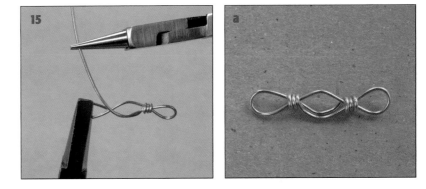

FAQ

How can I get jig designs to lie flat?

Large or intricate jig designs often appear bent after you remove them from the jig. With some designs, you can simply wiggle them into a flatter position using your fingers or flat nose pliers.

For a more dramatic effect, or when wiggling doesn't work, try hammering your design. You need to be careful not to hammer jig-made components too strenuously. They can easily be smashed and damaged. You can avoid this problem by using a nylon head hammer, hammering only on the outer edges of the loops in the design, or lightly hammering with a piece of suede or leather on top of the design.

CELTIC KNOT LOOPED CONNECTORS

These connectors make eye-catching focal pieces. Once you learn this basic approach, try creating them in other sizes and shapes using different diameters and arrangements of pegs.

1. Arrange six small pegs on the jig as shown.

2. Using wire directly from the spool or coil, place the wire horizontally beneath the top peg, leaving a tail about 1 inch long at the side.

3. Using one hand, anchor the wire against the jig.

4. With the other hand, bring the wire up and around the top peg and back down again.

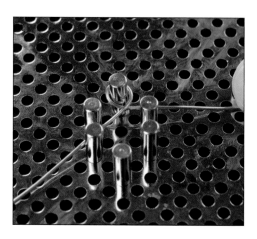

5. Bring the wire up, over, and around one of the side pegs.

6. Cross over the center of the formation and wrap the wire around the opposite peg, creating a sideways figure-eight.

7. Cross the wire over again and bring it down below the next peg on the other side.

8. Wrap another sideways figure-eight around this peg and the peg opposite it.

9. Bring the wire down and wrap it all the way around the bottom peg.

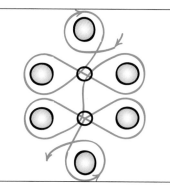

10. After removing the wire from the jig, use side cutters to trim the wire at the bases of the top and bottom loops.

11. Use flat nose pliers to wiggle each loop closed.

The completed Celtic knot looped connector is shown here (a).

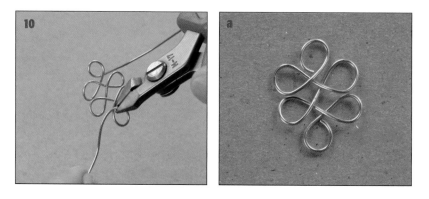

SPIRAL-END LOOPED CONNECTORS

You can add flair to your connectors by replacing the end loops with flat spirals. Follow these steps to add coil ends to a Celtic knot looped connector.

1 Arrange six pegs on the jig in the same formation as the Celtic knot looped connector.

2 Using wire directly from the spool or coil, place the wire end horizontally below the top peg, leaving a tail about 2 inches long at the side.

3 Using one hand, anchor the wire against the jig.

4 Perform Steps 6–8 under "Celtic Knot Looped Connectors."

5 After removing the connector from the jig, trim it off of the coil or spool, leaving 2 inches of wire tail on the connector.

6 Using chain nose pliers, fold-over the tip of one wire end in the direction shown.

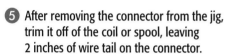
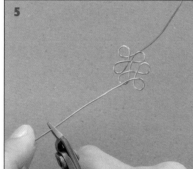

7 Begin spiraling the wire-end by performing Steps 4–7 for making spiral head pins in Chapter 6 (see page 134).

8 Continue forming the spiral until it reaches the connector.

9 Create a matching spiral on the other end of the connector, rolling the second spiral in the opposite direction to the first.

The completed spiral-end looped connector is shown here (a).

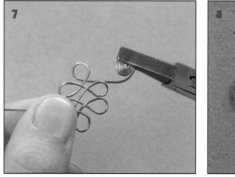
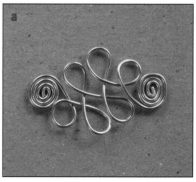

Form Ear Wires

Ear wires are easy to make and less expensive than their pre-made counterparts.

SIMPLE FRENCH HOOKS

1 Arrange one small, one large, and one medium peg on your jig, as shown.

2 Using 22- or 20-gauge wire directly from the spool or coil, use side cutters to make a flush-cut at the end of the wire.

3 Grasp the wire end with round nose pliers, and roll them away from you to create a loop.

4 Place the loop over the small peg on the jig, with the loop facing downward, as shown.

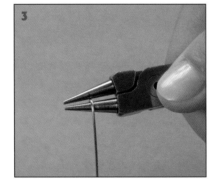

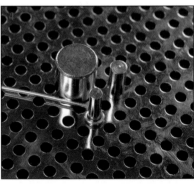

5 Wrap the wire around and over the large peg, and down between the small and medium pegs.

6 Pull the wire up slightly behind the medium peg.

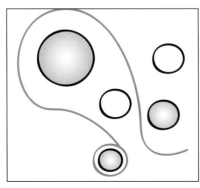

7 After removing the wire from the jig, use side cutters to trim the wire just past the final curve that you created in Step 6.

8 Repeat Steps 1–7 to create a matching ear wire.

9 To trim the second ear wire, hold it up against the first one to make sure that you cut it in exactly the same place.

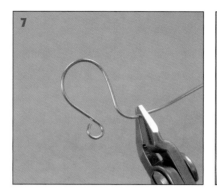
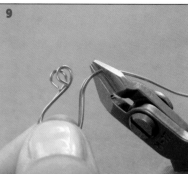

10 Place each hook on a bench block.

11 Lightly hammer the tops of the hooks in a direction moving away from you, until they are slightly flattened.

12 Optionally, turn the hooks around and lightly hammer the loops to stiffen them.

The completed hooks are shown here (a).

CONTINUED ON NEXT PAGE

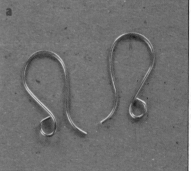

TIP

Deburring Ear Wires

Always *debur* your ear wires so that they will be comfortable to wear. Deburring is the process of removing sharp edges from an end of wire.

After removing each ear wire from the jig and trimming its end, use a needle file to smooth down the edges. Holding the file at a 45-degree angle, gently file all the way around the wire end. Then, lightly rub your finger over the end of the ear wire to see if it's smooth to the touch. If it's still scratchy, continue filing gently at an angle until the wire tip is completely rounded and smooth.

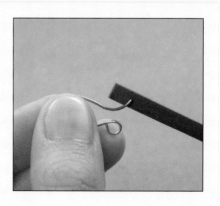

CURLED-LOOP FRENCH HOOKS

This style of French hook is a little more ornate than the simple version.

1. Perform Steps 1–2 under "Simple French Hooks" (see page 196).

2. Place the end of the wire on a bench block.

3. Slightly flatten the tip of the wire by lightly hammering in a motion that is moving away from you.

4. If needed, use a needle file to file the end of the wire smooth.

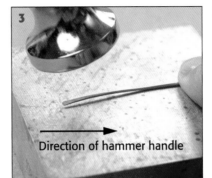

Direction of hammer handle

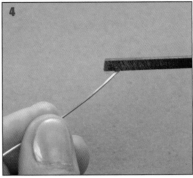

5. Grasp the wire end with the tips of round nose pliers, and roll them way from you to create a very small loop.

6. Turn the wire around so that the loop is facing you.

7. Grasp the wire with the round nose pliers just below the loop, and position the wire a little farther up on the nose of the pliers.

8. Roll the pliers away from you to create a second, complete loop.

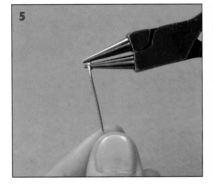

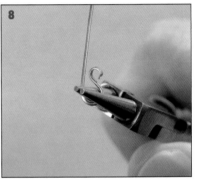

9. Before removing the pliers, gently pull the wire back and position it next to the first loop, as shown.

⑩ Place the second loop over the small peg on the jig with the loop pointing downward, as shown.

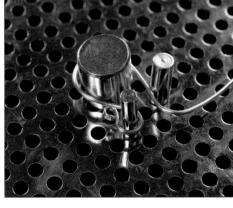

⑪ Complete the ear wire as you did in Steps 5–8 under "Simple French Hooks" (see pages 196–197).

⑫ Make a second ear wire to match.

The completed curled-loop French hooks are shown here.

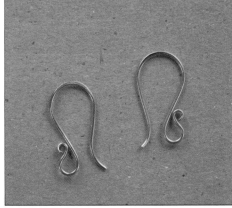

TIP

Customizing Ear Wires

You can give earrings a unique look by altering the design of their hooks. Try experimenting with different shapes, sizes, and embellishments. Just make sure that your hooks are easy to insert and comfortable to wear, and that they hold earrings in place securely.

Here are some ideas to try:

- Large, circular hoops made by using your largest jig peg.
- Hooks with wrapped loops instead of open loops.
- Extra-long, straight hooks.
- Hooks with beads above their loops.
- Square or triangular hooks.

Wire Jig Patterns

You can create your own unique components on a jig by experimenting with different peg sizes and configurations. When you discover a design that you really like, you may want to keep a record of it so that you can make it again. A good way to do this is to create a *jig pattern*.

DIAGRAMMING ON GRAPH PAPER

This is a very basic method for making a jig pattern. You simply draw in the locations of pegs in corresponding squares on graph paper.

Begin by arranging the jig pegs and wrapping wire around them to create your design. Place a piece of graph paper next to the jig, and copy the locations of each peg to matching squares on the graph paper. Allow each square to represent one space on the jig. Designate peg sizes by using varying sizes of circles or different letters, symbols, or colors on the paper. Use lines and arrows to show the path that the wire takes through the pegs. To use the pattern, simply arrange pegs in the jig to match your diagram.

PEG-HOLE PATTERNS

Another way to create a jig pattern is to use pegs to punch holes in a piece of paper. For best results, only use this method with a jig large enough to hold two separate arrangements of pegs at one time, or use two jigs.

Begin by arranging the pegs close to one side of the jig, and wrapping wire to create your design. Place a sheet of paper over the other side of the jig (or on a second jig). Using new pegs, re-create your design in the paper by pushing the pegs through it and into the jig holes. When you're finished, you'll have a template that you can place over your jig to re-create the design.

To designate peg sizes on a peg-hole pattern, try color-coding the outsides of the holes using colored pens. You can show the path of the wire using lines and arrows, as you would with a graph-paper pattern.

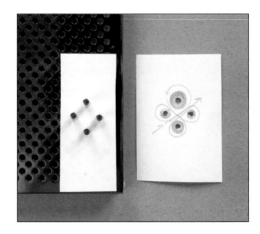

Some Wire-Jig Patterns to Try

Now that you know how to use a jig and jig patterns, try making these connectors by following the graph-paper patterns provided. When you get accustomed to them, try altering them to create your own designs.

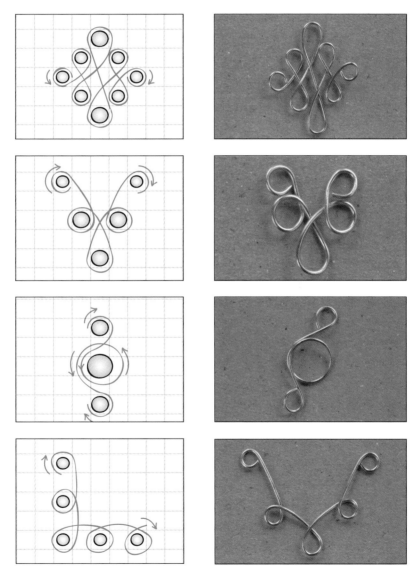

9

Macramé Knotting and Beading

Macramé and braided jewelry is fun and casual, and it can range from very simple to surprisingly complex. Many popular designs are made with natural fiber cords like hemp or jute. You can also knot and braid soft leather, satin, nylon, or cotton cord. You'll begin this chapter by learning some standard terminology, and then learn how to set up your knotting board and create the most common knots and braids.

When you make macramé jewelry, you work with multiple strands of cord that all have different purposes. The cords may be the same color, material, and size, but they have different names depending on their function. These names are used in most project instructions, and so it's good to become familiar with them.

WORKING CORDS

Working cords include all of the cords that you use as part of your design. There are two main types of working cords: *filler cords* and *knotting cord*s.

Filler Cords

When you begin a macramé jewelry project, your first step is to secure the *filler cords*. These are long, straight cords that you hold down, or *anchor*, so that you can tie knots around them using other cords.

Knotting Cords

Knotting cords (also called *tying cords*) are the cords you use to tie knots around filler cords. You can anchor them to your work surface with tape or pins.

ANCHOR CORD

An *anchor cord* (also called a *holding cord*) may or may not be part of a design. It is typically anchored at both ends, and you tie working cords directly to it.

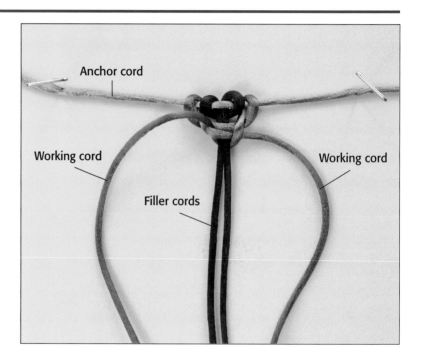

Anchor cord

Working cord

Working cord

Filler cords

WRAPPING CORD

You use a *wrapping cord* whenever you make a wrap knot (see page 213). It is a loose length of cord that wraps around a bundle of working cords to hold them together.

FAQ

How much cord do I need?

When you create your own designs, it can be difficult at first to estimate how much cord they will require. As a general guideline, begin with working-cord strands that are each at least 2½ to 3 times the desired length of your jewelry. (If you anchor your cords by folding them over, then each piece of cord needs to be twice this length.) Consider adding several additional inches if you plan to make a loop closure to finish your work.

Note that filler cords can be cut much shorter than knotting cords if they remain straight and unknotted throughout the design.

As you experiment with new ideas, always keep track of how much cord you actually use. Over time, you will develop a feel for the lengths of cord you need to create the styles of jewelry that you enjoy creating.

Set Up a Knotting Board

Your macramé work area can be either fixed or portable. If you don't need to move your work from place to place, you can anchor your cords to any heavy or immoveable object, like a table leg or an eye hook fastened to a wall. However, if you prefer a portable work area, or a setup that is simply more convenient, you can use a knotting board.

Types of Knotting Boards

You can buy a pre-made knotting board from a jewelry making supplier or you can make your own. If you're short on time or resources, you can even use a standard office clipboard in place of a knotting board.

PRE-MADE KNOTTING BOARDS

Pre-made knotting boards make macramé knotting easier, and they're relatively inexpensive. They are typically made of rigid fiberboard covered with paper and a layer of shrink-wrap plastic. Often, they are packaged with a supply of steel T-pins for anchoring cords. Most pre-made boards are marked on one side with a 1-inch grid that you can use to keep your work even and to make your jewelry to the desired length.

You can anchor your work to the board in various ways. The simplest method is to horizontally attach an anchor cord to the top of the board. Insert T-pins through the cord and into the board at both ends. Before you begin knotting, tie your working cords to the anchor cord. Another option is to tape a metal ring (like a washer or thin shower curtain ring) to the board and attach your working cords to it.

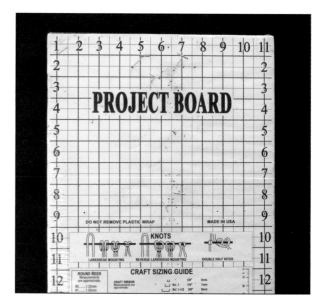

HOMEMADE KNOTTING BOARDS

You can make your own knotting board out of just about any material that is soft enough to insert T-pins and strong enough to hold them in place. Try a slab of dense foam board from a craft store or corkboard from an office supply store. If you'd like to add a grid of measured squares to your board, you can draw one out on heavy paper or light paperboard (or print one from a computer) and attach it to the board with pins or thumbtacks. You can use the same anchoring methods with a homemade board as you can with a pre-made board.

One of the nice things about a homemade board is that you can make it any size. You'll find that some projects are easier to complete on a smaller board than a larger one.

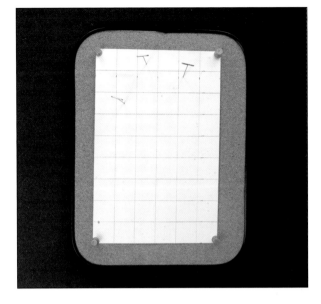

USING A CLIPBOARD

If you'd rather not purchase a pre-made knotting board or bother with making one, try knotting on a simple clipboard. Double-over a length of scrap cord and tie an overhand knot near the ends to create a loop. Clip it down to the board, with the knot just behind the clip. Use the loop below the clip as your anchor cord. Anchor the other ends of your cords, as needed, using masking tape.

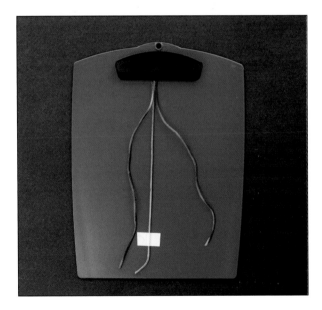

Learn the Basic Macramé Knots

You can make all kinds of interesting knotted patterns using combinations of several basic knots. To practice them, set up an anchor cord a few inches long, and prepare two 2-foot lengths of 2mm-diameter cord. Begin by using *lark's head knots* to secure the working cords to the anchor cord.

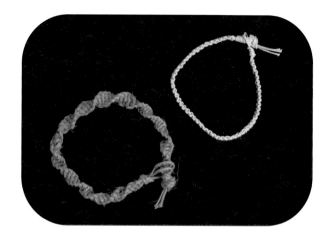

Lark's Head Knot

The lark's head knot folds over an anchor cord to create two strands of working cord.

1 Double-over the working cord and place the folded end on top of the anchor cord.

2 Tuck the folded end of the working cord downward beneath the anchor cord to create a downward loop.

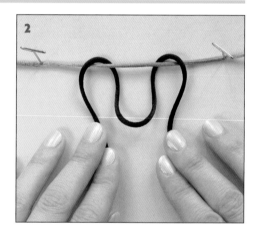

3 Insert both strands of the working cord into and through the folded portion.

4 Holding the top of the working cord with your fingers, gently pull down on its two strands to tighten the knot.

The completed lark's head knot is shown here. (a)

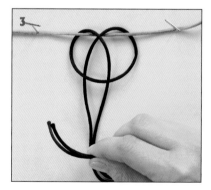

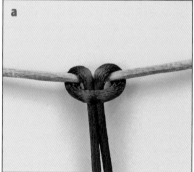

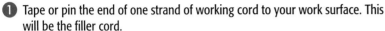

Macramé Overhand Knot

To make a *macramé overhand knot,* use a working cord to tie a simple overhand knot over a filler cord.

1 Tape or pin the end of one strand of working cord to your work surface. This will be the filler cord.

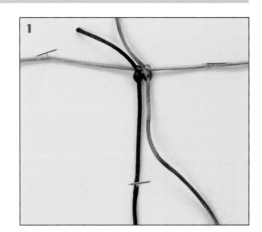

2 Position the other cord (the knotting cord) over the filler cord.

3 Tuck the end of the knotting cord beneath the filler cord to create a small loop.

4 Bring the knotting cord back to the other side of the filler cord, and thread it up through the loop.

5 Use your fingers to tighten the knot while positioning it up against the anchor cord or the previous knot in your design.

The completed macramé overhand knot is shown here. (a)

CONTINUED ON NEXT PAGE

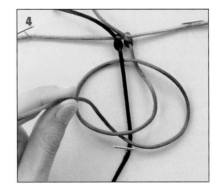

Half Knot

The *half knot* uses two filler cords and two knotting cords. If you repeat half knots, you will create a twisted rope pattern.

1. Attach two working cords to an anchor cord using a lark's head knot. Tie one knot over the other, as shown. You now have four strands of working cord.

2. Anchor the two middle strands to your work surface. These are the left and right filler cords, and the loose cords are the left and right knotting cords.

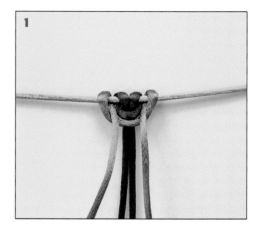

3. Tuck the right knotting cord beneath both filler cords.

4. Position the right knotting cord over the left knotting cord.

5. Bring the left knotting cord over both filler cords, and tuck it beneath the right knotting cord.

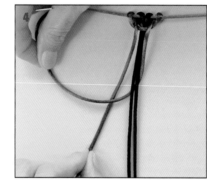

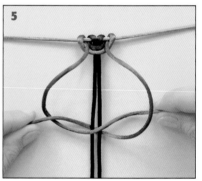

6. Simultaneously pull both knotting cords to their respective sides to tighten the half knot. The completed half knot is shown here.

7. Continue making half knots if you'd like to create a twisted rope.

Macramé Square Knot

The macramé square knot consists of two half knots tied in opposite directions.

1 Beginning with two filler cords and two knotting cords, tie a half knot.

2 Bring the left knotting cord under both filler cords.

3 Position the left knotting cord over the right knotting cord.

4 Pull the right knotting cord over both filler cords, and tuck it beneath the left knotting cord.

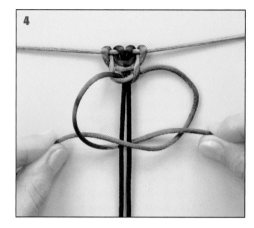

5 Simultaneously pull both knotting cords to their respective sides to tighten the second half of the macramé square knot.

The completed macramé square knot is shown here.

CONTINUED ON NEXT PAGE

TIP

Changing Macramé Square Knot Direction

On one side of the macramé square knot, the cord loops upward; on the other side, it loops downward. In the example above, the upward loop appears on the left side of the knot. You can make a macramé square knot facing the other direction—that is, with the upward loop on the right side—by beginning the half knot (see Step 1 under "Macramé Square Knot") with the left knotting cord instead of the right one. Then, perform Step 2 beginning with the right knotting cord instead of the left one.

Square Knot Picot

A *picot* is a length of cord that has been left loose between two knots. You can use it to create looped fringe along the sides of your work.

1 Tie one square knot.

2 Insert two T-pins into your work surface at an equal short distance from the filler cords on either side of the cords.

Note: *If you are not using a knotting board, skip this step and perform the next step as if there were T-pins in your work surface to help guide your knotting cords.*

3 Position both knotting cords around the T-pins.

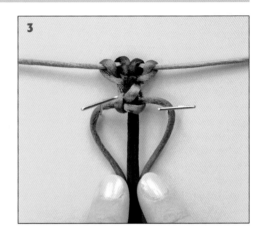

4 Tie another square knot below the T-pins.

5 Remove both T-pins.

6 Position the second square knot up against the first one.

The completed square knot picot is shown here. (a)

TIP

Correcting Mistakes

You may find that some knots that you attempt do not come out looking right, or you may occasionally lose your place in mid-knot and forget where you left off. When this happens, use a T-pin or awl to gently pull out each knot in reverse order until you reach a comfortable point to begin working again.

Wrap Knot

When you make a *wrap knot* (also called *gathering cords*), you wrap one cord (the wrapping cord) around a group of other cords to hold them neatly together. For practice, try wrapping one cord around a bundle of four cords.

1 Anchor the top ends of four working cords to your work surface. These are the filler cords for the wrap knot.

2 Cut another piece of cord about 17 inches in length. This is the wrapping cord.

3 Fold-over about 2 inches of the wrapping cord on one end to create a long loop.

4 Position the loop parallel to and against the filler cords.

5 Hold the base of the wrapping cord loop closed and against the filler cords with the fingers of one hand.

6 With the other hand, wrap the other end of the wrapping cord around all of the filler cords at the base of the loop, leaving about ½ inch of unwrapped tail at the bottom of the loop.

7 Continue wrapping around the filler cords, and the loop itself, in an upward direction until the wraps almost reach the top of the loop.

8 Insert the end of the wrapping cord into and through the loop, and pull it taut.

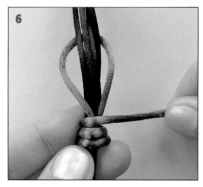
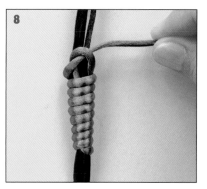

9 Release the top end of the wrapping cord from your fingers.

10 Pull on the bottom tail of the wrapping cord until the top of the loop is positioned completely inside the wraps.

11 Trim off the extra cord tails at both ends.

The completed wrap knot is shown here. (a)

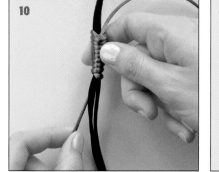

CONTINUED ON NEXT PAGE

Half Hitch Knot

To make a *half hitch knot*, you simply loop one cord around another cord. You can repeat half hitch knots to create a twisted rope effect.

1 Beginning with one knotting cord and one filler cord, bring the knotting cord under and then over the filler cord.

2 Tuck the end of the knotting cord back underneath itself.

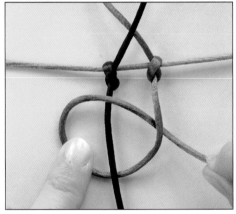

3 Pull the knotting cord to tighten the knot.

The completed half hitch knot is shown here.

ALTERNATING HALF HITCH KNOTS

Alternating half hitch knots are repeated half hitch knots that switch direction with each knot. They result in a flat rope.

 Make a half hitch knot.

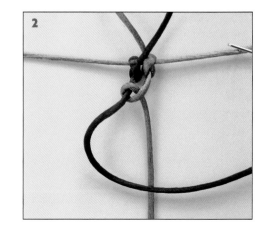

2 Remove the T-pin or tape from the filler cord, and use it to anchor the knotting cord instead. The original filler cord is now the knotting cord, and the original knotting cord is now the filler cord.

3 Using the new knotting cord, tie a half hitch knot around the new filler cord. This half hitch knot faces the opposite direction to the first knot.

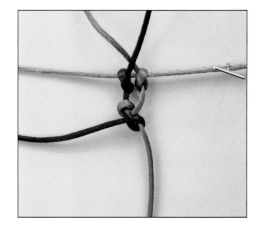

4 Remove the anchor from the filler cord, and anchor the knotting cord. The filler cord and knotting cord have switched roles again.

5 Make another half hitch knot.

6 Continue switching the filler and knotting cords and making half hitch knots to the desired length of rope.

A length of completed alternating half hitch knots is shown here.

Add Beads Between Macramé Knots

It's easy to string beads into macramé knotted designs. If you have beads with large enough holes, you can string them over all of the working cords just about anywhere in your design. If your beads' holes are not that large, or if you'd like a more integrated look, try the following techniques instead.

String Beads Lengthwise

Use this method to string a bead so that its hole runs lengthwise with the design.

1. Beginning with four working cords (two filler cords and two knotting cords), tie a macramé knot of your choice. This example shows a square knot.

2. Remove the pins or tape that anchor your filler cords.

3. String a bead onto both filler cords.

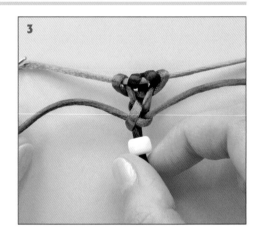

4. Re-anchor the filler cords.

5. Position the bead up against the knot that you made in Step 1.

6. Tie another knot at the bottom of the bead to continue the design.

   The secured vertical bead is shown here.

String Perpendicular Beads

Use this method to add a bead with its hole running perpendicular to the design.

1 Complete Steps 1–2 under "String Beads Lengthwise" on the previous page.

2 Holding the bead with its holes facing side-to-side (perpendicular to the cords), thread one filler cord sideways through the bead.

3 Pull the filler cord taut.

4 Continue holding the bead in place, and thread the other filler cord through the bead from the opposite direction.

5 Pull the second filler cord taut.

6 Re-anchor the filler cords.

7 Securely tie another knot up against the bead to continue the design.

The secured perpendicular bead is shown here.

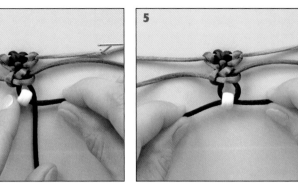

FAQ

How can I keep longer lengths of cord from tangling?

Some jewelry designs require that you use and keep track of multiple long lengths of cord. Cords can easily become tangled or fall out of place, which can cause some confusion.

When you work with longer cords, try making *butterfly bobbins to* keep them neat and orderly. Beginning about a foot away from where you will begin knotting, wrap one cord in a figure-eight pattern repeatedly around your extended thumb and index finger. Bring your thumb and finger slightly toward each other to remove the cord. Slip a rubber band over the center of the figure-eight where the loops of cord cross. Repeat this process for all of your lengthy working cords. Pull cord out of these bundles as needed when you work your design.

Braid Cords Together

You can braid together multiple strands of cord to create thicker and more decorative cording for your projects. You can also combine braids and knots in a single design. Here are the three most popular braids used in jewelry making.

Three-Strand Flat Braid

You are probably familiar with this simple braid, which is commonly used to braid hair. You can make it with three single cords or three groups of cords.

① Beginning with three cords anchored at the top ends, pick up the left and middle cords with your left hand.

② Using your right hand, bring the right cord over the middle cord and position it between the middle and left cords.

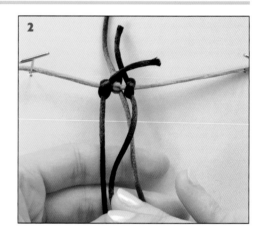

③ Bring the left cord over the original right cord.

④ Pull the cords gently to the sides to tighten the beginning of the braid.

⑤ Bring the cord that is now on the far right over the cord that is now in the middle.

⑥ Bring the left cord over the middle cord.

⑦ Continue bringing each side cord over the middle cord, tightening the braid as needed to keep it even.

A length of completed three-strand flat braid is shown here. (a)

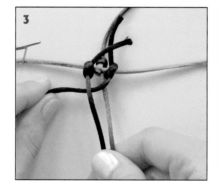

Four-Strand Round Braid

This braid is round with four even sides. First, set up the cords with an initial flat braid. Then make repeated round braids.

BEGINNNING THE BRAID

1 Beginning with four working cords anchored at their top ends, bring the second cord from the left over the second cord from the right, so that the two cords are crossed.

2 Cross the far-left cord under the second cord from the right.

3 Bring the far-right cord over and under the two cords that are closest to it, respectively.

ROUND BRAIDING

1 After beginning the braid, cross the cord that is now on the far left (green) beneath the next two cords to its right (at the point where they cross), and then back over the second cord it crossed under (orange).

2 Repeat this process on the other side. Cross the cord that is now on the far right (blue) beneath the two cords next to it (where they cross) and then back over the second cord it crossed under.

3 Pull the cords to tighten the developing braid.

4 Continue crossing each side cord under the two adjacent cords and back over one cord, alternating sides from far left to far right, and tightening the braid as you go.

A length of completed four-strand round braid is shown here.

CONTINUED ON NEXT PAGE

Six-Strand Round Braid

This braid is thicker and slightly more complex than the four-strand round braid. Again, begin with a flat woven braid, and then make the round braids.

BEGINNING THE BRAID

1 Beginning with six working cords anchored at their top ends, weave the third cord from the left (blue) over the cord to its right—under the next cord, and over the last cord.

2 Weave the second cord from the left (green) under the cord directly to its right, and over and under each subsequent cord to its right.

3 Finally, weave the first cord on the left over and under the cord directly to its right, and then over and under each subsequent cord to its right.

The three cords on the left are now crossed over and facing the right, and the three cords on the right are now crossed over and facing the left.

ROUND BRAIDING

1 After beginning the braid, cross the cord that is now on the far right (blue) beneath the next four cords to its left, and then weave it over and under the two cords to its right.

② Cross the cord that is now on the far left (orange) beneath the next four cords to its right, and then weave it over and under the two cords to its left.

③ Pull the cords to tighten the developing braid.

④ Continue crossing each side cord under the four adjacent cords and weaving it back through the next two in the opposite direction, alternating sides from far right to far left, and tightening the braid as you go.

A length of completed six-strand round braid is shown here.

TIP

Finishing Knotted and Braided Cord Jewelry

You can use a variety of standard methods to finish your knotted and braided cord designs. (For a review of common finishing techniques, see Chapters 3 and 4.) Knot-and-loop closures are especially popular because of their earthy, casual style. (See the Four-Strand Braided Leather Bracelet project in Chapter 11.) You can also attach pre-made findings by tying your cord ends into jump rings, or by gluing cord bundles or wrapped cord ends into fold-over or coil ends. Always be sure to decide on a finishing method before you begin a new project, and plan for any extra cord length or special knotting that it may require. As always, never be afraid to experiment. You just might invent a new finishing method to define your signature style.

chapter 10

Easy Projects

The projects in this chapter can be completed using the most basic jewelry making and beading techniques that you have learned. Keep in mind that the materials and design elements for each project are merely suggestions. You can substitute different components and incorporate other techniques to customize any of them to your own specifications. If you would like to make a project in a different size, be sure to alter the amount of materials you need accordingly. Some resources for finding the tools, supplies, and materials used in these projects are provided in the Appendix.

Funky Beaded Stretch Bracelet Set

Beaded stretch bracelets are quick and easy projects once you get the hang of them. They look especially stylish when worn in sets. This project uses a variety of larger vintage Lucite beads for a striking effect and comfortable fit.

TOOLS AND SUPPLIES

- Small, sharp scissors or nippers
- Small alligator clamp or Bead Stopper
- E6000 glue
- Paper towels
- Optional: Twisted wire needle (if you have trouble stringing the beads without one)

MATERIALS

These materials will make a set of five bracelets, each with an inside circumference of about 7 inches.

- About 6½ feet of clear .7mm stretch cord
- 16 round Lucite beads in marbled dark avocado (12mm)
- 4 Lucite rings in yellow opal (5mm x 15mm)
- 17 round Lucite beads in light olivine moonglow (11mm)
- 22 round Lucite beads in light olivine moonglow (8mm)
- 2 faceted round catseye glass beads in olive green (10mm)
- 15 round Lucite beads in brown-orange-green stripe (12mm)
- 13 round Lucite beads in lemon-and-white swirl (12mm)
- 4 round Lucite beads in lemon-and-white swirl (8mm)

How to Make the Funky Beaded Stretch Bracelet Set

The tasks required for this project are covered in Chapter 3.

① Following the bead patterns shown in the example, string and tie-off each bracelet, one at a time, using the alligator clamps or Bead Stoppers to keep the beads from falling off as necessary.

② Apply a drop of E6000 glue to the square knot on each bracelet, and slide each knot into an adjacent bead.

③ After the glue has fully set, use sharp scissors to trim off the cord tails.

FAQ

Where can I find unusual vintage Lucite beads like these?

Lucite beads are great for stretch bracelets not only because of their interesting style, but because they are very lightweight. However, you will not be able to find them at every bead store. Most Lucite beads are part of limited supplies of unused vintage materials that are collected by specialty suppliers. You can find them most easily by searching the Internet and by browsing online auction sites. A list of Internet vintage bead sellers and bead auctions is available in the Appendix.

Hill Tribe Silver and Gemstone Necklace

The Hill Tribe people of northern Thailand are renowned silversmiths. Their silver beads and jewelry are popular for their artistry and unique, rough-hewn style. This amazonite gemstone necklace features ornate Hill Tribe silver beads and a coordinating floral pendant.

Tools and Materials

TOOLS
- Small side cutters or nippers
  - Chain nose pliers
  - Flat nose pliers
  - Small alligator clamp or Bead Stopper

MATERIALS
These materials will create an approximately 16-inch necklace, including the clasp.

- About 18 inches of 19-strand, .015-inch-diameter beading wire
- 2 sterling-silver crimp tubes (2mm)
- 2 sterling-silver Wire Guardians
- 76 faceted briolette amazonite beads (6mm x 10mm)
- 44 Hill Tribe silver hollow-saucer spacer beads (2mm x 3.5mm)
- 2 Hill Tribe silver vertical floral beads (10mm x 12mm)
- 1 Hill Tribe silver flower pendant
- 1 Hill Tribe silver toggle clasp
- 2 sterling-silver jump rings, 18 gauge (6mm OD)

How to Make the Hill Tribe Silver and Gemstone Necklace

The tasks required for this project are covered in Chapter 3.

1 Affix an alligator clamp or Bead Stopper near the middle of the strand of beading wire.

2 On one end of the strand, string on one hollow-saucer spacer bead, one crimp tube, and a second hollow-saucer spacer bead, in that order.

3 String on a Wire Guardian.

4 Thread the beading wire back down through the beads and crimp tube.

5 With the beads still positioned beneath the Wire Guardian, use chain nose pliers to flatten the crimp tube.

6 Trim the beading wire tail at the base of the bottom spacer bead using small wire cutters or nippers.

7 Remove the alligator clamp or Bead Stopper from the beading wire.

8 String on two amazonite briolette beads and one spacer bead.

9 Continue adding two briolettes and one spacer bead until you have strung a total of 26 briolettes, ending with a final spacer bead.

10 String on one of the 10mm x 12mm Hill Tribe silver floral beads and one more spacer bead.

11 String on 12 more briolettes, with a spacer bead between each set of two briolettes, again ending with a final spacer bead.

12 String on the Hill Tribe flower pendant.

13 String on another spacer bead, and then string on the rest of the beads and the second Wire Guardian to match the first side of the necklace.

14 Thread the beading wire back down through the beads and crimp, as you did in Step 4.

15 Flatten the crimp tube with chain nose pliers.

16 Trim the wire tail as you did in Step 6.

17 To finish the necklace, use chain nose pliers in conjunction with flat nose pliers to attach a toggle clasp part to each end with jump rings.

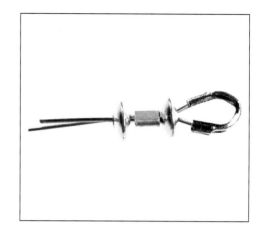

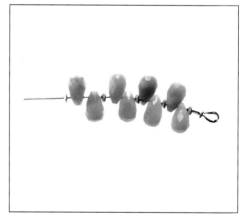

Memory Wire and Crystal Heart Finger Ring

This fun, casual finger ring features super-sparkly crystal components and small coils of memory wire. The example uses a crystal heart setting and crystal beads in topaz and clear crystal, but you can find similar settings and beads in a variety of colors and shapes.

Tools, Supplies, and Materials

TOOLS AND SUPPLIES

- 2 small alligator clamps
- Memory wire cutters (or heavy-duty household wire cutters)
- E6000 glue
- Paper towels
- Round nose pliers

MATERIALS

These materials will create one standard-sized memory wire finger ring.

- 2 full, separate coils of finger-ring-sized silver-tone memory wire
- 20 faceted crystal round beads in light Colorado topaz (3mm)
- 4 faceted crystal round beads in smoked topaz (4mm)
- 4 faceted crystal round beads in clear crystal (5mm)
- 4 round silver-plate memory wire end caps (3mm)
- 1 double-hole Swarovski crystal heart setting in clear crystal
- 2 blunt-cut ⅝-inch lengths of 20-gauge silver-tone wire

How to Make the Memory Wire and Crystal Heart Finger Ring

The tasks required for this project are covered in Chapters 3 and 6.

1. Glue an end cap onto one end of each of the two memory wire coils, and allow the glue to fully set.

2. String four Colorado topaz crystal beads onto each coil.

3. Use the round nose pliers to create a figure-eight-shaped simple clasp eye using one length of the 20-gauge wire, but make both loops in the wire very small and the same size. This component will serve as a spacer bar rather than a clasp eye.

4. String one loop of the separator bar onto one of the memory wire coils.

5. String the other loop of the spacer bar onto the other memory wire coil.

6. String another Colorado topaz bead onto each coil.

7. String one smoked topaz bead and one clear crystal bead onto each coil.

8. Thread one coil through the two top holes in the crystal heart setting.

9. Thread the other coil through the two bottom holes in the crystal heart setting.

10. String two clear crystal beads onto each coil, against the heart component.

11. String one smoked topaz bead and one Colorado topaz bead onto each coil.

12. Create a second separator bar with the remaining length of 20-gauge wire, and string it onto both coils.

13. String four more Colorado topaz beads onto each coil.

14. Attach an alligator clamp to each coil after stringing on the final bead.

15. Finish both coils by gluing on the remaining end caps.

16. When the glue has set, remove the alligator clamps.

Beaded Square Knot Hemp Bracelet

Create an earthy, casual hemp bracelet with some basic knots and ceramic and wood beads. The simple knot-and-loop closure eliminates the need for findings. You can use the same techniques to make a matching choker or anklet.

Tools, Supplies, and Materials

TOOLS AND SUPPLIES

- Sharp scissors or nippers
- Knotting board with T-pins (or a knotting board alternative)
- Masking tape

MATERIALS

These materials will make one approximately 7½-inch bracelet.

- 2 3-yard lengths of 20-pound test, natural hemp twine cord (1mm)
- 6 brick-colored kaolin ceramic beads (6mm x 7mm)
- 2 dark-brown wood latticework beads (5mm)
- 2 four-sided glazed ceramic tube beads in green and brown (19mm x 6mm)

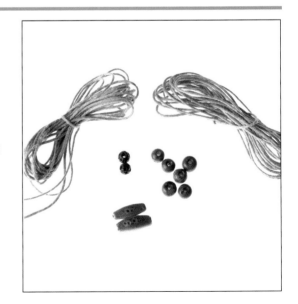

How to Make the Beaded Square Knot Hemp Bracelet

The tasks required for this project are covered in Chapter 9.

1. Align the two hemp cords next to one another and fold them together in half around a pencil.

2. Tie an overhand knot with all of the cords just below the pencil.

3. Remove the pencil from the cords. You now have a loop to use later as a closure.

4. Anchor the loop to your work surface.

5. Using two working cords and two filler cords, make two macramé square knots.

6. String a kaolin bead onto the filler cords and position it against the macramé square knots you just made.

7. Make three more macramé square knots.

8. String another kaolin bead onto the filler cords.

9. Make three more macramé square knots and add a third kaolin bead to the filler cords.

10. Make three more macramé square knots.

11. String one latticework wood bead onto the filler cords.

12. Make another macramé square knot.

13. String one long ceramic bead onto each of the two working cords (*not* the filler cords).

14. Make another macramé square knot.

15. Complete the second half of the bracelet by knotting and stringing beads in reverse order of the first side.

16. Tie all four cords into a tight double knot against the final macramé square knot in the design.

17. Use sharp scissors or nippers to trim off the excess hemp cords about an inch past the double knot. You can now secure the bracelet by slipping the double knot through the loop that you made in Steps 1–3.

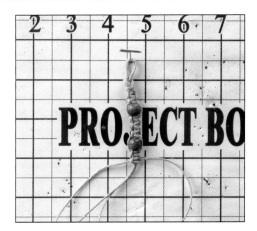

Cosmic Crystal Drop Earrings

Simple bead-drop earrings are especially easy to make. This design uses handmade eye pins, pre-made hooks, and funky Cosmic-shaped crystal beads for a high-fashion, designer look.

Tools and Materials

TOOLS

- Side cutters
- Round nose pliers
- Chain nose pliers
- Flat nose pliers (or a second pair of chain nose pliers)
- Chasing hammer
- Bench block

MATERIALS

These materials make one pair of earrings.

- 1 pair of sterling-silver lever-back earring findings
- 2 sterling-silver jump rings, 18 gauge (4.5mm OD)
- 2½ inches of dead-soft sterling-silver wire, 20 gauge
- 2 Cosmic crystal beads in indicolite (16mm x 14mm)

How to Make the Crystal Drop Earrings

The tasks required for this project are covered in Chapter 6.

1 Cut the wire into two equal, blunt-cut lengths, each about 1¼ inches long.

2 Use chain nose pliers to fold-over one end of each wire length to create simple head pins.

3 Place a bead onto each head pin.

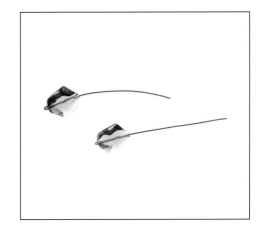

4 Use round nose pliers to create a simple loop at the top of each bead.

5 Use both pairs of pliers to open the jump rings.

6 Place a bead drop and earring finding on each jump ring and close it securely.

TIP

Experimenting with Bead Drop Earring Designs

The earrings in this project are simple yet striking. You can alter this basic design theme by using more elaborate head pins, like the paddles and spirals covered in Chapter 3. To add more beads to your design, use an eye pin instead of a head pin, and attach one or more additional bead drops to its loop.

Men's Rugged Leather and Bead Necklace

Men's jewelry typically has a rugged, masculine look. You can achieve this style easily by using leather cord and tribal-style, handmade beads. The beads in this project were made in Africa. Notice how the variety of materials in this design adds interesting texture to its basic color palette.

Tools and Materials

TOOLS

- Scissors or nippers

MATERIALS

These materials create one necklace that measures approximately 18 inches long.

- About 33 inches of brown Greek leather cord (1.8mm)
- 22 coco shell beads (2mm x 10mm)
- 10 dyed and painted bone beads (24mm x 9mm)
- 20 African handmade copper spacer beads (4mm x 6mm)
- 27 ostrich shell heishi beads (2mm x 10mm)
- 9 brick-red African glass heishi beads (2mm x 9mm)

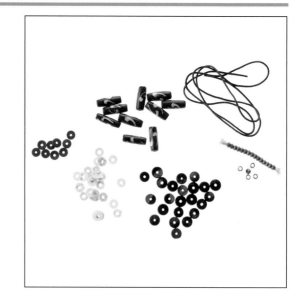

How to Make the Men's Rugged Leather and Bead Necklace

The tasks required for this project are covered in Chapter 3.

1 Tie a secure overhand knot about an inch from one end of the leather cord.

2 String on two coco shell beads.

3 Tie a second overhand knot against the coco shell beads.

4 String on the rest of the beads in the pattern shown.

5 Tie an overhand knot after the final bead.

6 Fold-over the remaining tail of cord to form a loop.

7 Tie a loose overhand knot in the doubled cord.

8 Position the knot close to the overhand knot that you made in Step 5, while adjusting it to create a loop slightly larger than the width of the two coco shell beads that you strung on in Step 2.

9 When the loop is the proper size, pull it tight.

10 Trim off the excess cord tail at each end of the necklace, leaving tails about 1 inch long.

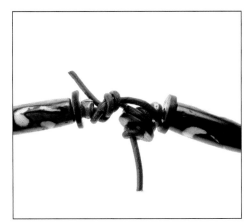

TIP

Alternative Endings for Cord Necklaces

Although this necklace design uses its own built-in clasp, remember that you can also use pre-made findings to finish your bead and cord necklaces. End pieces like coil ends and end caps are great alternatives, and they allow you to use jump rings to attach the clasp pieces of your choice. Review Chapter 3 for more information on using them.

Celtic Wirework Charm Bracelet

A basic double jump ring chain makes a perfect base for a charm bracelet. This design has a whimsical, Old-World theme with its Celtic knot and dragon charms. Spiral-end bead-drop charms add color and movement.

Tools, Supplies, and Materials

TOOLS AND SUPPLIES

- Side cutters
- Chain nose pliers
- Flat nose pliers
- Round nose pliers
- Optional: Knotting board with T-pins

MATERIALS

These materials make one bracelet that measures about 7½ inches long. For the silver-tone wire, you can use nickel silver, silver-colored copper, or sterling silver.

- 92 silver-tone jump rings, 18 gauge (7mm OD)
- 1 wirework simple hook clasp made from 18-gauge silver-tone wire
- 1 wirework simple clasp eye made from 18-gauge silver-tone wire
- About 30 inches of 24-gauge silver-tone wire
- 3 pewter dragon charms (23mm)
- 3 Celtic knot disc charms (14mm)
- 5 Celtic knot connectors (14mm)
- 9 Czech Fire Polish HurriCane Glass faceted round beads in amethyst-peridot-tortoise (6mm)

How to Make the Celtic Wirework Charm Bracelet

The tasks required for this project are covered in Chapter 6.

① Use 74 of the jump rings to make a double jump ring chain that contains 37 links.

② Attach the hook clasp and clasp eye to each end of the chain.

③ Use the 24-gauge wire and Czech glass beads to make nine wrapped bead drops with spiral ends.

④ Lay out the chain neatly on your work surface, with every other link facing the same direction.

> **Note:** *If you have trouble keeping the chain from twisting while you work, try anchoring it horizontally to a knotting board with T-pins.*

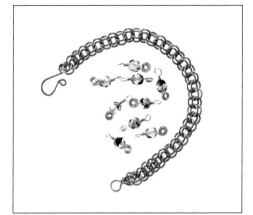

⑤ Beginning with the second link in the chain, attach a dragon charm to the bottoms of both rings in the link using one of the unused jump rings.

⑥ Skip the very next link, and attach a bead drop to the bottom of the following link (again using a jump ring).

⑦ Continue adding charms to the bottom of every other link in the order shown, ending with the third dragon charm.

⑧ Make one final cluster of three charms by adding the remaining charms to a jump ring and attaching it to the clasp eye.

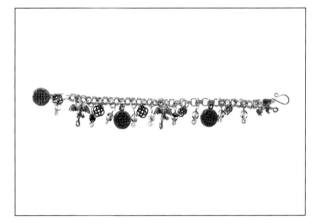

TIP

More Ideas for Charm Jewelry

The double jump ring chain is one of the simplest chains for attaching charms, but you can also use more elaborate chains for charm jewelry. "S" chains and double-wrapped loop chains both work well. You can even include simple or wrapped bead links within a chain to add color. This technique works especially well for charm necklaces, because their longer length allows the charms to be spaced more loosely. Finally, if you'd prefer a fringier look for your charm jewelry, try hanging multiple charms from each link. Just be sure to hold up your work occasionally to make sure that it has proper lay. (To review jewelry lay, see Chapter 2.)

Even-Count Flat Peyote Stitch Finger Ring

The even-count flat peyote stitch creates a smooth, flat, beaded fabric that is perfect for making finger rings. The basic technique involves stitching together the ends of the fabric to make a beaded tube. You can use this method to make just about any width of finger ring that you would like, as long as you complete the fabric with an even number of rows.

Tools, Supplies, and Materials

TOOLS AND SUPPLIES
- Sharp scissors or nippers
- Size 11 beading needle
- Thread conditioner

MATERIALS
These materials will make one size 7 finger ring.

- About 1⅕ yards of conditioned size B beading thread in gold
- 82 size 11/0 cylinder beads in metallic bronze
- 41 size 11/0 cylinder beads in metallic light bronze
- 123 size 11/0 cylinder beads in metallic olive
- 41 size 11/0 Japanese triangle seed beads in matte metallic dark brown
- 41 size 11/0 cylinder beads in metallic hematite

How to Make the Even-Count Flat Peyote Stitch Finger Ring

The tasks required for this project are covered in Chapter 5.

1 Thread the needle onto the conditioned beading thread, and fold over the first few inches of thread so that you can weave using the single-strand method.

2 String on and secure a stop bead about 6 inches from the end of the thread.

3 String on one metallic hematite bead, one matte metallic dark brown triangle bead, three metallic olive beads, one metallic light bronze bead, and two metallic bronze beads.

Note: Feel free to change the order of the colors for a slightly different look.

4 Slide all eight beads up against the stop bead.

5 String on another metallic bronze bead and thread back through the second-to-last bronze bead in the first row to complete the second row of even-count peyote stitch.

6 Weave each successive row using the even-count flat peyote stitch.

7 After finishing the final row, tie an overhand knot around the nearest woven thread.

8 Bring the two sides of beaded fabric together.

9 Stitch together both sides in a zigzag pattern, back and forth through each protruding bead on either side of the fabric. (The sides will come together like a zipper.)

10 To secure the seam, zigzag stitch back down through a few more beads, and then weave-in your thread as usual.

11 Remove the stop bead from the beginning end of thread and use the needle to weave-in that thread as well.

TIP

Making a Ring with the Right Angle Weave

The even-count flat peyote stitch creates a smooth, dense weave of fabric. For a ring with a looser, more netted look, try using the right-angle weave instead. Just be sure to experiment with thread and needle sizes before you get started. You'll need to pass through some beads three times (when connecting the ends of the fabric), so you may want to weave with a single strand, rather than a double strand, of thread. For more information on the right-angle weave and selecting thread and needles, review Chapter 5.

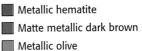

- Metallic hematite
- Matte metallic dark brown
- Metallic olive
- Metallic light bronze
- Metallic bronze

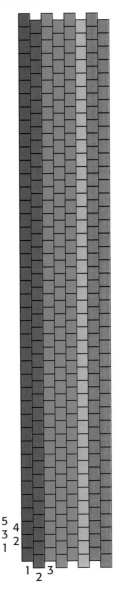

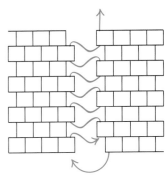

Dancing Bell Daisy Chain Bookmark

Because of their small size, seed beads are a favorite medium for making eye-catching bookmarks. This project uses the daisy chain stitch to create a thin, flat length of beaded fabric. Dancing bell charms at each end add weight and movement.

Tools, Supplies, and Materials

TOOLS AND SUPPLIES

- About 1½ yards of conditioned size D beading thread in chartreuse
- Size #11 English beading needle
- Sharp scissors or nippers

MATERIALS

These materials make one bookmark that measures about 7 inches long, not including the charms.

- About 168 size 11/0 Japanese seed beads in lavender
- About 28 size 11/0 Japanese seed beads in amethyst
- About 84 size 11/0 Japanese seed beads in lime green
- 2 silver-tone split rings (6mm OD)
- 6 silver-tone dancing bell charms

How to Make the Dancing Bell Daisy Chain Bookmark

The tasks required for this project are covered in Chapter 5.

1. Attach three charms to each split ring and set them aside.

2. Thread the needle and position it several inches from one end of the thread.

3. Fold-over the short end of the thread and hold the needle onto the thread with your thumb and index finger.

4. String on and secure a stop bead about 10 inches from the end of the thread.

5. String on six lavender beads.

6. Thread back down through the first bead to begin the daisy chain stitch.

7. String on one amethyst bead to form the center of the first daisy.

8. Thread back down through the fourth bead you strung on in Step 5 to continue the stitch.

9. To begin the green stripe in the design, string on one lime green bead, two lavender beads, and another lime green bead, in that order.

10. Continue the stitch by threading down through the fifth bead you strung on in Step 5.

11. String on another lime green bead to form the center of the first green stripe.

12. Continue the daisy chain stitch, following this pattern, until you have about 7 inches of completed fabric.

13. After the last daisy, make an overhand knot around the nearest thread between two beads.

14. String on six lime-green beads for the top loop.

15. Slip one split ring (with three charms) onto the thread and over the beads that you added in Step 14.

16. Weave back through the last daisy and up through the loop one more time (to strengthen it).

17. Weave-in the thread end and trim it off as usual.

18. Close the loop by weaving back into the last couple of daisies.

19. Remove the needle and use it to carefully remove the stop bead from the other end of the bookmark.

20. Thread the needle onto the 10-inch thread tail at that end.

21. String on six lime-green beads to make the bottom loop.

22. Slip the other split ring over the lime-green beads that you added in Step 20.

23. Weave through the first daisy and back through the loop one more time.

24. Weave-in and trim this end of thread to complete the project.

chapter 11

Intermediate Projects

The projects in this chapter involve slightly more complicated techniques than those in Chapter 10. You can use them to practice intermediate skills like working with multiple strands, creating elaborate wirework designs, weaving more substantial beaded fabrics, and developing more complicated macramé work and braids. As with the projects in Chapter 10, some resources for the tools, supplies, and materials used in these projects are listed in the Appendix.

Multi-Strand Tin Cup Anklet

This project uses traditional tin cup styling to create a casual anklet that is lightweight, secure, and comfortable to wear. The multiple strands are finished using the traditional beaded tassel-making technique.

Tools, Supplies, and Materials

TOOLS AND SUPPLIES

- Knotting awl, darning needle, or knotting tool
- 1 handmade folded-card tin cup necklace spacer with a length of ½ inch.
- Alligator clamp (for securing the spacer)
- Sharp scissors or nippers
- Bead reamer
- E6000 glue

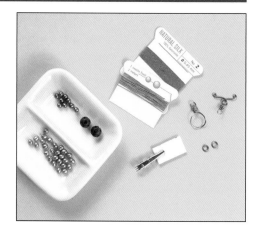

MATERIALS

These materials will make one anklet that measures about 10½ inches long.

- 1 2-meter card of size No. 2 jade green silk cord with attached twisted-wire needle
- 1 2-meter card of size No. 2 beige silk cord with attached twisted-wire needle
- 2 carved latticework wood beads (10mm)
- 25 chartreuse green off-round pearl beads (5mm)
- 9 light-bronze round seed pearl beads (4mm)
- 2 brass or gold-tone jump rings, 18 gauge (4mm OD)
- 1 wirework toggle clasp (T-bar and eye) made with brass or gold-tone wire

How to Make the Multi-Strand Tin Cup Anklet

The tasks required for this project are covered in Chapter 4.

1. Remove all of the jade green silk cord from its card and give it a couple of gentle tugs to help straighten it out.

2. Tape off the cord about 6 inches from the end.

3. String on one of the wood latticework beads.

4. Use the folded-card spacer and the knotting tool to make a knot in the cord ½ inch away from the wood latticework bead (to review how to use the folded-card spacer, see page 79).

5. String on the first chartreuse pearl bead, following the pattern of beads used in the example.

6. Make another knot to hold the bead in place.

7. Continue using the folded-card spacer to space and knot nine more chartreuse pearl beads.

8. Clamp the folded-card spacer to the cord after the last set of knotted beads.

9. String on the second wood latticework bead.

10. Tape off the strand on the other side of the wood bead and remove the spacer. (It's fine for now if the wood bead slides down away from the tape.)

11. Trim the cord about 6 inches away from the tape that you applied in Step 11.

CONTINUED ON NEXT PAGE

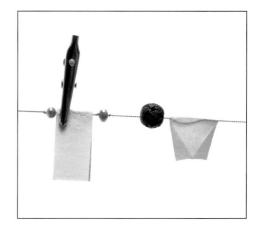

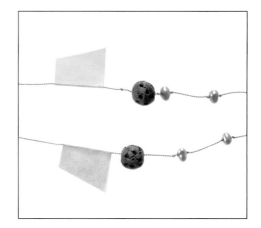

12 Remove all of the beige cord from its card, and tug it a little to help straighten it.

13 Tape it off about 6 inches from the end as you did with the first cord.

14 Thread the cord through the wood latticework bead that you strung onto the first strand in Step 4. Now both strands are strung through the first wood bead together, and both are taped off behind the wood bead.

15 Use the folded-card spacer card and the knotting tool to make a knot ½ inch away from the wood latticework bead. Continue adding beads and knots to complete the strand.

16 When you finish all of the knotted beads for the second strand, clamp on the folded-card spacer again.

17 Thread the cord through the wood bead on this end (the one that you strung onto the first strand in Step 10).

18 Tape off the second strand on the other side of the wood bead, as you did with the first strand.

19 Use this same method to add the next strand of cord following the pattern in the example. Now all three strands are knotted and beaded, and their ends are strung through each of the two wood latticework beads.

20 Beginning with one end, remove the tape from all three strands.

21 Thread a jump ring over all three cord ends. Make a double overhand knot to secure the jump ring in place.

22 Place a tiny drop of E6000 glue on the knot.

23 Slide the wood bead over the knot.

24 Repeat Steps 21–24 on the other side of the anklet.

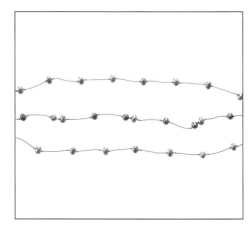

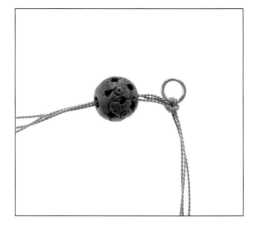

25 Allow the glue at both ends to set.

26 Trim off the extra cord tails at the inside edge of each wood bead.

27 Attach the clasp parts to the jump ring.

Beaded Multi-Knot Hemp Choker

This design uses high-quality bleached hemp cord to create small, tight knots with a more even look than natural twine. The pale cream color of the cord nicely accents the blue and green ceramic beads, and the lightweight fish-vertebrae beads add texture.

TOOLS AND SUPPLIES

- Sharp scissors or nippers
- Yard stick and/or ruler for measuring
- Knotting board with T-pins (or a knotting board alternative)
- Masking tape

MATERIALS

These materials create one choker that measures about 14½ inches long. (To make it longer, increase the number of square knots at the beginning and end.)

- 6 yards of .9mm, 10-pound test bleached hemp twine cord
- 6 fish-vertebrae beads (4mm x 8mm)
- 4 kaolin ceramic beads in chartreuse (6mm x 7mm)
- 2 four-sided glazed ceramic tube beads in blue and brown
- 1 carved black jade convex-tube focal bead (15mm x 12mm)
- 2 copper jump rings, 18 gauge (6mm OD)
- 1 wire fold-over clasp made with 20-gauge copper wire
- 1 wire-wrapped clasp eye made with 20-gauge copper wire

How to Make the Beaded Multi-Knot Hemp Choker

The tasks required for this project are covered in Chapter 9.

1 Cut the hemp cord into the following lengths:

- 1 4-yard length (for the working cords)
- 1 1½-yard length (for the filler cords)
- 2 9-inch lengths (for the wrapping cords)

2 Fold-over the 4-yard and 1½-yard lengths in half and hold them together.

3 Use a lark's head knot to attach the cords to one jump ring.

4 Anchor the jump ring to the knotting board.

5 Make a ¼-inch-long wrap knot around all four cords just below the jump ring, and trim off the cord tails.

6 Make about 1 inch of macramé square knots.

7 String a fish-vertebrae bead vertically onto the filler cords.

8 Make about ⅞ inch of half knots.

9 String another fish-vertebrae bead vertically onto the filler cords.

10 Make about ⅞ inch of macramé square knots.

11 String a kaolin ceramic bead horizontally onto the filler cords.

12 Make another ⅞ inch of half knots.

13 String a four-side ceramic bead vertically onto the filler cords.

14 Make about ⅜ inch of macramé square knots.

15 String on another vertical fish-vertebrae bead.

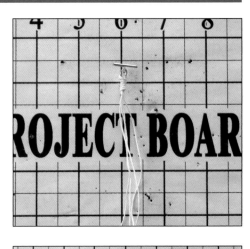

CONTINUED ON NEXT PAGE

16. Make another ⅜ inch of macramé square knots.

17. String on another horizontal kaolin ceramic bead.

18. Make two macramé square knot picots.

19. String the jade focal bead vertically onto the filler cords.

20. Complete the second half of the choker by knotting and stringing beads in reverse order of the first side.

21. String on the second jump ring.

22. Fold-over all four cords about ½ inch away from the last macramé square knot.

23. Using the wrap cord, make a ¼-inch-long wrap knot around all four cords between the last macramé square knot and the jump ring, and trim off the excess cord tails.

24. Open each jump ring and attach the clasp and clasp eye.

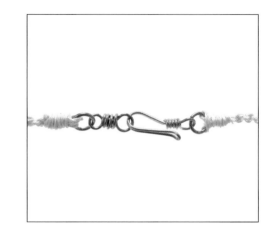

Organza ribbon makes an elegant base for wire pendants that are made with a jig. This design features a spiraled variation of the Celtic knot connector, accented with pretty, wrapped gemstone briolettes.

Tools, Supplies, and Materials

TOOLS AND SUPPLIES

- Sharp scissors
- Side cutters
- Round nose pliers
- Flat nose pliers
- Chain nose pliers
- Wire jig
- Masking tape

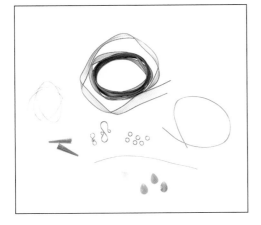

MATERIALS

- Enough ½-inch wide, olive organza ribbon to create a three-strand necklace in the length of your choice using end cones
- 3 faceted natural agate briolettes, 1 pale and 2 dark (8mm x 12mm)
- 1 faceted carnelian briolette (8mm x 12mm)
- About 11 inches of 26-gauge gold-colored copper wire
- About 4½ inches of gold-colored copper wire, 20 gauge
- 1 approximately 8¼-inch length of gold-colored copper wire, blunt-cut at both ends, 18 gauge
- 4 gold-colored jump rings, 18 gauge (4mm OD)
- 2 gold-colored jump rings, 18 gauge (4.5mm OD)
- 2 gold-tone end cones (19mm x 6mm)
- 1 wirework "S" hook made from 18-gauge gold-colored copper wire
- 1 wirework clasp eye made from 20-gauge gold-colored copper wire

CONTINUED ON NEXT PAGE

How to Make the Briolette Pendant Ribbon Necklace

The tasks required for this project are covered in Chapter 4.

MAKE THE BAIL

1. Using 18-gauge wire directly from the coil or spool, wrap the end of the wire around a large peg in the jig to create a large loop.

2. Use side cutters to trim off the excess wire and make the end of the wire blunt.

3. Use your fingers to close the loop.

4. Trim the loop off of the coil or spool, making a blunt cut about 14mm below the loop.

5. Using round nose pliers, make a small loop below the large loop, facing the opposite direction.

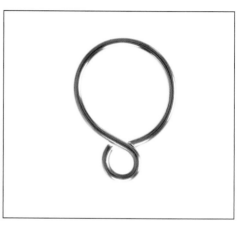

MAKE THE PENDANT

1. Arrange medium pegs on the jig in the Celtic knot pattern (see page 194).

2. Place the 8¼-inch length of 18-gauge wire horizontally beneath the top peg, with 1½ inches of wire protruding from one side, as shown in the example.

3. Hold the wire tail against the jig surface with one hand as you create the Celtic knot pattern with the wire.

4. Remove the wire from the jig.

5. Create a matching spiral on the other end of the connector, facing the opposite direction to the first.

6. Using the 26-gauge wire, convert all four briolettes into wrapped drops.

7. Use jump rings to attach the two dark natural agate briolette drops and the carnelian drop to the lower portion of the pendant, as shown.

8. Attach the bail by securing the upper spiral of the pendant to the small loop on the bail, and slip the loop of the pale carnelian drop onto the small loop of the bail before closing it.

ASSEMBLE THE NECKLACE

1. Align the three strands of organza ribbon.

2. Attach an end cone to one end of the strands by using the 20-gauge wire to make an eye pin (see Chapter 6).

3. String the bail over all three strands of ribbon.

4. Attach the second end cone to the other end of the ribbons, making sure that all three ribbons are equal in length.

5. Attach the "S" hook and clasp eye to the ends of the necklace using the 4.5mm OD jump rings.

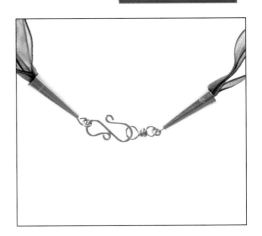

Gothic Bead Lace Collar Necklace

This project uses an embellished version of the beaded lace pattern and Czech glass fire polished beads for a draped, romantic look. This design is called a *collar necklace* because it is very short and is worn against the neck. If you'd like to make it longer, simply increase the number of 4mm beads you string on at the beginning and end of the upper strand. If Gothic is not your style, you can replicate the design using beads with more vibrant colors.

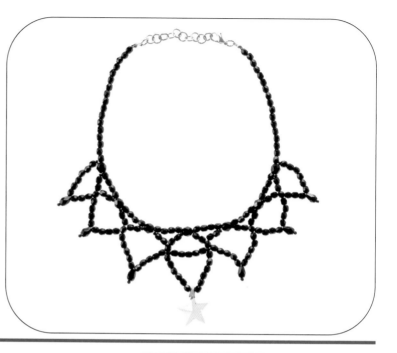

Tools, Supplies, and Materials

TOOLS AND SUPPLIES

- Size #10 beading needle
- Sharp scissors or nippers
- Masking tape
- E6000 glue

MATERIALS

These materials make a collar necklace that is adjustable between about 12½ and 14 inches long.

- One 23-inch length of conditioned size B beading thread in black.
- One 1½-yard length of conditioned size B beading thread in black.
- 101 round Czech glass fire polish beads in black (4mm)
- 7 Czech glass fire polish beads in black (6mm)
- 6 faceted teardrop Czech glass fire polish beads in black (7mm x 5mm)
- 26 size 11/0 Czech seed beads in black
- 1 crystal star pendant in golden shadow (20mm)
- 1 silver tone prong bail
- 2 silver-tone clamshell bead tips
- 12 silver-tone jump rings, 18 gauge (5mm OD)
- 1 silver tone lobster clasp

The tasks required for this project are covered in Chapters 3 and 4.

1 Attach the bail to the star pendant by inserting the prongs into either side of the pendant hole and squeezing them closed with your fingers.

2 Set the pendant aside.

3 Align one end of the 23-inch strand of thread with one end of the 1½-yard strand.

4 Tie two double overhand knots, one on top of the other, with both strands, about one inch from the ends.

5 String one bead tip onto both strands, and use the glue to secure it over the knots.

6 Thread the needle onto the upper strand of thread, and fold-over a few inches of thread so that you can hold it onto the needle with your fingers.

7 String on 17 4mm beads and one 6mm bead.

8 String on four more 4mm beads and another 6mm bead.

9 Repeat Step 6 five more times.

10 String on 17 4mm beads to complete the upper strand.

11 Remove the needle and tape off the end of the upper strand about 3 inches past the final bead.

12 Thread the needle onto the lower strand of thread.

13 String through the first 18 beads in the upper row.

14 Bring the needle out again and pull the thread taut.

15 String on one seed bead and six 4mm beads.

16 String on one teardrop bead and another seed bead.

17 Pull the thread taut again, and string back up through the teardrop bead.

18 String on six more 4mm beads and another seed bead.

19 String back through the next bead on the top row and out again, and pull the first lace loop taut.

20 Slide-over the beads in the top row that are to the right of the bead you strung through in Step 17, and tie an overhand knot around the top strand of thread to secure the first loop.

Note: Use the needle to help position the knot.

CONTINUED ON NEXT PAGE

㉑ Slide-back the upper beads, and continue the design by following the pattern below, tying an overhand knot around the upper strand after you complete each lace loop.

Note: *Before you string on the pendant, string on two seed beads to support the bail.*

㉒ When you reach the center drop, first string the shorter loop (1) then string up to the top and back down again to create the longer one (2).

㉓ When all of the lace loops are complete, string back through the last 17 beads in the upper strand.

㉔ Carefully remove the tape from the top strand.

㉕ Finish both thread ends with a single bead tip, like you did in Step 1, using the needle to help you position the final knots inside the bead tip.

㉖ Attach the lobster clasp to one of the bead tips using jump rings.

㉗ Connect the rest of the jump rings to make the extender chain, and attach it to the other bead tip.

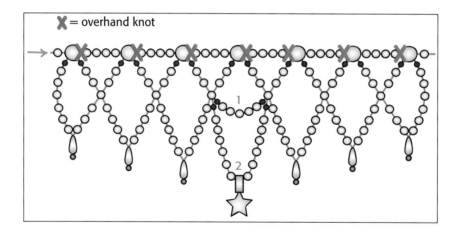

Loom weaving is a fun way to create longer lengths of beaded fabric with neatly aligned rows. In this project, a band of fabric becomes a bracelet when you finish it with pre-made clamp ends.

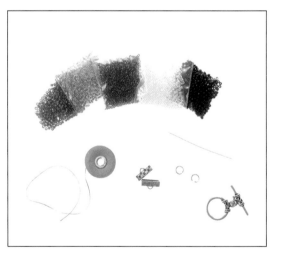

Tools, Supplies, and Materials

TOOLS AND SUPPLIES

- A beading loom that is long enough to accommodate about 7 inches of beaded fabric, plus ⅛-inch of selvage at each end
- 1 size #12 beading needle that is about 2 inches long
- Sharp scissors or nippers
- E6000 glue
- Toothpick
- Flat nose pliers
- Thread conditioner
- Optional: Sticky note to help you keep your place in the pattern

MATERIALS

These materials will make one bracelet that measures about 7 inches long.

- 354 size 11/0 Japanese seed beads in opaque black
- 154 size 11/0 Japanese seed beads in transparent earth brown
- 46 size 11/0 Japanese seed beads in white-lined translucent light brown
- 51 size 11/0 Japanese seed beads in rose-lined crystal clear
- 32 size 11/0 Japanese seed beads in transparent-light-pink with aurora borealis finish
- About 7 yards of size B beading thread in black
- 2 silver-tone metal clamp ends (13mm)
- 2 silver-tone jump rings, 18 gauge (5mm OD)
- 1 silver tone toggle clasp

CONTINUED ON NEXT PAGE

How to Make the Cherry Blossom Loomwork Bracelet

The tasks required for this project are covered in Chapter 5.

 Set up the loom with 10 vertical rows of warp thread.

2 Using a separate length of conditioned thread, weave on all 71 horizontal rows of beads, following the pattern shown on the next page, with about ⅛ inch of selvage at each end. (You can use a sticky note to mark your place at each row in the pattern as you work, to help you keep your place.)

3 Seal the last few rows of each selvage with E6000 glue, and allow the glue to dry.

4 Trim the design off of the loom.

5 Apply glue to the first ⅛-inches of beads at both ends of the design.

6 Use a toothpick to fold each selvage against the back of the design to glue it in place.

7 When the glue has dried beneath the selvage, apply another drop of glue to the selvage on the back of the design, and to the first ⅛-inches of beads on the front of the design at each end.

8 Insert each end of the design into one of the metal clamp ends.

9 Use flat nose pliers to gently squeeze each clamp end closed, being careful not to break any of the beads inside.

10 After the glue has fully set, use jump rings to attach the toggle clasp parts to the ends of the bracelet.

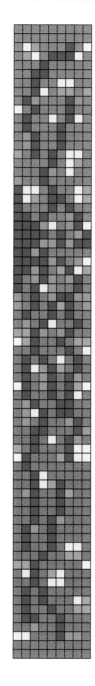

■ Opaque black

■ Transparent earth brown

■ White-lined translucent light brown

☐ Rose-lined crystal clear

■ Transparent-light-pink with aurora
borealis finish

Byzantine and Turquoise Drop Earrings

The Byzantine chain is usually used in bracelets and necklaces, but you can also use it to make chunky drop earrings. In this design, a short length of sterling-silver Byzantine chain is accented by a turquoise cube bead drop.

Tools, Supplies, and Materials

TOOLS AND SUPPLIES

- Chain nose pliers
- Flat nose pliers
- Side cutters
- Chasing hammer
- Bench block
- Needle file
- Safety pin

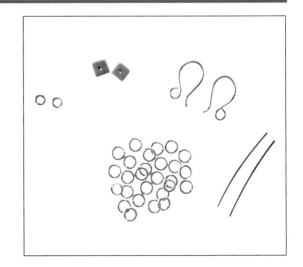

MATERIALS

These materials will make one pair of earrings.

- 28 sterling-silver jump rings, 18 gauge (5.5mm OD)
- 2 sterling-silver jump rings, 18 gauge (4mm OD)
- 2 wirework earring hooks made from 22-gauge sterling-silver wire
- 2 natural blue turquoise beads (6mm)
- 2 ⁷⁄₈-inch lengths of 20-gauge dead-soft sterling-silver wire

How to Make the Byzantine and Turquoise Drop Earrings

The tasks required for this project are covered in Chapters 6 and 7.

1. Use both sets of pliers, the safety pin, and the 28 6mm OD jump rings to create two lengths of Byzantine chain containing 14 jump rings each, as shown in the example.

2. Connect the top two rings in each length of chain to each earring hook using the two 4mm OD jump rings.

3. Use the hammer and bench block to convert each of the ⅞-inch lengths of 20-gauge wire into paddle head pins.

4. Smooth the edges of the paddles using the needle file.

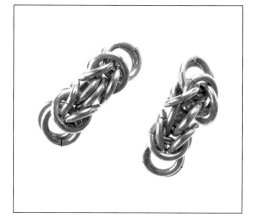

5. String each turquoise bead onto each head pin.

6. Use the side cutters to trim each head pin about ¼-inch above each bead. (Be sure to make blunt cuts.)

7. Use round nose pliers to create a loop above the bead on each head pin.

8. Attach each head-pin loop directly to the bottom two rings in each of the Byzantine chains.

Wirework Bead Cuff Bracelet

This cuff bracelet design features double-twisted wire, double-wrapped wire beads, and ornate, handmade sterling-silver beads from Bali. You can make it using copper wire as shown, or sterling-silver wire for a more formal look.

Tools, Supplies, and Materials

TOOLS

Note: Because 14-gauge wire is thick and takes extra force to bend and cut, always use strong, good-quality tools when you work with it.

- Round nose pliers
- Heavy-duty side cutters
- 2mm round mandrel
- Bracelet mandrel (or bracelet mandrel substitute)
- Needle file

MATERIALS

These materials will make one medium-sized, adjustable cuff bracelet.

- 1 8¼-inch length of 14-gauge copper wire
- 3 29-inch lengths of 20-gauge copper wire
- 3 7-inch lengths of 18-gauge copper wire
- 2 12-inch lengths of double-twisted copper 20-gauge wire with 15 twists per inch
- 2 sterling-silver scroll-design Bali beads (12mm x 7mm)
- 2 sterling-silver daisy-spacer Bali beads (2.5mm x 8mm)

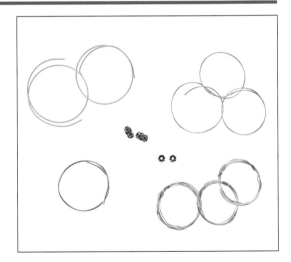

How to Make the Wirework Bead Cuff Bracelet

The tasks required for this project are covered in Chapter 7.

1 Create three double-wrapped wire beads using the three 29-inch lengths of 20-gauge wire, the three 7-inch lengths of 18-gauge wire, and the 2mm mandrel.

2 Wrap each 12-inch length of double-twisted wire snugly around the mandrel to create two 1¼-inch coils.

3 Use round nose pliers to create a loop at one end of the 14-gauge wire.

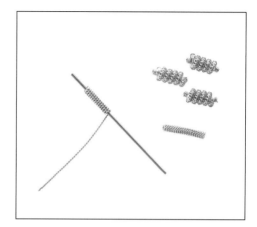

4 String each component onto the 14-gauge wire in the order shown.

5 Use the round nose pliers to create a loop at the other end of the 14-gauge wire.

6 Use a bracelet mandrel (or bracelet mandrel substitute) to bend the bracelet into a round shape.

7 Perfect the cuff-bracelet shape by bending the bracelet gently inward with your fingers.

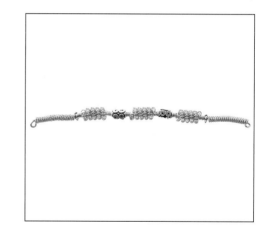

Modern Square Stitch Table Mat

The square stitch is a fun weave for creating decorative household items as well as for jewelry. In this project, a large sheet of beaded fabric becomes a trendy table mat. It makes a nice base for a candle and candle holder, and you can even use it as a wall hanging.

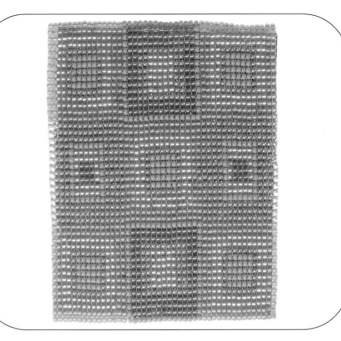

Tools, Supplies, and Materials

TOOLS AND SUPPLIES

- Size #10 beading needle
- Sharp scissors or nippers
- Thread conditioner

MATERIALS

These materials will make one coaster that measures approximately 5 inches long by 4¼ inches wide.

- About 17 yards of size D beading thread in chartreuse
- 528 size 8/0 cylinder beads in fuchsia-lined crystal
- 520 size 8/0 cylinder beads in matte silver-lined orange
- 212 size 8/0 cylinder beads in silver-lined orange
- 472 size 8/0 cylinder beads in matte silver-lined chartreuse
- 293 size 8/0 cylinder beads in opaque turquoise green
- A sheet of adhesive-back foam in black that measures about 4⅞ inches long by about 4 inches wide.

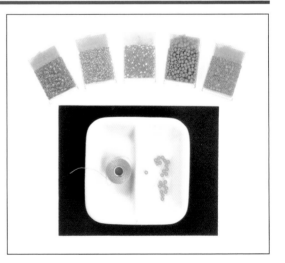

How to Make the Modern Square Stitch Table Mat

The tasks required for this project are covered in Chapter 5.

1 Thread the needle onto 2 or 3 yards of conditioned beading thread.

2 Fold-over the end of the thread a few inches past the needle, and hold it against the needle with your fingers.

3 String on a stop bead and secure it about 8 inches from the end of the thread.

4 Weave the entire square stitch pattern shown, beginning at the bottom-left corner.

Note: You will begin to run out of thread several times before finishing the pattern. Whenever you have only 6–8 inches of thread left to work with, weave-in and begin a new piece of thread as usual.

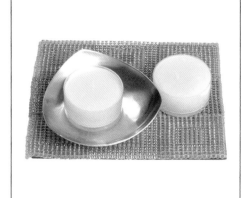

5 Weave-in and trim the thread when you finish the pattern.

6 Return to the beginning of the pattern and remove the stop bead.

7 Weave the thread tail into the first two rows of the pattern, and trim off any excess.

8 Align the beaded fabric with the adhesive foam sheet, and press it into place on one side of the fabric.

The bottom of the mat, with the foam sheet in place, is shown here.

CONTINUED ON NEXT PAGE

This bracelet is made up of beaded framework links that are made using a jig and round nose pliers. Copper is a good choice for this design because it is soft enough to bend at a larger gauge, and it is much more economical than sterling silver.

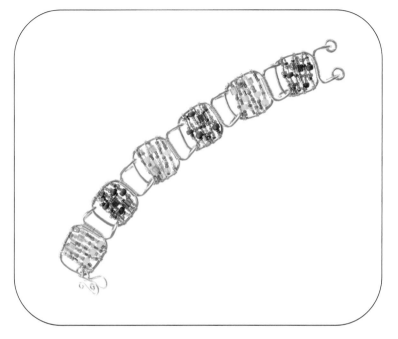

Tools and Materials

TOOLS

- Wire jig made of metal
- Round nose pliers
- Heavy-duty side cutters
- Needle file
- Chain nose pliers
- Flat nose pliers
- Nylon jaw pliers

MATERIALS

These materials will make one bracelet that measures about 7½ inches long.

- 6 10-inch lengths of 24-gauge copper wire
- 6 12-inch lengths of 24-gauge copper wire
- 6 5½-inch lengths of 14-gauge copper wire
- About 375 mixed-color Czech glass seed beads in a variety of sizes
- 2 jump rings, 14 gauge (10mm OD)
- 2 wirework hook clasps made with 16-gauge copper wire, with loops large enough to fit loosely over 14-gauge jump rings

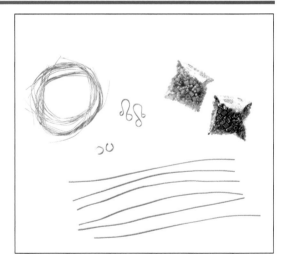

CONTINUED ON NEXT PAGE

Beaded Framework
Link Bracelet *(continued)*

How to Make the Beaded Framework Link Bracelet

The tasks required for this project are covered in Chapters 3, 7, and 8.

MAKE THE LINKS

1 Arrange four medium-sized pegs on the jig in a square formation about ⅜ inch apart.

2 Center one 5½-inch length of 14-gauge wire along one side of the square formation.

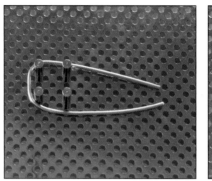 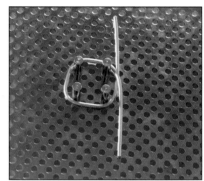

3 Bend the 14-gauge wire around all four pegs, as shown. One side of the square will have double wire.

4 Remove the wire from the jig.

5 If necessary, use flat nose pliers or nylon jaw pliers to straighten the sides of the square you just made.

6 Holding the double wire together with your fingers, use a 10-inch length of 24-gauge wire to wrap both wires together at the center, creating about a ½-inch length of wraps.

7 Trim off any extra 24-gauge wire at each end of the wraps, and use chain nose pliers to flatten the ends against the 14-gauge wire.

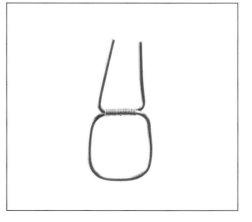

8 Grasp one end of the wrapped wires with flat nose pliers and bend the 14-gauge wire tail to a 90-degree angle.

9 Repeat Step 8 on the other end of the wraps.

10. Use a needle file to smooth the edges of the wire tails, as needed.

11. Using a length of 12-inch 24-gauge wire, wrap the link with coordinating mixed Czech glass beads, leaving a space of about ⅛ inch at each end of the link. Use the nylon jaw pliers as needed to straighten the wire as you work.

12. Repeat these steps to complete a total of six framework links.

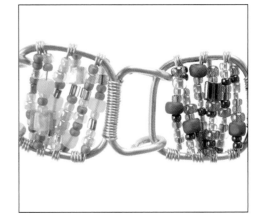

CONNECT THE LINKS

1. Using round nose pliers, convert both 14-gauge wire tails on each framework link into loops that point in the same direction.

2. Use flat nose pliers to gently open each loop.

3. Connect the links by inserting non-looped ends into looped ends, and using flat nose pliers to close each loop as you go along.

ATTACH THE CLASP

1. Attach the two 14-gauge jump rings to the non-looped end of the last framework link.

2. Attach the two 18-gauge wire-hook clasps to the loops on the first framework link. You can now fasten the bracelet by inserting the hook clasps into the jump rings on the other end.

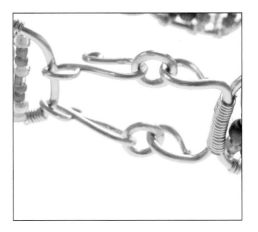

Four-Strand Braided Leather Bracelet

Leather is a traditional, yet challenging, cord medium for round braids. You will need a little more finger dexterity with leather than with smaller, softer cord, but the results are worth the effort. If you would like to make this design using the six-strand round braid instead of the four-strand braid, be sure to switch to a smaller-diameter cord.

Tools, Supplies, and Materials

TOOLS AND SUPPLIES

- Knotting board with T-pins (or a knotting board alternative; a clipboard works especially well for this project)
- Sharp scissors, nippers, or side cutters

MATERIALS

These materials will make one bracelet that measures about 8 inches long, not including the fringe.

- 2 2¼-yard lengths of 1.8mm leather cord in brown
- 2 Hill Tribe sterling silver coiled rings (8mm OD)

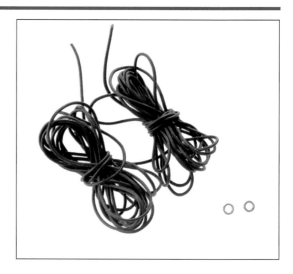

How to Make the Four-Strand Braided Leather Bracelet

The tasks required for this project are covered in Chapters 3 and 9.

1 Align both lengths of leather cord and fold them over at their centers.

2 Tie a temporary overhand knot with all four strands near the cord ends.

3 Tie another overhand knot to create a loop at the folded-over end of the cords, using the knot from Step 2 as a guide to determine the size of the loop. The loop should fit over the knot from Step 2, but not too loosely or too tightly.

4 Remove the overhand knot that you made in Step 2.

5 Anchor the loop securely to the knotting board.

6 Braid 7½ inches of four-strand round braids.

7 Tie an overhand knot with all four cords against the end of the round braids, and pull it tight.

8 String each of the two Hill Tribe sterling silver rings onto separate strands of cord tail, securing each with a single-strand overhand knot.

9 Cleanly trim the end of each fringe piece at an angle, about a ½ inch away from each overhand knot.

10 Trim the other two fringe strands, at similar angles, to the desired length.

chapter 12

Expanding Your Horizons

You are now familiar with the most common beginning-level methods, techniques, and styles of jewelry making and beading. You can continue this journey by choosing a specialty, learning from and exchanging ideas with other artisans, or even by starting a business. This chapter provides some ideas on how you might take your hobby to the next level.

As you work through this book, you will find that certain methods and styles of jewelry making and beading appeal to you more than others. Over time, you may want to expand your skills in those areas or narrow your focus to even more specialized themes. Here's a look at some of the more advanced jewelry making and beading niches that you can explore.

Jewelry by Preston Reuther

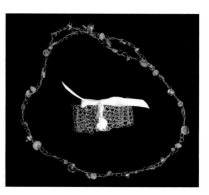

ADVANCED BEAD WEAVING

There are limitless creative possibilities to explore in the area of bead weaving. You can learn more complex weaves and create designs with complicated shapes, textures, and color patterns. Many beadwork artists incorporate dimensionality into their designs to make beaded objects and vessels. If you decide to become an advanced bead weaver, you can even take your skills beyond jewelry making to create unique, quality pieces of artwork.

WIRE SCULPTURE

Wire sculpture is a specialized style of wirework that involves multiple strands of wire and elaborate, flowing wire embellishments. You can create ornate, sturdy bracelets and rings, or wrap beads and stones to make eye-catching pendants, drops, and settings. Just like the wirework techniques covered in Chapters 6, 7, and 8, these methods do not require solder. Some appear to hold shape almost by magic.

WIRE KNITTING AND CROCHET

You can knit and crochet with very small-gauge wire to produce beautiful mesh-like wire fabric. These techniques are especially popular for making wide-band or rope-shaped bracelets and chokers. It's good to have some basic yarn-knitting and crochet skills before you give these methods a try with wire.

WIRE WEAVING

Wire weaving, as its name indicates, is the process of weaving with wire. You can learn to weave wires around, over, and across one another to create dense, textural designs. If you enjoy wrapping beads into a framework (see "Wrap Beads within a Framework" in Chapter 7), then you might also like this technique.

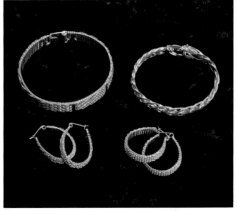

Jewelry by Linda Chandler

MAILLE WEAVING

Maille (or *chain maille*) was a popular metal fabric used in suits of armor during the Middle Ages. You can make maille-inspired jewelry by weaving together jump rings in various three-dimensional configurations. Some weaves result in chains similar to the Byzantine chain in Chapter 7 (see page 178). Others form slinky, tactile sheets of metal fabric.

ADVANCED CORD WORK

Chapter 9 covered some of the most basic macramé knotting and braiding techniques. If you enjoy working with cord, you can learn more advanced knots and complex ways of arranging them. You might also try *cord weaving*, where you weave together multiple strands of cord to create wide bands of fabric. Many fiber artists combine weaving with macramé and beads, and even set stones, to create amazing, artistic jewelry designs.

CONTINUED ON NEXT PAGE

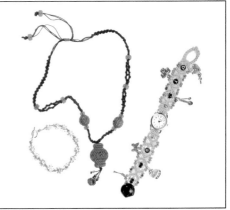

Jewelry by Sherri Haab

POLYMER CLAY

Polymer clay is a soft, malleable material made from a type of plastic. It contains special ingredients that allow it to permanently harden in a regular kitchen oven. You can use polymer clay to create beads, pendants, and other jewelry components. By layering colors and manipulating textures, you can mimic the look of elaborate glass work and natural materials like bone and wood. Polymer clay is relatively inexpensive, and it's easy to get started and experiment with at home.

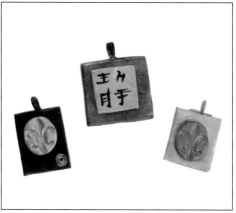

Pendants by Lisa Shea

METAL FABRICATION

Metal fabrication is the process of cutting, bending, hammering, shaping, and connecting metal to create original jewelry and jewelry components. Most of these methods are traditional techniques for making jewelry. Today, metal fabrication is used to create artistic one-of-a-kind or limited-edition jewelry. Some beaders and wirework artisans use basic metal fabrication techniques, like sawing and torch soldering, to expand their design possibilities.

GLASS AND CERAMIC BEAD MAKING

If you love beads and aren't afraid to work with advanced equipment, then you can learn to make your own beads out of glass or ceramic clay. *Lampworking* is one of the most popular methods for making artistic glass beads. It involves using a torch to melt glass on metal rods, and then allowing the glass pieces to cool very slowly (or *anneal*) in a kiln. If you prefer the look of ceramics, you can learn to make beads and other components using ceramic clays, which you fire in a kiln to harden.

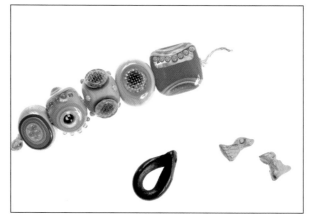

Lampwork beads by Sarah Moran

WAX CARVING AND CASTING

Much of the mass-produced jewelry that you see at retail stores was made by *casting*, or molding, metal. However, you can also use casting to create artistic, one-of-a-kind or limited-edition jewelry. *Lost wax casting* is a popular casting method. To begin, you carve a design into special wax (or form a wax copy of a finished piece), which is then used to create a mold. Molten metal is poured into the mold and specially processed to harden in the shape of the design. Because this requires working with very hot materials and specialized equipment, casting is not a practical technique for most home studios. However, you can contract an outside casting company to have your wax or fabricated designs cast offsite.

METAL CLAY

Metal clay contains precious metal, like silver or gold, combined with an ingredient that keeps it soft until it's heated to a very high temperature, or *fired*. You can use metal clay to create all kinds of jewelry and components that look like they might have been fabricated or cast. Metal clay is relatively expensive, but many artists find that its special attributes are worth the investment.

Jewelry by Sherri Haab

JEWELRY DESIGN

Technically, you are acting as a jewelry designer any time you devise and create a new piece of jewelry. If you enjoy the design phase of this process more than the craft phase, you might consider making design your primary focus. Designers typically compose their designs manually on paper or by using special computer programs. The results can be fabricated or converted to wax models and then cast.

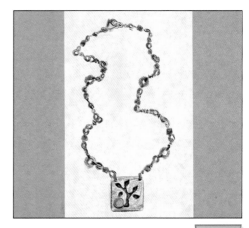

Find Advanced Help and Training

If you have access to the Internet or a local library, it's easy to find resources to help you advance your skills. There are three general categories of learning opportunities that you can pursue: self-learning, local classes and workshops, and professional training programs.

Self-Learning

Many jewelry artisans are completely self-taught, and others started out learning on their own before exploring more structured options. You have already begun self-learning by reading this book. Here are some other resources that you can investigate.

SPECIALTY BOOKS

Search online or at your local library or bookstore for more printed books on jewelry making. You can find books devoted to each of the specialized paths described in this chapter. The major booksellers' Web sites typically offer detailed book descriptions, reviews, and topical lists of titles to help you find what you need. For a short list of recommended titles to start with, see the Appendix.

E-BOOKS AND E-COURSES

Some jewelry making teachers offer e-books that you can download from the Internet to your computer, or distance-learning courses that you can take online. If you enjoy working at the computer, these can be convenient options. To find them, run some searches online or post queries about your interests in topical Web site forums.

MAGAZINES

There are a number of printed magazines devoted to beading and jewelry making. Most are published monthly or bi-monthly, and each issue contains new projects, instructions, and tips. You can find them at bead shops or hobby stores, and you can subscribe to them for home delivery. See page 284 for a listing of the most popular publications.

TOPICAL WEB SITES

Some Web sites offer free information, projects, newsletters, and even forums where you can post questions and comments for other jewelry artisans. These are great opportunities to continue learning while networking with people from all over the world who share your interests. For a listing of recommended jewelry making Web sites, see page 285.

LOCAL CLASSES AND WORKSHOPS

Hands-on jewelry making classes and workshops are available in most communities. Beading, bead weaving, and wirework classes are offered at many bead shops and at some craft stores. You can often find metalworking courses offered by community colleges or local parks and recreation departments. To find private offerings at studios or institutions, check your phone book or ask for references at a bead shop or art gallery.

PROFESSIONAL TRAINING PROGRAMS

If you're interested in a full-time jewelry making career, consider investing in a professional training program. These programs are offered by both public and private institutions, and they have structured curricula to help you achieve specific career goals. Most schools award certificates or degrees after the completion of the required coursework. See page 285 for a list of schools and program directories.

As your jewelry making skills develop, you may begin to receive requests for jewelry from family and friends. For some crafters, these personal transactions eventually develop into jewelry selling businesses. There are many potential venues for selling handcrafted jewelry, from outdoor markets to the Internet. Here are some guidelines to help you decide whether a jewelry business is right for you.

DO A LOT OF RESEARCH

Before you get started, you should spend many hours researching all aspects of your business idea. Learn how small businesses work and what it takes to operate one. Investigate other similar businesses. Are they succeeding? Why or why not? Determine how much of a time and financial commitment your business would require in order for you to reach your goals. The resources on page 285 are good places to get started.

FORMULATE A PLAN

Take the time to develop a written business plan that organizes and applies the information that you discovered during your research. If you would like to borrow money to start your business, potential lenders will probably want to see this plan when you apply for a loan. Even if you don't borrow money, the business plan will help you make informed business decisions and give you a better sense of control during challenging times.

DEVELOP YOUR SKILLS

Most artisans start out making jewelry that is of lower quality, but still fun to wear and experiment with. Give yourself enough time to fully develop your skills before you begin selling jewelry. The jewelry that you sell needs to be of professional quality in every way: it must be sturdy, wearable, secure, and made with quality materials. Over time, you will see your designs improve. You can build an excellent reputation for your business by offering top-notch work from the very start.

DEFINE YOUR STYLE

There will be many other artisans making and selling jewelry that is similar to yours. To succeed in this crowded market, and to avoid violating other artisans' copyrights (see page 34), you need to discover ways to set your designs apart from the rest. This doesn't mean you must invent a completely new jewelry idea. Simple, unique touches that you develop through experimentation can make your work more recognizable and increase its appeal.

NETWORK WITH OTHER ARTISANS

Take every opportunity you can to communicate with other jewelry artisans and to become involved in the jewelry making community. There are aspects of the business and craft that you can only learn from experience—or from someone else who has experienced them. You'll find that many artisans are happy to share their knowledge and offer support and encouragement. See the resources on page 283 for some good ways to find them.

SET REASONABLE EXPECTATIONS

Unfortunately, most small jewelry businesses have difficulty succeeding. Competition from importers who sell similar, inexpensive jewelry is one challenge. Additionally, many artisans have trouble reaching enough target customers. To avoid frustration, try to set reasonable expectations. (You know that saying, "Don't quit your day job.") This may mean allowing your business to begin small and to evolve very slowly. As your knowledge, skills, and reputation grow, your chances of success will become increasingly better.

Appendix

Reference Materials

Resources for Tools, Supplies, and Materials

Here are some resources for finding the tools, supplies, and materials needed to complete the tasks and projects in this book.

LOCAL BEAD SHOPS

Many cities and towns have one or more local bead shops. You can find them by contacting your chamber of commerce or checking the phone book. Some Web sites and magazines also provide lists of bead shops by city or state. Most bead shops carry a variety of beads as well as beading tools, stringing materials, findings, pre-made components, wire, and basic wire-work tools. Bead shop employees are especially knowledgeable about jewelry making and beading, and they can provide valuable tips and advice. Many bead shops also offer onsite classes.

JEWELRY MAKING SUPPLY STORES

Jewelry making supply stores typically carry some beads, but their primary offerings are tools, equipment, and supplies for jewelers. This is where you can find all of the tools and materials that you need for wirework. If you don't have a local jewelry making supply store, you can search the Internet or request a print catalog from one of these well-known U.S. companies:

- Rio Grande (www.riogrande.com; 800-545-6566)
- Contenti (www.contenti.com; 401-421-4040)
- Kingsley North (www.kingsleynorth.com; 800-338-9280)

E-COMMERCE WEB SITES

You can also purchase beads and other jewelry making supplies over the Internet. Find them by using your favorite search engine or by checking directories and ads in beading and jewelry making magazines. Although shopping for supplies online can be convenient and fun, keep in mind that colors may be slightly inaccurate on computer monitors. (Because of this, when you're shopping for a very specific color of bead for a project, your local bead shop might be a better option.) Here are some popular beading and jewelry making supply e-commerce sites, some of which also offer print catalogs:

General Beads and Supplies

- Fire Mountain Gems and Beads (www.firemountaingems.com)
- Rings & Things (www.rings-things.com)
- Shipwreck Beads (www.shipwreckbeads.com)
- Fusion Beads (www.fusionbeads.com)
- ArtBeads.com (www.artbeads.com)

Bead-Weaving Beads and Supplies

- Foxden Designs (www.foxdendesigns.com)
- Bead Cats (www.beadcats.com)

Bead-Weaving Graphs and Patterns

- Bead-patterns.com (www.bead-patterns.com)
- Shala's Beadworks (shala.addr.com)

Vintage Beads

- Beadin' Path (www.beadinpath.com)
- Beadroom.com (www.beadroom.com)

Beading Wire

- Beadalon (www.beadalon.com)
- SoftFlex Company (www.softflexcompany.com)

Wirework Supplies and Instruction

- Wire-sculpture.com (www.wire-sculpture.com)
- Spider Chain Jewelry (www.spiderchain.com)

Shows

At bead shows, large numbers of bead and supply vendors come together to offer their latest wares. They typically are held at exhibition centers in major cities, and most are open to the public. Bead shows can be great places to find new bead designs at reasonable prices, but be prepared to buy in bulk. Most beads are sold by the strand, and vendors often refuse to sell in smaller quantities. Feel free to haggle over prices, especially when you plan to purchase multiple strands from a single vendor. Here are some of the largest bead shows held in the United States. Check their Web sites for scheduling information:

- Annual Show in Tucson (www.colored-stone.com/tsg)
- Bead Renaissance Show (www.beadshow.com)
- Gem Faire (www.gemfaire.com)
- International Gem & Jewelry Show (www.intergem.com)
- The Whole Bead Show (www.wholebead.com)

Community and Educational Resources

These resources can help you stay up-to-date in the world of jewelry making and beading. You can also use them to investigate specializations and further your skills.

MAGAZINES

Beading and jewelry making magazines are very useful resources for keeping abreast of trends, techniques, and new products. They provide step-by-step projects, advice, and interesting stories about fellow crafters. Even the ads in these magazines can be fun to browse through; you can use them to find inspiring beads and materials that you otherwise wouldn't know are available. Most magazines are available at local bead shops, craft stores, bookstores, and by subscription. Here are a few of the most popular beading and jewelry making magazines:

- *Bead & Button Magazine* (www.beadandbutton.com)
- *Beadwork Magazine* (www.interweave.com/bead/beadwork_magazine)
- *Lapidary Journal Jewelry Artist* (www.lapidaryjournal.com)
- *Art Jewelry* (www.artjewelrymag.com)

BOOKS

If you enjoy learning at your own pace using books, you have lots of titles to choose from. Some are collections of projects that share common themes, and others are structured as reference materials with tips and information. Here are some suggested titles that you may enjoy:

- *Metal Clay and Mixed Media Jewelry: Innovative Projects Featuring Resin, Polymer Clay, Fiber, Glass, Ceramics, Collage Materials, and More* by Sherri Haab
- *Beaded Macramé Jewelry: Stylish Designs, Exciting New Materials* by Sherri Haab
- *Woven Wire Jewelry: Contemporary Designs and Creative Techniques* by Linda L. Chandler and Christine R. Ritchey
- *Creative Techniques For Polymer Clay Jewelry* by Nanetta Bananto
- *The Complete Metalsmith: An Illustrated Handbook* by Tim McCreight
- *Making Glass Beads* by Cindy Jenkins

VIDEOS AND DVDS

You can also learn new techniques by watching instructional videos or DVDs. Here are some to consider:

- Artgems Instructional Beading Videos (http://artgemsinc.com/VideoLive)
- Joan Babcock's Micro-Macramé and Cavandoli Knotting DVD (www.joanbabcock.com)
- Preston Reuther's Sculptural Wire Techniques Packages (www.wire-sculpture.com)
- Victoria Lansford's Russian Filigree Instructional DVD for Metalsmiths (www.victorialansford.com/filigreed.html)

WEB SITES

The Internet is a great place to communicate with other beaders and jewelry crafters all over the world. There are many Web sites and blogs devoted to providing free information and enhancing the jewelry making community. Many of these Web sites offer instructions, projects, and book and product reviews as well as forums, chat rooms, and e-mail newsletters. You can find them by searching online. Here are some examples:

- About.com Beadwork (beadwork.about.com)
- About.com Jewelry Making (jewelrymaking.about.com)
- BellaOnline.com Beadwork (beadwork.bellaonline.com)
- BellaOnline.com Jewelry Making (jewelrymaking.bellaonline.com)
- Ganoksin (www.ganoksin.com)
- Bloglander Jewelry Making Blog (www.bloglander.com/jewelrymaking)

SCHOOLS AND PROGRAMS

If you'd like to take your beading or jewelry making skills to an advanced level, consider enrolling in a hands-on educational program or workshop. You can find local classes by searching online, checking the Yellow Pages for jewelry schools, or inquiring at a bead shop or jewelry making supply store. Magazines also usually contain ads or listings for popular programs. Here are some resources where you can find more information:

- BellaOnline.com Jewelry Making Courses Directory (www.bellaonline.com/subjects/8106.asp)
- GIA Career Fair (careerfair.gia.edu)
- MJSA Education Guide (www.mjsajournal.org/pub_education.php)

BUSINESS RESOURCES

If you're interested in learning more about selling your beadwork and jewelry creations as a business, these resources can help you get started:

- American Craft Association (www.craftassociation.com)
- Home Jewelry Business Success Tips (www.home-jewelry-business-success-tips.com)
- Jeweler's Resource Bureau (www.jewelersresource.com)
- U.S. Small Business Administration (www.sba.gov)

Index

Read Less–Learn More ®

Teach Yourself VISUALLY™ books...

Whether you want to knit, sew, or crochet . . . strum a guitar or play the piano . . . create a scrapbook or train a dog . . . make the most of Windows Vista™ or touch up your Photoshop® CS3 skills, Teach Yourself VISUALLY books get you into action instead of bogged down in lengthy instructions. All Teach Yourself VISUALLY books are written by experts on the subject and feature:

- Hundreds of color photos that demonstrate each step and/or skill
- Step-by-step instructions that accompany each photo

- Tips and FAQs that answer common questions and suggest solutions to common problems
- Information about each skill that is clearly presented on a two- or four-page spread so you can learn by seeing and doing
- A design that makes it easy to review a particular topic

Look for Teach Yourself VISUALLY books to help you learn a variety of skills—all with the proven visual learning approach you enjoyed in this book.

Make terrific crafts

NEW! Quick Tips series

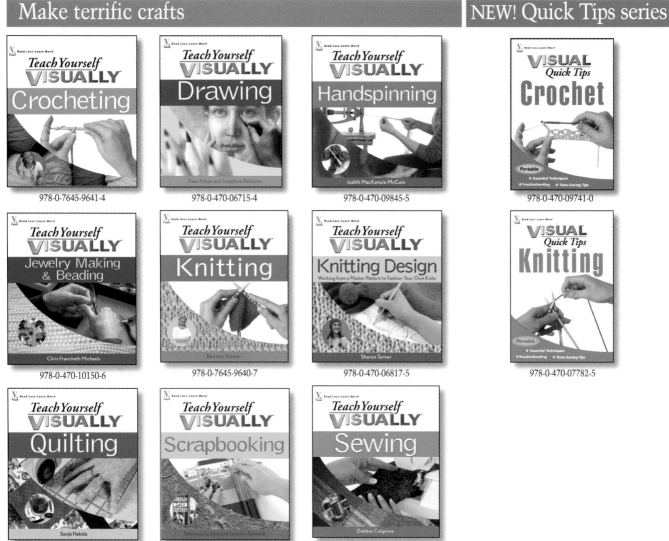

978-0-7645-9641-4

978-0-470-06715-4

978-0-470-09845-5

978-0-470-09741-0

978-0-470-10150-6

978-0-7645-9640-7

978-0-470-06817-5

978-0-470-07782-5

978-0-470-10149-0

978-0-7645-9945-3

978-0-471-74991-2

designed for visual learners like you!

Make beautiful music

Make Rover behave

978-0-470-04850-4

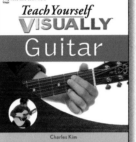

978-0-7645-9642-1

Teach Yourself VISUALLY Piano

978-0-471-74990-5

978-0-471-74989-9

Make improvements in your game

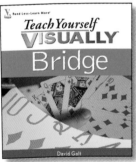

978-0-470-11424-7

978-0-470-04983-9

Teach Yourself VISUALLY Golf

978-0-470-09844-8

Teach Yourself VISUALLY Poker

978-0-471-79906-1

Make the most of technology

Teach Yourself VISUALLY Computers 5th Edition

978-0-470-16878-3

Teach Yourself VISUALLY Microsoft Office Excel 2007

978-0-470-04595-4

Teach Yourself VISUALLY Adobe Photoshop CS3

978-0-470-11452-0

Teach Yourself VISUALLY Microsoft Windows Vista

978-0-470-04573-2